The Peculiar Business of labor law

and thoughts on the U.S. Constitution

(formerly Dog Law)

Donald H. Wollett
with Susan G. Crowell

Winding Road Press
Newfield, New York

The Peculiar Business of Labor Law and thoughts on the U.S. Constitution

Winding Road Press
New York 14867

DEDICATION

My co-author, Susan Crowell, was my teacher. She doesn't think of herself that way, but I do. She taught me that everything begins at home. This is true not only of baseball, but also in life. She took me through my high school years and my years at the University of Chicago. She taught me about my years in the Navy during WWII, and how the important thing about combat is not the fighting, but the working together, especially on a small ship. She taught me the moral values of courage in the context of racial integration. How she knew all this I don't know. I could go on about everything Susan has taught me with each chapter of of this book, but a separate chapter would be needed. With each chapter Susan taught me about my friends, my advisories, but mostly myself. This was a gift Susan had, that she gave to me. I can think of no one else to whom I owe so much. And it is my honor to dedicate *The Peculiar Business of Labor Law and Thoughts on the U.S. Constitution* to her.

CONTENTS

DEVISING A BARGAINING SYSTEM 225

THE ELEPHANT'S TAIL 233

ACKNOWLEDGEMENTS

We would like to thank those who reviewed different versions of the manuscript with a gentle, but firm hand. Robert McKersie, Duane Beeson, Richard Booth, and perhaps most of all the extreme patience of John (Jake) Kelliher.

PREFACE

*T*he *Peculiar Business of Labor Law and Thoughts on the U.S. Constitution* is about football scandals, strikes, protests, racism, social movements, workplace disputes, and public sector fiscal woes. It is about everyday people who encounter laws they do not understand and jurists who pronounce judgments on crimes they do not understand. It is about my professional life a labor lawyer and teacher of labor and constitutional law and what drove me toward greater cooperation in my practice of law.

My chronicle starts with the intellectual and humanist understanding of law at the University of Chicago law school in 1939. As a law student, I was not interested in torts and contracts, though I would end up teaching these courses as many law professors do at one time or another.

The fact is, I had not planned to be a lawyer, rather an actor or a minor league baseball player like my dad.

Those idle ambitions disappeared when dry legalese came to life. My professors gave me intellectual reasoning, an insatiable curiosity about relationships, and a belief in civility that touched something of value in my nature.

My labor law trajectory started during my Navy years. I learned as a young captain of a sub chaser that I valued my men. I determined that their trust depended upon my fairness. To achieve that trust the rule of reason had to co-exist, and sometimes over-ride military law. The result of my lesson was a smooth running ship.

I became a teacher of Constitutional Law because no one wanted the job. As I lived through momentous events over the next decades, I came to know law not as a doctrine, but as our lives teeming with thoughts, emotions, grandeur, notions of power, and few resolutions on contemporary issues.

During my early career I directed the Arthur Garfield Hays Program at New York University. Post graduate students and I sorted out meanings of justice and injustice and possible causes of the latter, whether that was reliving Nazism through the memories of Arthur Garfield Hays who loved America's legal institutions but also observed how jurists abdicated the rule of law, or experiencing the entrenched beliefs of a Louisiana legislature that denied the existence of the 14th Amendment following *Brown v. The Board of Education.*

My awakening to non-adversarial approaches to law occurred during a trial in the 1950s when I represented the Armour Meatpacking Company in the Midwest concerning a matter of plant closures. This was a slam-dunk and back-to-New York City kind of trial and somewhat boring until I considered that the audience consisted of mostly quiet, stolid women and children who intently followed tedious, technical matters for no discernible reason. Then I understood that if I won, and I knew I would, their husbands would have no jobs and the families would probably lose everything.

An extraordinary bilateral cooperative venture between labor and management intervened in the form of a joint committee that devised ways to guaranteed portable seniority for laid-off workers whatever the planned plant closures.

As Director of the Office of Employee Relations under the Governor Hugh Carey Administration, I used the Armour model in a trade with New York State's largest union for a no-money mandate that was imposed on public sector unions due to a severe fiscal crisis. The Continuity of Employment Committee created a vision of job security for the future through extraordinary research efforts and with the use of demonstration projects.

The Committee was the first of its kind in the country to seriously look at the role of government in relation to job security. The three-year project quietly ended during Governor Hugh Carey's second term and appeared to disappear. However, some of its legacy remained.

As a senior partner in a large New York law firm. I recruited a select team of talented young lawyers to help me turn the National Education Association into a serious union that could engage in collective bargaining against stronger and more experienced union competitors.

During that time K-12 teachers taught me that the power of social movement brings the courage to change. This experience convinced me that there would never be equity between labor and management without the human right to a strike threat.

I was involved in teachers' strikes in places such as Newark, New Jersey, Flint Michigan, Los Angeles, and Hawaii. The teachers were always more than their union. They were individuals deciding to walk the line.

I became their loyal advocate in New York. New Jersey, and California. In Huntington, New York, the end-result of the public school teachers' grueling and brave protest against the whims of an ignorant school board was one of the most innovative, comprehensive, and inclusive labor contracts for teachers in existence.

I ended my academic career and conducted labor arbitrations full time. Grievance arbitrations in the private and public sectors revealed a record of cases involving the breakdown of human relations. The right remedy came from judicial discretion and honoring the living contractual arrangements owned by the parties. Fairness over the matter of just cause came from cooperation between those deemed natural adversaries.

Abraham Lincoln believed, as did Justice Oliver Wendell Holmes, Justice Learned Hand, and others, that *stare decisis* and the letter of the law, if devoid of reality, should not dictate the final judgment of a case, and in truth it does not. The law is alive as I relate in my stories. It is our search for justice and fairness. We should not have to live under the weight of laws and court interpretations we do not understand and pay a price for deeds we do not understand.

We have the right to live simply under the aspirations found in the Bill of Rights which can be both flexible and codified. It is what I have learned and what I would like to share about my professional life . So, I raise my lance because every dog should have its day, and tell a few stories along the way.

While Edward Hirsch Levi is gone now along with other great figures in law, I thank my former law professor at the University of Chicago because he taught a young brash student about "dog law," a concept introduced by Jeremy Bentham, who in his day was one of the most articulate opponents of the limited use and the misuse of common law.

The Peculiar Business
of Labor Law and
Thoughts on the U. S.
Constitution

THE PURPOSE OF THE UNIVERSITY IS NOTHING LESS THAN TO PROCURE A MORAL, INTELLECTUAL, AND SPIRITUAL REVOLUTION THROUGHOUT THE WORLD, ROBERT MAYNARD HUTCHINS, UNIVERSITY OF CHICAGO PRESIDENT.

1

Principles of engagement

We lived in Peoria Illinois. My mother was a Midwestern liberal. She was determined that I learn how to express ideas. When I was very young, she had me take speech lessons from moonlighting teachers and speech therapists.

Thanks to my mother I learned to articulate complex ideas. I joined my high school debate team and my speech on the *Nine old Men* sitting on the US Supreme Court brought me the prestigious "Original Oratory Championship of the State of Illinois" at a competition in Lincoln.

I wrote articles in high school and became editor-in-chief of the high school newspaper, *Opinion*, a 16-page tabloid printed weekly at a local newspaper. We had an editorial department and our own print shop where we produced mats for type. The roar of the press and the first proofs put ink in my veins. I would be a newspaperman someday.

My high school journalism teacher, Earl English, taught me about plain language. He was relentless when it came to hyperbole or gratuitous displays of language. "Wollett," he would say, "'opined' is unnecessary. Just say 'said' then actually say something." For the most part, I followed his teaching.

I was also involved in local theatre in high school. I began to think that I had enough talent to be an actor.

I finished high school fifth in a class of 500 and went on to Bradley Polytechnic Institute (later named Bradley University) for the next two years without any idea of what I was going to be. I walked the same route past the school of horology where disabled WWI veterans assembled watches. I had lost my way and time was ticking.

One day I stopped in front of the school of horology and thought it was time to move on, but to what? I could be an actor. I was active in the Peoria theater. I loved my family, but I needed to get away.

The University of Chicago

It had never occurred to me to study law. However, I had heard that the president of the University of Chicago, Robert Hutchins, had initiated a new law school program. I could get a law degree in two years and be done with school. Then I would be free to go wherever I wanted.

I accepted a scholarship and traveled the 160 miles to Chicago. I was young, eager, and about to be on my own.

My sister, parents, and I had made annual treks to Chicago's South-side, close to where the University was located, to visit my Uncle Bob, a comptroller for the YMCA college. We were welcomed by my aunt and our three cousins on Thanksgiving or Christmas Day. The

Hyde Park area next to the University of Chicago, had been middle-class white and gentrified. It was real Norman Rockwell scene. When I arrived at the University I found that my uncle had left the neighborhood and moved his family to a safer part of South Chicago that was still identifiable as Hyde Park.

By 1938, the University of Chicago was an enclave bordered by fading elegance along the north side of the University. The beautiful old homes in the area were run down. There were obvious signs of growing poverty. Crimes, mostly theft, had increased significantly. The majority of the poor in the neighborhoods were struggling African American families.

Looking west, the University of Chicago lined both sides of the Midway. Originally planned as a haven for middle class and upper class families, the Midway, created in 1891, represented a transition between the declining Hyde Park area and the continual modernization of the University of Chicago, new dorms and that sort of thing.

Numerous new University buildings had been constructed on the south side of the Midway. Venerable buildings, including many neogothic structures, were still in place on the north side. Rockefeller Chapel was located on the east side of the quadrangles. It was a beautiful cathedral with sermons every Sunday.

The law school was on the north side of the building and housed in Stuart Hall, a Gothic-style building located on one of the campus' main quadrangles.

When the University of Chicago was founded about 75 years before, William Rainey Harper thought it was a bad idea to build a new college. He envisioned a college that would be part of the University and he wanted it in the Middle West. Many of his supporters and funders were opposed to combining a university with a college. They also resisted the idea of having a college in the ill-bred city of Chicago.

His vision bore fruit. Over the years the University of Chicago graduated students of diverse persuasions. Thanks to the University's founders, its students were endowed with values such as continuous learning. President Robert Hutchins' philosophy of education included inclusiveness and openness. Consequently, many students from working class families had unusual access to higher education. Like me they worked their way through school. Even though I had a scholarship, I worked 35 hours a week checking library books.

I had felt isolated and alone during my first year, however my social life improved in my second year when I moved into The International House on the north side of the campus and earned money waiting on tables in a short-order coffee house called the Telling Room. Thanks to my job as a waiter I socialized with people from around the world. I joined a lively student group that met at the student union on Sunday nights.

President Robert Hutchins (left) and Professor Edward Levi (right).

LEARNING LAW

One of the taglines popular with University of Chicago students was that the University of Chicago was a nonsectarian university founded by a couple of Baptists, quickly transformed into a Protestant, a Presbyterian or an Episcopalian institution, I've forgotten which, then into a secular institution.

William Rainey Harper's vision engendered a special intelligence among a diverse student body, including the sons and daughters of many blue collar workers, that was unmatched in the country. I recently read in 2013 that the University of Chicago had created a program that would allow under-privileged high school students to attend the University and graduate without a student loan debt. It seems that William Rainey Harper's vision lives on.

In 1939, there were leanings of all degrees left, right, and center. Thanks to John D. Rockefeller, Jews such as Mortimer Adler were able to teach Catholicism and atheists received the teachings of St. Thomas Aquinas. I experienced this primordial soup as an eclectic oasis blended with the Midwestern values of decency and honesty. There was no sense of entitlement due to some inherited standing or social status.

President Robert Hutchins believed strongly in research and academic pursuit. This contributed to an extraordinarily diverse, motivated, and highly competitive student body.

While working in the library, I had noticed that a number of books were kept out past the return date. I cornered a student one day and asked him why he failed to returned his book on time. He answered, "because, if I keep it out it isn't available to anyone else." That's how competitive the student body was.

After many years teaching and contributing to the growth of law schools in different parts of the country, I concluded that the most successful schools relied on smart, hardworking students who bought into meritocracy. That was the University of Chicago during my student years.

THE LAW SCHOOL FACULTY

In my second year, I still had no idea what my practice area would be. The University was weighted toward economics in its law teachings so I followed this course and very briefly became a political and economic conservative. Given my liberal disposition and upbringing, this surprised a lot of people, including myself.

However I had a persuasive teacher. During my first year, President Robert Hutchins had to deal with some faculty unrest caused by Professor Henry Calvert Simons, who was a brilliant, out-of-the-box thinker when it came to economics. President Hutchins decided the solution was to park him in the law school.

Professor Simons was a persuasive speaker. He could turn any socialist into a libertarian. Professor Simons' *Positive Program for Laissez-faire* further sharpened my oratorical and writing skills as I roundly argued for capitalism and the free market, despite the fact that I was probably always a socialist of some sort at heart.

Another of my professors, Malcolm Sharp was brilliant and he inspired his students to think of the law in association with matters that should influence the making of law.

He was a gentle and complex man. He frequently described himself as both a teacher and a learner. His store of knowledge spanned numerous disciplines. Professor Sharp presented a law of economics that was inseparable from anthropological concepts such as social change. He introduced me to concepts such as the right to break a contract. Children spit on their hands and make an agreement, but the trouble always begins with the offer....where certainties are obfuscated by unnamed facts.

Listening to him, I wondered why I was in law school when I understood so little. I felt better when I learned that most students had a problem grappling with his teachings. Later, many of Professor Sharp's precepts proved critical to my work as a labor negotiator.

Whatever the subject, his thinking was that knowledge had to be useful. Furthermore, the only "useful" lawyers were those who had a capacity to think on their feet, however complex the question.

This utilitarian view was captured at his memorial service held several years later, against his wishes I might add. He had instructed that he did not want a service because it was not "useful." Despite Malcolm's Sharp's request, the living wanted eulogies. The faculty and students needed to pay homage to a great teacher. A eulogy from one faculty member went like this,

When speaking with alumni about Malcolm, I often encountered a well-remembered bemusement about his classes. Sometimes it seems that only the most respected and admired of teachers evoke this sense of confusion. It is captured in a student verse described as 'affectionate malice.

> Malcolm, Malcolm, you are welcome
>
> With your ivy-covered mind
>
> Though no one can understand you,
>
> You are good and wise and kind."

William Crosskey was another of my professors. He and Malcolm Sharp had been close friends. The two educators staunchly defended historical interpretations of the Constitution.

He enthralled students with elegant arguments.

Professor Crosskey challenged fledgling legal minds to put aside their awe of the "greats" and great ideas so that we might think critically.

Professor Crosskey, incisively challenged the orthodoxy of *The Federalist Papers* and the lack of scholarship into the intent behind the constitution, which was captured in his three-volume tome, *Politics and the Constitution in the History of the United States* (He and Malcolm Sharp were staunch defenders of historical interpretations of the Constitution).

An alumnus of his teachings recalled Professor Crosskey's grand entrance into his classroom on the first day of school when without missing a step, he launched a satirical dismissal our icons:

> You have all heard, gentlemen, that James Madison is the father of the Constitution; that Oliver Wendell Holmes, Jr., of Massachusetts was our greatest Supreme Court Justice; and that Louis Dembitz Brandeis was the leading authority on the jurisdiction of the federal courts. Before I finish this summer, I propose to demonstrate to you that Madison was a forger - he tampered with the notes he kept of the debates at the federal constitutional convention in order to suit his own political

advantage and that of his party. Holmes undoubtedly knew a great deal about old English law, but he was not the most eminent authority on American constitutional history. As for Brandeis, his opinion in *Erie v. Tompkins* demonstrates that he did not understand the true meaning of the judiciary provisions in Article III of the Constitution.

I took labor law and torts from Professor Charles O. Gregory. Everyone, including students, called him "Charlie." Professor Gregory was one of the great pioneers of labor law. He introduced us to the power of the courts and such matters as injunction devices. He co-authored a widely published book on torts which became the most important classroom book on the subject in law schools across the country, He also introduced a conceptual framework for labor law in his book titled, *Labor and The Law* with an acuity that I could only aspire to.

DOG LAW: THE BEGINNING

Edward H. Levi was possibly my favorite professor. He taught jurisprudence and later became president of the University of Chicago. He was the author of the seminal work, An Introduction to Legal Reasoning.

Professor Levi believed the law relied too much on behaviorism before the ideas of behaviorist John B. Watson became popular. In his view, a behaviorist perspective of law meant that a person had no soul and no mind, only a brain that responded to external stimuli. This explained our country's adherence to a poorly fitting and antiquated system of law, especially in terms of how we came to define evidence.

Professor Levi introduced me to "dog law." The concept had been introduced by Jeremy Bentham, a critic of common law, more than a century ago.

Professor Levi said,

The basic pattern of legal reasoning is reasoning by example...in which a proposition descriptive in the first case is made into a rule of law and then applied to the next similar situation. A method...necessary for the law, but [with] characteristics which under other circumstances might be considered imperfections.

Exploring the meaning of justice through Socratic dialogue was an accepted practice used by many law professors in my student and early teaching days. This was not an erudite exploration. For example, a portion of my educational experience in law school dealt with practicalities surrounding power. In the dialogue between Socrates and Tharymysus, Socrates asks what is justice; justice is power. In preparation for the world of practice, we learned through reviewing case law and other means that in the real world what power gets away with might be considered justice.

This meaning of justice cast a large shadow over my golden years of learning the law. I studied the intricacies of laws meant to hold a civil society together and listened to Winston Churchill on the radio at night. The sound of marching feet grew louder and the law seemed to be held together by fragile threads.

INDIANA UNIVERSITY

My two years at the University of Chicago earned me a Bachelor of Arts, which was sufficient to graduate from law school in those days. I wanted to continue, but I ran out of money. Luckily, the Indiana University wanted me and gave me a lectureship in the school of business so I no longer had to worry about finishing law school. I kept the credits I had earned so far. I would be a bona fide lawyer in less than a year.

As it turned out, the University of Chicago urged me to stay and even promised me the financial aid to do so. However, I decided to go ahead and transfer to Indiana University since I had a secure job waiting for me. I deeply regretted leaving the University of Chicago, but under the deanship of Bernard Gavit, the law school at Indiana University was one of the most highly ranked in the country. The University where I would finish my education also had a top law school faculty, though I found the student body at Indiana University less invigorating compared to the University of Chicago student body.

Bernard Gavit, dean of the law school, taught civil procedure. I did not take courses from him, but we became good friends. He was ultimately responsible for my finding first job on the West Coast following the war.

I took tort law from Fowler Harper, and administrative law from Frank Horack. I learned criminal law and legal philosophy from Jerome Hall, who turned out to be my favorite teacher at Indiana.

Professor Hall was a tall thin man with black rimmed glasses and a wild shock of hair. He was a gentle person but he adamantly refused to allow a student's performance to be less than their best. He never raised his voice, rather he offered a penetrating and slightly fearsome stare, which was worse.

Edward Levi once described the mission of a university as "a search for [the] basic knowledge to preserve and to give continuity to the values of mankind's many cultures." Professor Jerome Hall subscribed to this view as did other law professors at Indiana University. He defined legal education as a changing landscape produced by cultures with many stories.

In 1952, he wrote an open letter to Indiana University calling for the formation of a school of cultural legal education. He envisioned a rigorous curriculum that provided interdisciplinary perspectives that would be explored based on collaborations of students from different disciplines.

Professor Hall presented justice not as absolute power, but in the following manner:

> I leave it to your imagination to bound the limits of the work that needs to be done if law, the eternal guardian of life, is to fulfill its mission. There is more than abiding interest and love of wisdom to encourage such a culture. For it is out of these incursions into the thought of the ages that a higher and fuller measure of justice is achieved. It is by this contact with culture and chiefly with the social sciences that the jurist who-none-the-less keeps his ear to the ground during his own days, and his fingers on the pulse of his own times, creates a nobler and

a wiser vision of justice. And in doing this, is he not fulfilling the highest hopes of humanity for whom justice will forever be the most distinctive, the most human and the most inspiring of human qualities?

My student experiences with the two law schools influenced my later belief that cooperation was essential to finding justice. However, as events would have it, the voices of my professors who called for more social science perspectives faded with time in the law business. Following WWII, market-driven principles took over. Meantime, I joined the fight to save humanity and learned more about justice at sea.

I HAD THE FIRST STRIKE OF MY CAREER. MY MOST VALUABLE CREW MEMBERS, THE SIGNALMAN, THE RADIOMAN, AND THE QUARTERMASTER, REFUSED TO LEAVE WITHOUT THE MISSING CREW MEMBER, NO MATTER WHAT THE CONSEQUENCES.

2

Rules of War

I received my law degree in the summer of 1942 and went to midshipman's school at Northwestern University to study navigation, seamanship, and communications. I graduated at the top of my class.

After attending boot camp at Notre Dame for three weeks, I enlisted in the Navy's officer training program. My most difficult task was surviving algebra and trigonometry.

I wanted to serve on a destroyer. Instead, I was assigned to small craft training in Miami Florida where I was trained in antisubmarine warfare. I learned how to handle a 110-foot sub chaser (SC) and 170-foot patrol crafts (PC).

My leadership training happened at sea.

I had been aboard the SC1063 as an officer for about two years when its captain ordered us to abandon ship in the middle of the night. It was cold and dark and the ship was taking on water. She was sinking fast even as I turned out his order.

No crew member was lost, but I fell overboard. The boson's mate, a big roughneck from Georgia, quickly rescued me from the deep. It must have gone against his grain to rescue an officer, but he never hesitated.

Remarkably, the SC1063 was salvaged and substantially rebuilt at a shipyard in Houston and we sailed again with a new captain. This time we ran aground when the new captain cut a sea buoy at Key West and put the ship up on a coral reef.

The crew was aware that our captain cared more about chasing women and getting drunk than running a ship. Nevertheless, we were under his command so we had no choice. Though I knew little about ship handling, navigation, or handling a drunken captain, I ended up running the ship. I learned a lot about leadership with this experience.

Unfortunately, while the crew and I survived the captain's command, our ship had developed a bad reputation.

I had hoped to change that and assume command of the SC1063 when the captain was relieved of duty. Instead, the subchaser was turned over to yet another captain. He was a decent fellow and more competent than his predecessors.

A few weeks later, I was given my own ship. I was 25-years-old and captain of the SC511.

Exercising mercy

I had learned something about giving orders when I covered for the captain of the SC1063. Now, I had to learn how to execute orders, knowing no one else was to blame if something went wrong.

Navy rules worked well enough until I was forced to dramatically increased the SC511's speed to avoid being hit by a merchant vessel on my first trip down the Florida Keys. I ordered the machinists to open up the valves to the heat exchangers. There was no machinist on duty in the control station to receive my order. Consequently, the valves were not thrown open and the starboard was destroyed. It cost the Navy about $100,000 to replace the engine. Even worse, we missed two scheduled convoy assignments.

An admiral directed me to convene court martial proceedings against the wayward machinists. I complied. There was no question about their responsibility or their liability. However, I kept thinking that the facts did not support *absolute* responsibility or liability.

I decided to assess their guilt on my terms rather than exclusively relying on naval rules. My motive was that I did not want to lose any of my men if I could help it, either overboard or to a court martial, because I had not fairly considered all the facts.

I had fully acknowledged the rule that the commanding officer must take responsibility for his failure to carry out his authority. However, I had extended this rule beyond precedent when I decided that my predecessor had failed to carry out his authority. He had not instructed the machinists on how to move from watch to watch or how to transfer authority from one machinist to another when they had to go to the head.

In other words, I had invoked an unprecedented interpretation I made up on the spot. The failures of the commanding officer are not to be attributed to those who must obey him. They are to be attributed where they belong, which in this case was to management. It did not matter to me that this was a previous management. So I invoked this rule, and on that basis reduced the machinists' punishment.

While I considered this a just and fair decision, my belief was not shared by the admiral of the Gulf Sea Frontier who was provoked into writing the only letter I had ever received from an admiral. Unfortunately, it was a letter of disapprobation. His interpretation was that I did not have the guts to be tough.

He was wrong. I knew I had the guts. It was just that I truly believed that a local, fully informed execution of punishment was best, particularly at sea where people lived and worked together under uncertainties and in close proximity.

My judgment did not violate our mission which was to protect, to defend, and to win the war. Treating the crew fairly through my considered judgment, given the circumstances, won the respect and trust of my men, which in turn helped win the war, which purpose was after all to defend a democracy that protects our due process rights.

Anyhow, in that instance we missed our convoy assignment and I did not do what the admiral wanted me to do. Nevertheless, the sub chaser ran smoothly under my command, thanks to a well operating team, and we never missed another assignment.

In the final analysis, my capacity to deliver justice and fairness depended upon my ability to encourage initiative and to build skills among my crew members. My crew was eager to learn new skills and I was eager to teach them. For example, I set up an extra-mural class in celestial navigation, which was my area of expertise. This kind of practical skill building also built leadership.

The value of encouraging this kind of initiative came home to me south of New Orleans when the hedgehogs failed to fire off missile racks.

One of my gunner's mates, with the concurrence of the other gunner's mate, took it upon himself to voluntarily defused a live missile. I would have ordered him to do this, but he did it on his own volition without hesitation in response to a crisis situation.

The gunner's mate who defused the missile was one of those who had participated in my celestial navigation class. He learned enough so that he could have taken over navigating the ship if something happened to me.

There were leadership lessons ahead for me involving a balance between authority and negotiations with the crew that gave me early insights into labor relations.

My chief petty officer on the SC511 was regular Navy. He was very good at what he was trained to do, but he had an annoying habit of not finishing a job. My predecessor had consistently given into his excuses for unfinished work. As things stood, the officer was not much use to me.

One morning at 6 a.m. we were scheduled to go out beyond the sea buoy and rendezvous with other escort vessels in order to pick up a convoy in the Gulf. Four ships would leave Key West at about the same time in tandem. I worked on navigational items such as checking the charts and the rendezvous points until about 2 a.m. in the morning. When I finally finished, I was exhausted. I had taken an apartment in Key West off base so that I could spend some time in the comfort of an apartment rather than in my sack on the ship and that is where I headed to get a few hours sleep before we sailed.

The chief petty officer stopped me as I was about to leave the ship and said, "Captain, the injectors on the diesels are not firing properly. I had to pull all of them and they are spread out on the deck in the engine room. We can't leave at 6 a.m. because the engine is down." I said, "that's an alibi, that's an excuse, and it's not good enough. We are leaving at 6 a.m.."

He warned me, "We'll have to go out on one engine."

I responded, "If we go on one engine, by God, we'll go on one engine. Just make sure that port engine is ready to go. I promise you that if it isn't ready we'll go out anyway."

He said, "You wouldn't do that." I said, "Yeah, I would. Try me. I'm going home . I'll be back at 4 a.m. or 5 a.m. If we go on two engines, fine. If we go on one it won't be fine, but we'll do it."

At around 5 a.m. I returned to the ship and my officer found me and announced with pride, "Miracle, I got the port engine going." I did not think it was a miracle.

So we went to sea at 6 a.m. firing on both engines. As I looked back on that episode while writing this book, I wondered. Where did I find the courage as a young and untried youth to take that kind of risk and hang tough? Though it could be done without too much danger in this case, I had no desire to go out on one engine, but I knew myself well enough to know I did not make empty threats. I also knew my crew. I had never doubted that the chief petty officer could pull it off because I knew how competent he actually was. I also knew that he had not wanted to go to sea because he had a girl friend in Key West.

Anyway, it was an uneventful trip and my chief petty officer never pulled that on me again. He also finished his jobs. Some of his loss of initiative had come from boredom. The fact was he was overqualified for his position on the SC511 and he wanted to serve on a bigger ship. I believed he would do well with the change so I approved his request for promotion and within a month or two he was gone.

The collective spirit of war

My next leadership experience involved an episode in the Port of Cuba's second city fifty or sixty miles up the coast from Guantanamo Bay, where we were temporarily operating. Captain Fuqua, my operational manager there, had told me that he would permit me to go take my ship up the coast and that my men could have an overnight liberty in the second city of Cuba, which was not a bad little place. So off we went, but with a warning. The commander made clear that we had to be shipboard at a designated time. He said, "Wollett, you have to be back the next morning by 8 a.m., no delay, no fooling around. It's 8 a.m. We're escorting a convoy down to Panama. You've got to get the hell out of here and go out and pick up a task force."

"Okay," I assured him, "That's fine, captain. We'll be back." I let as many guys go ashore as I could without jeopardizing the ship's safety and warned them unequivocally when they had to return.

"We're leaving at 6 a.m. in the morning I mean six o'clock. I do not mean one minute after six o'clock. If you're not here we're going to leave you behind, so, show up on time."

The next morning at 6 a.m., I had all the crew on the forward deck along with my leading boson's mate, but one guy was still missing. I reminded the crew of my earlier warning and told them we were leaving without the missing crew member. This stance led to the first strike of my career, at least a facsimile of a strike. My most valuable crew members, the signalman, the radioman, and the quartermaster, refused to leave without the missing crew member no matter what the consequences.

I said, "I gave you an order. This is mutiny." They did not seem to care. They were confident that I could not leave without them because they were not replaceable.

There I was, young and naive, facing my first credible strike threat. I did need them. These particular crew members were highly skilled. I negotiated and gave them 45 minutes to find the missing crew member.

That was the best compromise I could make. I was not making an empty threat. I would have had a hell of a time getting back to Guantanamo without them, but I would have done it. Ultimately, I knew I could not allow them to defy my authority. At the same time, I did not want to leave the wayward crew member behind.

They found their mate in a whorehouse arguing with the madam about a payment he owed her, and they did so within the 45 minute time limit.

There was no preferred right or wrong in this situation. It would be wrong to be late getting back to Guantanamo Bay. It would be wrong to go to sea without my communications department. It would be wrong to leave a crew member behind. It would be wrong to not exert my authority. However, we negotiated and it came out all right. We made a deal. That was as optimal as it was going to get.

I personally admired the loyalty among the crew to one of their own. It was an example of solidarity. However, I had to clearly justify my decision to compromise my authority, at least to myself.

My next leadership test involved another chief petty officer. This more than anything involved the uncertainty of measuring the character of a person.

The crew member had ended up on my ship as a punishment under Navy rules. He had been disciplined for hitting a solider over the head with a full bottle of whiskey in a barroom brawl in Corpus Christi Texas. The man he attacked sustained a skill fracture and died. Under Texas law, the chief petty officer was charged with murder and acquitted, possibly because of the rampant racial prejudice at the time. The guy he killed was Hispanic.

The Navy was not satisfied with civilian law and charged him with gross misbehavior. He ended up in the brig.

He was a model prisoner during his years as an inmate in the

Portsmouth Naval prison in New England so he was given an opportunity, along with other model prisoners, to accept a combat assignment. If he stayed clean, the Navy would forgive the remainder of his sentence.

I told the ex-prisoner that his past was of no concern to me. I intended to treat him the same as the rest of the crew.

We went to British Samoa for an overnight liberty. The new crew member could not believe it when I actually gave him shore leave.

I had made a bad call. The next morning at muster he was not there. After questioning some of the crew members, it turned out he was on the ship, lying incapacitated in the forward berth quarters. I found him flat out hung-over with a bruised eye that was swollen shut.

Within an hour, a whaleboat came along aside carrying three British officers. They asked me if the errant crew member was on board. I answered, yes. They said, "Well, you need to release him to us. He tore up a bar in Nupia British Samoa. Did a lot of damage. Beat up a couple of natives and we want him. We're bringing charges against him."

I refused to turn him over. I said, "He is on my ship so he's my responsibility. However, I'll go with you as an American naval officer to check the situation out."

After investigating the incident I found that he had indeed engaged in a drunken brawl and he had beaten up a guy, causing some serious damage. I made a deal with the British officers and agreed that I would pay for the damages.

As far as I was concerned the matter was ended. It could have been worse except for the fact that the person who was beaten up had beaten my guy even more severely.

However an officer on my ship refused to let go of the matter. He said that the law said we had to report the incident to the commandant in America Samoa because the crew member had broken his probation. He had to be returned to the Portsmouth Naval prison to serve out the rest of his sentence.

I disagreed. He had proven to be an excellent crew member who, whatever his past history, had made a single mistake while on my ship. He needed to be punished, but I was not going to be responsible for his serving ten more years in prison over a barroom brawl.

The officer objected to my decision and we had a heated exchange. I was never one for unnecessarily pulling rank, but I made an exception in this case. I convinced him that if he wanted to make an issue out of this I was willing to go before the commandant and fight it out, but he needed to remember that I held the ultimate power because I outranked him and I would exercise that power if he insisted on treating the crew member unfairly. I made my point and the officer let go of the matter.

The crew member in question went on to have a stellar career in the Navy. He never moved beyond seaman first class, but he knew more about the activities and responsibilities of a deck jockey than anyone on the ship. In fact, he showed good leadership qualities and ended up being the top dog, though without formal authority and without a portfolio.

DRINKING WITH THE ENEMY

The enemy is faceless in war, particularly these days. This was also true at sea. Your enemy is less than human. It is a gray ship that passes in the night or a shape rising from the sea.

In the aftermath of WW11, former enemies attempted to restore meanings abandoned in the inhumane process of war. It has been that way throughout the history of armed combat.

I was alone on deck at 1 a.m. in the morning, surrounded by a vast sea. The sea was not terribly rough that night.

The radar was not operational for some reason. The forward lookout alerted me that he thought he had picked up a surface submarine about a mile north of us.

Key West was an important port primarily because it was a training area for submarine warfare. Two or three American submarines operated in the area. The word was that if you saw a submarine on the surface make sure it is not one of ours. In other words, do not attack without full information. German subs had been fairly active in the area.

I checked the submarine sighting out and sure enough, there was a sub sitting there, barely moving. It was too dark to see its insignia. I sent off a recognition signal and she responded properly, identifying herself as American. That response coupled with the knowledge that this was a sanctuary for American sub training caused me to let it go.

I headed for port and tied up at the place assigned me by the port director. The engines were down and I was ready to head out to my off-base apartment when two intelligence officers came aboard and questioned me, "Captain, did you see a submarine about a mile north of the sea buoy around 1 am in the morning?"

I said, "Yes."

"Did you exchange recognition signals with it?" I answered affirmatively.

Then they asked, "Did she respond properly?"

"I answered positively again.

"So you assumed she was American?"

"That's right."

"Well, Captain," said one of the intelligence officers, "I hate to tell you this, but there were no American submarines out there tonight. It must have been a German U Boat."

My reaction was, "holy shit..."

The standard doctrine on my ship was if we ever caught an enemy submarine on the surface, we would ram them. Of course, my ship would have been destroyed, but my crew and I would have gladly traded one 110-foot wooden ship for a German submarine threatening shipping in the Gulf of Mexico.

Years later, when I was teaching at the University of Washington, I had a class of 10 German students under a contract between the State Department, our law school, and the U.S. State Department. We were at peace with Germany and these young students were going to be lawyers that would help rebuild Germany. I taught these students constitutional law, labor law, and other courses. In the process, I got to know some of them well.

One student was from an aristocratic Prussian family. He was bright and spoke excellent English. I spoke a little German, though not eloquently.

We became beer-drinking friends. One night we were shooting the breeze in a local pub, this is four or five years after the war. We started comparing notes about what we had done in World War 11. I told him I had been in submarine warfare and he said he had served on a German submarine tasked with destroying American shipping. We exchanged notes, where, when, and so on. The evidence grew as we talked. We concluded that there was a better than 50 percent probability that he had been on the submarine in my sights that night.

I thought, I would have killed this guy at the drop of a hat four years ago and he would have killed me. We were blood enemies brought to that point by our respective countries. Now we were beer-drinking pals.

That leads me to a precept that is critical to remember involving negotiations between "natural" adversaries. There is always tomorrow.

Altogether, 111 ships under the American flag were lost in the Gulf Sea Frontier, mostly in 1942 and 1943, including Merchant vessels and tankers. By the end of 1943, the German submarine menace was over. We had beaten them through our convoy system and our pesky little over-armed splinter fleet, though we would have had a hell of a time if a submarine had stayed on the surface and done battle with us. Nevertheless, the numbers in the convoy system caused the Germans to quit. It is a little known chapter of WW11 but it did happen.

It is interesting that our base of operation during WW11 was technically in Key West, but many of our adventures began in Guantanamo Bay, Cuba, a beautiful harbor guarded by submarine nets.

Guantanamo Bay symbolized our war against the German submarines and our ultimate victory. Today, Guantanamo Bay is a dirty word because of choices made by the Bush Administration. However, we were proud to be associated with Guantanamo Bay then because that spot represented an honorable victory. Whatever has happened in the 21st century, this memory of Guantanamo Bay still belongs to those WW11 veterans who hold it close in their memories.

When I left the Subchaser 511 and headed for a new assignment in the Pacific after 16 months of service in Gulf of Mexico, I was the object of a Navy ritual, which was to give a salute to the departing officer. To my surprise, two crew members made a cradle with their arms and carried me ashore followed by the rest of my crew. As far as I know, this was not part of the ritual.

I asked half-jokingly, "What are you doing, trying to get rid of me?"

One of the men that had carried me answered, "No Captain, you carried us for over a year, now it's our turn."

The Navy taught me the obedience of command. The experience also taught me that applying military rule and serving justice through fair judgements are not always the same thing. I had learned something else that made me an excellent negotiator in later years, always be prepared to back up your words with action.

As I subsequently told my students over the years, credibility is like virginity. It is easy to lose and impossible to get back. If you bluff, you lose. I would have left port on one engine.

I WANTED MY LAW STUDENTS TO USE KNOWLEDGE TO THINK INDEPENDENTLY ON THEIR FEET AND PERHAPS THROUGH THEIR ACTIONS SERVE SOME SOCIALLY USEFUL PURPOSE.

3

TEACHING LAW

The war was over and I was now a civilian.

I took advantage of my friendship with Dean Bernard Gavit at Indiana University and asked him to help me find a teaching job close to the sea on the West Coast. He told me that he had limited connections in the western states, but he was able to arrange for me to meet with Judson Falknor, dean of the University of Washington law school in Seattle, Washington, Ray Allen, president of the University, and Nelson Ahlstrom, the University's comptroller.

I was nervous. I had a wife and a new son to take care of and there were many young lawyers back from war and looking for work.

I usually wore bow ties because the collars of my few dress shirts were frayed. I did not feel that a bow tie was appropriate for a job interview so I wore my one straight tie.

I was inordinately pleased with my attention to detail until I walked in the room and saw that all three men wore bow ties. I vowed never again dress to please someone else. I would probably get it wrong.

I was hired on the spot and headed for Seattle with my family.

Seattle was often called the Emerald City. I saw why. It was green, fresh, and relatively easy going compared to the eastern cities. It seemed like a good place to raise my new son, Fritz. Thinking of the times I went to games to watch my dad, I immediately sought out the baseball park where the Seattle Rainiers played. It was a beautiful little ballpark located in the south part of town.

The University of Washington had been established in 1861 with the formation of a marine fishery school. Its law school in 1947 was small with a handful of professors.

I did not start my career at the University of Washington teaching. Instead, I worked in admissions. This was a perfunctory job because at that time anyone who had graduated from an accredited institution with a bachelor's degree was accepted into law school.

It was a transition time for law schools. Particularly small ones like the UW law school. Most schools had experienced a 65 percent student loss because of the war as well as faculty members who were drafted to serve in positions around the world. As the war wore on, the remaining students and faculty struggled with limited resources.

The majority of law schools were unprepared for the exponential increase in students with new needs and a range of orientations following the war. Students flooded the campuses, especially veterans who attended law schools under the GI Bill.

The University of Washington was experimenting with a law school admissions test, but it had not been adopted yet. We had not figured out how to weigh criteria to decide who was accepted into the law school. There was a large gap between getting in and staying in. At the end of the first year, a student might become one of the 35 percent of the class dropped for poor performance.

In terms of admission standards, many believed that the quality of higher education was declining with the groundswell of new students. Dean Falknor, along with other university administrators representing law schools around the country, published an opinion in the *Columbia Law Review* warning that once the veneer of the few best and the brightest students was stripped away, the student body as a whole represented a less than stellar performance.

MY NEW JOB

Eventually, I persuaded Dean Judson Falknor to hire me as an acting assistant professor. I subsequently taught business law and a half-assed labor relations course in the college of business and economics with the promise that I would become full- fledged member of the law faculty the following year.

The University had a three-year law curriculum. The first-year curriculum was torts, contracts, real property, and criminal proce-dure. Torts was my least favorite subject, however, thanks to the teaching of Charles O. Gregory at the University of Chicago, I had a solid and insightful foundation on the subject. Most importantly, I followed the example of my former law professors and made the subject interesting and relevant.

I also incorporated practicalities as well as a sense of ethics in my teaching style. Lyle Bryant, my former economics professor at Bradley, had taught me that the first thing to ask yourself as a teacher is why am I teaching this and why am I teaching it this way. I had not forgotten this lesson. I wanted my students to have reasonable chanc-es at future employment to fill immediate needs. I also wanted them to be able to reflect on how and why they practiced law. I did not want my students to think like a lawyer for the sake of a high-paying job. I wanted them to know the law and then use their knowledge to think independently on their feet and perhaps through their actions sometimes serve some socially useful purpose.

The students liked my classes. It occurred to me that I was a good teacher.

POST-WAR VALUES

I'm not sure how much I enhanced my students' chances in terms of the post-war changing mores of the marketplace given my views on the purpose of a legal education. A high degree of specialization had evolved in law schools even as law schools became more nation-alistic and market-driven.

The discovery during World War II was that universities in general could be "useful," particularly in promoting technological advances. The emphasis was on learning to think like a lawyer as though law were a science according to changing market conditions, which did not make much sense to me.

Taxation and labor law were taught in the second and third years of law school as specialty courses. Criminal Procedure was the only introduction to Constitutional Law. It was quite a change from the value placed on constitutional law occurring during my student days.

I concluded, despite the concerns of Dean Falknor and other university administrators and my own belief that the student body defined the school that, at this juncture, the quality of the incoming student population was less of a detriment than the fact that attitudes were changing from intellectual and humanistic focus to market-driven values. This trend could not be blamed entirely on the loss of resources during WWII. Whatever the reason for the changes in law school education, the economic motives were largely removed from the social values I had been exposed to during my student years.

THE NEW LABOR LAW

I was becoming known as one of a handful of labor law experts in the country during a period when labor law was barely a consideration. There were no guidelines and no precedent. This gave me a unique opportunity to develop a curriculum. I designed labor law courses on arbitration, negotiations, and mediation.

I published a number of papers on seminal subjects related to labor law. I had a particular interest in federal jurisdiction because of Section 301 of the *Taft-Hartley Act*. Harry Wellington and I co-authored an article in the [1]*Stanford Law Review* on the subject. Our article was introduced in a U.S. Supreme Court decision which held that an executory promise to arbitrate was specifically enforceable.

---

1   Wellington, Harry H. and Wollett, Donald H., "Federalism and Breach of the Labor Agreement" (1955). Faculty Scholarship Series. Paper 1966.http://digitalcommons.law.yale.edu/fss_papers/1966

This monumental decision was greatly responsible for the growth of the labor arbitration business. Justice Frankfurter cited our article with approbation. It represented some of my best law review writing.

I had a unique opportunity to shape students' attitudes about labor law. I wanted my students to understand labor law as a distinctly different area of law with a particular perspective on human relations. Most of my students would never meet John L. Lewis, or later Jimmy Hoffa. They would, however, sit at a bargaining table and negotiate contractual arrangements. They would have to deal with compulsory arbitration, strike activities, and whatever else headed their way. Labor law students would also have to be well-versed given the rapid proliferation of statutory language that was impacting this area of practice.

I wanted to send a message to students that they had to be more than a lawyer, whatever their area of law. They had to both educate and mediate. It was clear to me even back then that labor law was a particularly odd fit within an adversarial legal system. I was not the only person in higher education who felt that way. Noting that labor law represented some extreme differences compared to other areas of law, administrators and faculty from different law schools met in 1988 to consider how labor law might be better situated in law school education based on how labor and management actually operated.

CONSTITUTIONAL LAW

While torts and taxation became highly valued subjects, no one wanted to teach the Constitutional Law course. It was nebulous and it was not lucrative in terms of future practice.

Then John Scholly came along and rescued the subject from criminal law until he died unexpectedly from a stroke and I inherited his classes.

I had two problems with my inheritance. First, Scholly died in the middle of the term. Second, he had used his own book to teach the class and it was the only one like it on the market. The problem for me was that his book was not arranged topically or by subject matter.

Instead, it was arranged by epochs: The Taney Court, the Marshall Court, The Hughes Court, the Warren Court, et al.

Students probably learned a lot about American history by studying his writings on the political effects of court decisions. However, they learned little about critical thinking and contemporary understanding. In general, the work deviated from more useful standards that had emerged for teaching constitutional law. I could not change reading materials in midstream so I had to work that much harder while maintaining a full course load.

I continued teaching the Constitutional Law course during the next year and forever after throughout my teaching career. I went on to teach the subject at New York University, Louisiana State University, and at other universities, but I never used Scholly's book again. Many good teaching materials had become available, including my own work.

Homegrown communism

In the post-war era, an increasingly competitive stance with Russia over economic security and a race for scientific innovation and new technologies brought about vilification of "the enemy."

The State might have been tucked away in the furthest northeast corner of the country, but Wobblies, Butts, and other rabble rousers reached the rest of the country with a call-to-arms in the face of hysteria and gross travesties that occurred due to largely unfounded fears about communism, particularly associated with labor.

Albert Canwell, a so-called "journalist" operating out of Spokane, had been publishing a rag that had few followers. This changed when he decided to root out communism in Washington State. Still even with his growing following, my view was that he could print all the hyperbole he wanted without doing much harm.

I had second thoughts regarding my initial impression of his impact on audiences after his election to Washington State's House of Representatives, The once obscure representative from Spokane Washington made impassioned speeches warning of the dangers of communism, now with the support of law.

Washington State passed a law barring communists from holding public office or working in the public sector. The law remained in effect until it was declared unconstitutional by the U.S. Supreme Court in 1967.

Strong warnings were contained in reports, published by the House UnAmerican Activities Committee regarding inquisitions that had taken place in the Northwest. According to these reports, communists were lawless. They knew nothing about due process and would never tolerate anyone who disagreed with their philosophy.

However, due process considerations appeared to mean little to Rep. Albert Canwell, many members of the Washington State Legislature, the University of Washington administration, and even to organizations that purportedly existed to protect human rights and constitutional affairs. This included the American Association of University Professors (AAUP), which had supported academic freedom since 1918. The AAUP expressed dismay over the occurrence of constitutional violations during what became known as the "red hunt", yet took no action. The same could be said of the American Civil Liberties Union (ACLU). Meantime the power of the Canwell Committee grew.

I had some history defending Washington Pension Union (WPU) members. However, there was nothing I could do to stop Rep. Canwell from going after the WPU under the label of communism.

The Canwell Committee's attacks on the WPU significantly impacted the Seattle community. WPU had protected pensions for the elderly and raised funds for under-privileged children. The organization had engaged in reciprocal activities through coalition building in order to efficiently represent a nexus of issues, causes, communities, and organizations. The only way this nonprofit network was allowed to continuing functioning in the face of gross accusations was because the Washington legislature contained enough liberal Democrats who had power and who were concerned with addressing the range of social problems that had amassed following the war.

Additionally, demonstrations took place on the streets of Seattle protesting red scare tactics and the loss of constitutional, rights. Lawyers such as John Caughlan and Kenneth MacDonald, a civil liberties lawyer, turned over their careers in order to represent accused and actual communist party members, and later civil rights activists. Sympathy grew for the people and organizations who were targeted by the committee.

These social forces proved to be problematic for Rep. Canwell and his committee. The Canwell Committee had to refocus or risk losing its momentum. They did this by selectively targeting groups. After all, not all demonstrators could be communists.

The committee, which operated within the Republican controlled state legislature, shifted from the prospect of moving large numbers of reds into prisons to embarrassing liberals at the University of Washington and in the legislature. President Robert Hutchins had dealt with the same tactic at the University of Chicago before WW11. The committee targeted the weakest link which was professors in higher education since it was doubtful that the general population would be much interested in their plight given a general national distrust of intellectuals.. Union members and university professors alike were ordered to appear before the Canwell Committee.

The Canwell hearings bore little resemblance to an inquiry. As the chief inquisitor, Canwell would bang his gavel over any perceived offense to his unwavering belief that fugitive communist types lurked in the shadows and on the Capitol steps. Aided by the highway patrol, victims and their lawyers who appeared to disagree with his beliefs, were indiscriminately thrown out of the courtroom.

John Caughlan recalled that the hearings were,

> ...an amazing display of the arrogance of small people who suddenly feel invested with the power of the state... The honest thing, Caughlan concluded, would have been for me to tell my] clients that a lawyer will do them no good in these proceedings because due process didn't apply here.

The University of Washington Board of Regents and university president, Ray Allen, refused to defend either alleged pink or red faculty members.

When Senator Thomas Bienz, a Republican from Spokane, claimed that 150 communists or communist sympathizers taught at the University of Washington, the University administration assured him that it would recommend dismissal of anyone "found by the Canwell Committee to be engaged in subversive activities."

Three faculty members were brought before the UW Faculty Tenure Committee operating under the University's shared governance structure. The committee recommended that two of the three suspected communists keep their job. The third should be fired for "lying" about his affiliations. Historically, faculty committee recommendations carried some weight however in this case President Ray Allen, and the Board of Regents ignored the committee's recommendation and fired all the professors. The University of Washington became the first university in the country to actually fire professors accused of communism. One professor went on welfare, the two others went on to relatively menial jobs. None of them taught again

President Ray Allen's reasoning behind the firings reflected the typical thought of the day regarding the greatest danger of communism:

> Freedom is the most important ingredient of a university and of a democracy and a member of the Communist Party is not a free man... Educational institutions can prosper only as they maintain free teaching and research... a member of the Communist Party is ... a slave to immutable dogma and to a clandestine organization masquerading as a political party.

Shock waves from Washington State reached a good friend of mine, Vern Countryman, who was dismayed about what was happening in his home state. Vern had become a nationally known bankruptcy scholar who had been mentored by William O. Douglas and a respected academic.

Vern was a vigorous supporter of academic freedom. Having grown up in the Seattle area, he wrote his only book on the subject, titled, *UnAmerican Activities in the State of Washington: The Work of the Canwell Committee (1951)*, while an assistant professor at Yale.

He was denied tenure because of this book and other writings. Yale's president, A. Whitney Griswold over-rode the law school's recommendation for tenure, claiming that the book did not have sufficient academic quality.

Many law school faculty members knew that the academics behind the book were good and that Countryman's loss of tenure had to do with his strong political views on red hunt happenings in his home state. During those red hunting years, I remember sitting in a faculty meeting the year I taught at Harvard. President Griswold, was also at the meeting when Vern referred to the president's selective liberality, "gentlemen, we have too many conservatives on this committee, we need some liberals." Someone said, "you mean like Vern Countryman." Vern answered roundly, "yes."

Vern was down, but not out. He resigned and joined the Harvard Law School Faculty where he went on to a great career.

Faculty members in higher education did not generally mount much of a protest against what was happening to fellow faculty members and others across the country. When the word spread concerning what had happened to Vern, Addison Mueller, a friend, was the only contemporary to offer a serious protest. Mueller had graduated first in his class at Yale and was well-known for shaping contract law. His book, *Contract in Context* (1951) was widely used by law students across the country.

When Countryman was denied tenure, Mueller resigned and urged the law school faculty to walk away with him, even at the risk of losing their tenure. There were no takers. Addison Mueller later joined the UCLA faculty and did quite well.

THE LOYALTY OATH

In 2013, Washington State still had a cold war loyalty oath. Attempts to take it off the books that year failed. Around 13 states still have laws for anti-subversive oaths.

As professors or k-12 teachers, we were required to swear that we were not a "subversive person." We would not "commit, or advise, teach, abet or advocate another to commit or aid in the commission of any act intended to overthrow or alter, or assist in the overthrow or alteration, of the constitutional form of government by revolution, force or violence." "Subversive organization" and "foreign subversive organization" were defined in similar terms and the Communist Party was designated as a subversive organization.

The idea of swearing fealty to the government was not new, but it was and is still used preemptively with no clear and present danger in sight.

I cannot remember whether I signed a loyalty oath or not while teaching at the University of Washington, but I must have. Signing a loyalty oath didn't seem like a big deal, but if you did not sign you would be fired. That is how Charles (Chuck) Davenport, a fellow professor at the University of California Davis, remembers it. You sign a bunch of papers, you keep your job, and you go on to more important matters. It is only later that you see the import of the act on what this country stands for - such things as freedom and democracy.

The question of loyalty oaths is not an artifact of history. In fact, looking at 2013 in the post 9/11 world the practice seems to be on the rise as proposed bills come before the different state legislatures. The subject surfaces targeting different groups, ranging from debate in 2011 as to whether Israel should impose a loyalty oath or whether U.S. organizations should impose loyalty oaths on other organizations helping sex workers as a condition of aid or support. In 2006, Ohio re-invigorated a subversive portion of the loyalty oath. Arizona considered a 2013 bill where all high school students must sign a loyalty oath in order to graduate. The language read, "I take this obligation freely." Logic apparently escaped the Arizona legislature. Clearly, it is not "freely" if one can't graduate because he or she refuses to take the oath.

During the McCarthy era, my friend and fellow faculty member, Arval Morris, represented professors and others who protested signing a loyalty oath in *Baggett v. Bullitt*. This was a class action suit for a judgment declaring unconstitutional 1931 and 1955 state statutes that required loyalty oaths from teachers and other state employees as a condition of employment. The suit was brought by the ACLU and the University of Washington's chapter of the American Association of University Professors(AAUP) and included members of the faculty, staff, and students.

The 1955 loyalty oath for University of Washington professors and other state employees incorporated provisions of the State's 1931 Subversive Activities Act. The act was useful to those who would curtail academic freedom because it was vague and open-ended. It was trotted out during the Canwell Committee hearings.

Arval Morris, Byron Coney, and Kenny MacDonald became involved when a three-judge District Court held that the Washington State statutes did not violate the First and Fourteenth Amendments where the constitution offers Americans the freedom of speech and association, except associations with people conducting a criminal act, and speech that extends to "fighting words," inciting a riot or other forms of speech that might lead to violence. As we know, these days the term "criminal act" has undergone significant change.

I should note that language contained in 21st Century Patriot Act is similar to language found in the 1931 Subversive Activities Act with the addition of perhaps more frightening elements found in vague definitions such as "material support." Today, all this preemption is confusing and not only beyond the ken of average people, but of people such as myself who supposedly know the law. Any of us might or might not find ourselves an enemy of the state because we are on the wrong side of a moral judgment.

Anyway, *Baggett v. Bullitt* dragged on for seven years until in 1962 the Supreme Court handed down a decision calling for an injunction. The injunction was dissolved and the University of Washington board of regents gave faculty members 30 days to sign a loyalty oath or be fired.

Following another injunction, the Supreme Court decided in 1964 that the loyalty oath was unconstitutional. A number of states fell in line with the Court's decision. On the day of the 1964 Supreme Court ruling, Arval Morris told *The Seattle Times* with his usual passion that the decision "reaffirmed an honored tradition in American law," which he depicted as the "conviction that governmental coercion of opinion is a mistake."

It is a "mistake" we continue to repeat.

The real threat to this country was not communism, but from within. On one occasion Dean Judson Falknor asked for my advice regarding a student group. By this time he had become a friend and I was half in love with his daughter, Sara. A group of students had informed him that they wanted meeting space in the law school for a new student chapter of the National Lawyer's Guild (NLG). This was a radical organization in that era's terms. Jud was concerned because he did not want the same problems of student unrest that the University of California system was experiencing.

The NLG had visions of becoming a viable liberal and humane alternative to the American Bar Association (ABA), which it viewed as placing too great an emphasis on property rights and laissez-faire economics over human rights. The NLG was a strong proponent of the New Deal philosophy. In many ways the organization was ahead of its time. For instance, it was the first racially integrated bar association in the country while the ABA was still segregated at the time.

While I liked some of the group's ideals, I was primarily concerned with protecting Jud's interest, which was to maintain a smooth running institution.

I was informed by a reliable source that the students' demand was instigated by the NLG because it was struggling to survive. One member in particular hoped to embarrass the law school with the knowledge that Jud, a prominent and conservative Republican who had once run for lieutenant governor, would refuse the students' request. If Jud said, "no," then the lawyer and his political cohorts could claim a violation of academic freedom, freedom of association, and all those good things.

I informed Jud of this and suggested that he circumvent the lawyer's plan and give the students whatever they wanted. I assured him that the student's hoped for organization on campus would not happen. Jud agreed, but said that I had to be their faculty sponsor and their advisor. The first organizational meeting was pathetic. Almost nobody showed up and the organization died

However, my brief involvement in the NLG made me the object of investigation years later when I was under consideration for a political job. I learned for the first time that I had two strikes against me in the marketplace. I had attended one meeting of the North American Committee for the Preservation of Spanish Democracy and I had served as a student advisor to the NLG, which had been labeled at some point as a left wing organization and placed on the Attorney General's subversive list. This stuff seemed absurd at the time. It seems less absurd these days.

I was somewhat disturbed over these incursions into my rights and the rights of others so I, Kenny McDonald, and other Seattle lawyers successfully reactivated the Washington Chapter of the American Civil Liberties Union (ACLU).

Threats to the Constitution, including loyalty oaths that imposed strict rules on even indirect associations in words or deeds with organizations suspected of communism, along with a growing consciousness of racial discrimination, radicalized students and many professors across the country. I was still teaching at the University of Washington when student unrest reached a point where it was a serious management issue for many school administrations.

Clark Kerr, the president of University of California, Berkeley, and I had initially come to know and respect each other over some Pac-10 antics engaged in by our respective schools. I empathized with Clark's situation. He had upheld academic values and maintained a manageable administration despite widespread criticism. This included containing student unrest to a reasonable extent. I doubt if history has truly captured all the routine details of Clark Kerr's management challenges including the agonizing he shared with me over what to do about the widespread use of the word "fuck."

Unlike President Ray Allen at the University of Washington, Clark Kerr roundly defended 60 of his professors accused of communist affiliations because they refused to sign a loyalty oath. He gained a lot of media attention and was further vilified as a result. Partly because of this support, UC Berkeley professors held onto their academic careers, unlike the sad fate of the three University of Washington professors.

As far as I know, I never became a communist, but then similar to the word "terrorist" it is a convenient term, so maybe I did. I did become pinker as I aged.

I THOROUGHLY STUDIED ALL THE CASES, INCLUDING EVERY FOOTNOTE. ARCHIE COX HAD TRAINED HIS LAW STUDENTS TOO WELL. THE FOOTNOTE BATTLE BEGAN.

4

Second String at Harvard

I took over Archibald Cox's classes of around 70 second and third-year students for almost a year while he serve on the War Labor Board during the Korean War.

I had come to know Archie after enticing him to come to the University of Washington as a visiting professor. He accepted and taught

torts and labor law. Archie's Ivy League teaching style was a new experience for my students. He was one of the foremost experts on the Socratic method and demanding of students.

We became close friends and spent some our spare time exploring Washington State which thrilled Archie.

ARCHIBALD COX

Archie helped direct my career by sharing his valuable connections. He also encouraged me to become actively involved with key organizations on the forefront of labor relations. This included the Labor Law Group (LLG) founded in 1947. The LLG was instrumental in formulating the new field of labor law education. I also joined the Labor and Employment section of the American Bar Association at Archie's urging. He served six terms as secretary for the group and I served the position for two terms.

Dean Erwin Griswold at Harvard once described Archie as one of the few men who could do it all. This was an apt description.

Archie was more than a lawyer. His interest in public service took him into governmental and political realms. His strong sense of commitment came from a family heritage that had passed down the belief that a lawyer's duty was public service.

Archie was in demand as a consultant. He offered a deep and well- tested knowledge of behavior that helped others see the bigger picture in labor relations. For instance, he knew how big union guys actually behaved which gave him a good sense of what was coming down the pipeline. Few lawyers or academics possessed that kind of street knowledge.

He believed that a good lawyer had a responsibility to educate others. This could be challenging. On one occasion he attempted to educate the Kennedy Administration about how labor leaders behaved. He warned the Administration that overlooking winks and nods in its negotiations with big labor would lead to union ploys akin to Khrushchev banging his shoe, but no one listened.

Khrushchev, he said, had it right: cut off the smallest possible slice at a time. Sometimes it was a way of achieving broader goals that perhaps you couldn't achieve if you sought to achieve them in broad legal terms. This maxim guided his work and mine.

Archie often reminded me that when it came to grievance arbitrations, disciplinary cases always turned on facts peculiar to the grievant.

Archie's obituaries were all over the Internet. Most accounts highlighted his role in the Saturday Night Massacre when Archie stood up to Nixon and refused to accept abridged damning tapes. That incident is how he is frequently remembered. When I think of that event, I think of his positive influence in so many other areas. From my perspective as a teacher it is reassuring to know that many hundreds of students passed through Archie because his ethics were impeccable.

Summarily, his contributions to labor law as perhaps the leading expert on the subject during a particular era; before and immediately after passage of the National Labor Relations Act (NLRA) are incalculable .

THE FOOTNOTE BATTLE

Archie's students included Derek Bok, who later taught labor law at Harvard, became its Dean, and finally president of Harvard, and Harry Wellington who eventually became dean of the law school at Yale. These students represented the caliber of many of Archie's students.

I suspected his students would be a tough sell and they were. They adeptly challenged everything I had learned about law.

The night before I taught my first class I said to my wife, "Mary, I've heard that Harvard law students are the pick of the New England Brahman crop. I am going to find out if that is true."

I introduced myself to the students with an analysis of decision by Associate Justice Felix Frankfurter. I chose Justice Frankfurter partially because he was my hero and more to the point because he was a Harvard product. Archie had taken his class as a student at Harvard and argued before him on several occasions.

Following the lead of my former professor, William Crosskey, I made sure everyone was awake by immediately disassembling Justice Frankfurter's logic associated with particular cases. Perhaps what I should have remembered was the genesis of the class intellect. As Archie knew, we are products of our training and we pass this history on to our students.

Archie had been first in Felix Frankfurter's classes. Professor Frankfurter's style was to take the few top students and direct most of the questions to the hierarchy of students. This meant that most of the questions were directed to Archie. He recalled that was around 50 to 60 percent of the questions. The second top student would have the next highest percentage of questions, then the third and so on. Whatever questions remained went to the rest of the students.

Justice Frankfurter had a particular style both as a professor of law and as a justice. Archie described it this way:

Frankfurter could be most annoying with his questions I was inclined to think that the case was one of those that might very well turn on whether I came out even with Felix Frankfurter in the oral argument, whether he'd demolish me with his questions or whether I stood my ground sufficiently that if it were called a debate or a prizefight, it would be a tie.

...As I was about halfway through developing the first point, Felix asked --he raised the second major point. And I said, as I regularly did, 'our answer to that will be thus and so. I planned to develop it in the second part of my argument.' Ordinarily, a law professor would let you go back to the thread of your agreement. But not Frankfurter. He persisted. It got so bad that I did something I would not ordinarily do. I said, 'your honor, to answer your honor in full requires me to cease developing my argument on the first half of the case, and shift to the second, and I assure you I will come to it.' No, he insisted that I deal with his part then and there.

And that is exactly what Archie's students did to me in the footnote war.

I invited questions as I typically did. Several students asked me general questions about my lecture. This was followed by more questions about some of my specific criticisms of Associate Justice Frankfurter's decisions.

One student demonstrated his skill by offering supportive arguments for a Fifth Circuit decision regarding a case and set forth a well-developed position contrary to Justice Frankfurter's decision. The student then went on to make some argumentative comments, substantiating this with footnotes. He implied that, in relation to my criticisms, I did not know what I was talking about.

After the first student's challenge, another student asked me about another case and delved into more footnotes. This onslaught went on for about a half an hour.

This was the only group of law students I had run across that had the wherewithal to conduct a careful reading of footnotes.

But I wondered, why footnotes? Perhaps the students wanted to know whether this young professor was just glib or whether I was someone from an obscure law school who actually knew the subject of labor law. What better way than the detail found in footnotes.

I had hoped to make a good impression on my first class to establish the tone of my visiting professorship. But at this point I was feeling a bit disassembled. I had thoroughly studied all the cases I planned to present, including every footnote. I believed I was ready to respond to any sensible response. I was unprepared for the students' volleys.

The student siege felt orchestrated. I began to suspect a well-planned conspiracy. I took a chance and called the class on what I viewed as a footnote war. I said that I believed that they had conspired to back me against a wall. The students confessed they had.

Twelve of Archie's student had divided all footnotes and pertinent questions addressed in the casebook among themselves. The remainder of the students were out of the loop but appreciated the entertainment. The revelation that I had been set up was followed by a lot of laughter, including mine. Archie had taught them well.

I had won their respect. The word spread among the rest of Archie's students that I was credible. I was not a megalomaniac like the professor in "The Paper Chase." I knew my subject. I did not make students look bad. I had no displays of temper, real or contrived. I promoted healthy exchanges between people who wanted answers in order to learn more. I also made an effort to learn my students' names. I treated the students as adults.

After my introduction to Archie's students, my Harvard teaching experience went well. Through the practice of inquiry, we learned something each day about each other and some critical understanding of our respective positions. This helped us get along, which is the point of law in my view.

I was sorry when Archie returned to Harvard to reclaim his class. I had enjoyed myself and though my time was short at Harvard I had made a difference. I exchanged letters over the years with students such as Derek Bok and enjoyed following their respective careers. My friendships with several students including Derek Bok and Harry Wellington, continued throughout my retirement.

RETURNING TO SEATTLE

During my tenure at the University of Washington Law School I had developed, as far as I know, the first curriculum of its kind in any law school.

Cornelius (Neil) Peck, an assistant professor, had been hired to replace me while I was gone. Neil took over my torts classes and carried forward the courses that I had initially established in the law school, including labor law, arbitration, and a course in negotiations.

Neil and I became close friends. In 1962, he co-authored a supplement to my book, *[1]Labor relations and the Law, 2nd edition*. Benjamin Aaron and I had compiled a first edition which was published in 1960 as part of a series introduced by the Labor Law Group.

Neil and I served on many committees together as more or less kindred souls. Neil was a gentleman and a scholar and one of the finest teachers I have ever known.

Like Archie Cox, Neil made heavy use of the Socratic method to particularly address a point of ignorance. A student once told me that Neil's teaching style intimidated him. Neil grilled students and forced them to think based on the reality that there is always more than one answer.

---

1   Wollett, Donald H. & Aaron, Benjamin. Labor Relations and the Law. Little, Brown & Company, 1960.

THE STARS SWEPT THE FLOOR AT HALF-TIME...
IT WAS GOOD THEATRE.

5

SKIRMISHES WITH THE NCAA

Telegram - To: Donald Wollett School of Law, University of Washington, Seattle, From: Brad Booth – "Congratulations: when the law goes to hell you can make a fortune as a salesman."

All university faculty must be involved at some point in extracurricular activities. I met that obligation when President Dr. Henry Schmitz, appointed me chairman of the finance committee of the Associated Students of the University of Washington (ASUW).

My job was to represent the University in the Pacific Coast Conference and with the National Collegiate Athletic Association (NCAA).

I was for the most part a genial fellow, well-liked and generally respected. My perennial bow tie and off-the-cuff humorous, and sometimes irreverent, comments spiced up the local media.

I had a large private office and my own secretary. These perks along with my media interactions relieved some of the boring aspects of academic life, e.g., faculty meetings.

Football and, to a much lesser degree, basketball subsisted on the passion and patriotism of fervent alumni, some with deep pockets. Despite the carefully cultivated fiction that the sports programs were run by academics, administrators and faculty usually went along for the ride.

The faculty representative for football was an odd creature. In those days, it may not be true now, the faculty representative held an exalted position as the president's exclusive agent. I could only be over-ruled by the president himself. To emphasize the scope of my power, it was fashionable to run a full-page portrait of the faculty representative in the football program for home games.

I was the go-to person when anything broke in the media, especially scandals surrounding student-athletes. I was quoted in the national media not because of my role in the rapidly evolving field of labor law or as a reflection of my efforts to help build the University of Washington law school, but because of college football scandals.

DEEP POCKETS

I use the term "student-athlete" because it is a familiar term, though not necessarily reflective of a balance between access to academic opportunities and athletic prowess.

The term did not exist until the Wisconsin widow of Ray Dennison, a player for the Fort Lewis A&M Aggies, sued for workman's compensation and lost. The Colorado Supreme Court ruled that since the college did not benefit from football there was no entitlement to compensation. The NCAA at that point invented the nebulous term "student-athlete" to support its position. Until then there were no student-athlete grants-in-aid or scholarships. It did not take long for these revenue sources to come into play with their accompanying scandals.

What we did at the University of Washington was to provide football and basketball players with phony jobs subsidized by alumni. I have forgotten the rate of pay but it was far in excess of what they were worth to the extent that they were worth anything.

It was good theatre. Football and basketball stars swept the floor at half-time to demonstrate that our athletes were hard-working students earning their way through school when the truth was they were getting money from the infamous Greater Washington Advertising Fund, which had been slipping cash to university football players on a regular basis. It was not a fortune, to be sure, but any amount was illegal under Pacific Coast Conference and NCAA rules.

THE MERCY STRATEGY

As the new faculty representative, my first legal argument of notable interest regarding the University's scandalous behavior was a hearing by the infractions committee of the NCAA held in Lexington, Kentucky.

Abe Kirwan, a history professor and former football coach, who later became president of the University of Kentucky at Lexington, chaired the committee which had been impaneled in 1951 before NCAA had any legitimacy in regard to football infractions. This meant the committee had been formed without the full convention of NCAA schools. The panel was not inclined toward forgiveness or due process for that matter.

I came before the committee to respond to charges that the University of Washington had violated NCAA rules governing financial aid to athletes. I had nothing to say to the panel - no confessional, no brilliant legal thinking. The University was guilty as charged and the whole matter seemed like a joke. All I could do was ask for the committee's mercy while swearing that we had learned our lesson. We would never, ever do it again. Of course, we did.

The University of Washington was not the only transgressor. The University of Southern California, the University of California, Los Angeles (UCLA), and the University of California, Berkeley, were punished by the NCAA and the Conference for similar offenses. We were all put on probation and declared ineligible for bowl games. UCLA received the severest punishment when the board suspended it for six months. Stanford remained disgustingly clean.

Harvey's Dilemma

The fallout from the UW football scandals was much more than a media event. It affected (or in some cases infected) good people such as the University's athletic director, Harvey Cassill. Harvey was one of the straightest people I had ever met.

Harvey was someone who saw football as a way to build character. In my view, he was an excellent athletic director for that reason. Despite his unwavering allegiance to his players, he never allowed them to escape their responsibility to the University.

For example, Harvey's job included reporting expenses to me when I was chairman of the ASUW finance committee. In one instance, the team's return from a football game over in eastern Washington against Washington State was delayed by bad weather so the team spent an extra night in a motel in Corte d'Alene Idaho. The rates were cheap, but Harvey presented me with a bill for several thousand dollars. When I questioned the unusual expense Harvey said that the team members had destroyed their hotel rooms while they were celebrating their victory. The room assigned to our star quarterback and running back were the hardest hit.

Harvey was furious with the team members because he felt they had dishonored the University. He wanted the players to be punished and he reasonably expected that would happen. However, when he approached Howard O'Dell, who was the coach at the time, with the demand that the two star football players be punished, the coach refused his request. He explained to Harvey that since they were the stars on the team, disciplining them would damage the morale of the entire team. Harvey did not buy this argument. He was outraged and refused to back away from his demand for some form of punishment.

I had already left for my visiting professorship at Harvard when this occurred. Nevertheless, I kept a long distance eye on happenings in Seattle. I suspected that Harvey would lose the dispute.

I viewed the confrontation as symptomatic of more serious divisions within the UW football program. I had already guessed that there would be casualties and that one of these casualties might be Harvey.

As the University's football news filtered to the East over the next weeks, I came to believe that, somewhat ironically, the Huskies' coach, Howard O'Dell, was in even deeper trouble over the incident. After refusing Harvey's request to punish the stars, the general impression among academics and the public was that O'Dell had allowed the players to dishonor the university and therefore in a very real sense the State of Washington.

As the press, including national publications such as *Time Magazine*, exploded on the subject of illegal payments to football players at the University of Washington and elsewhere, Harvey ended up in the middle of the University's scandals as one of the perpetrators.

Was he entirely blameless? I was never sure. but I believed that he was innocent for the most part. I am sure the national exposure cut him deeply.

Since there was no real evidence of his guilt, I had always wondered whether it was Harvey Cassill's extraordinary loyalty to the University of Washington that caused him to resign in the face of scandals involving under the table compensation or was he was forced to resign.

In any case, Harvey had backbone, but he also had what seemed to me to be an excessive loyalty to the institution that led to a strong belief that the University could not do anything wrong. This blind spot colored his judgment and eventually heightened his sense of betrayal. It was painful to watch.

The way the story unfolded was that Harvey had fired a University of Washington alumnus named Johnny Cherberg who was O'Dell's successor as football coach for reasons unrelated to any scandals. But, after Johnny was fired, he misplaced his good judgment and publicly accused most of the team and team supporters of illegal payments. He also singled out some wealthy alumni who had been careless about displaying their transactions of money to players. His accusations were generally true, but the fallout was not necessarily fair.

The press never understood, or perhaps even cared about, the real reason Harvey terminated Cherberg. It had nothing to do with alumni money to players. Cassill had fired Cherburg because after a game that we should have tied or perhaps won, Cherburg slapped a player for a misplay and this cost us the game. One of Harvey's rules was that coaches never physically abuse players. They run them, but they do not touch them. Johnny Cherberg did not follow the same rule.

I cannot recall all the charges and counter charges that were made, but it was scapegoatism. Cherberg ended up being a fall guy and so did Harvey, though there was no real evidence either was guilty in relation to the student-athlete scandals. The official university line regarding under the table compensations from alumni was that the University had been the victim of errant behavior by a couple of employees. Cherberg was fired.

Harvey Cassill was not fired probably only because he took the University off the hook by resigning. I had some cause to suspect that the real truth was somewhere up the line of authority and involved both the Board of Regents and the University's vice president. However, I do not think President Henry Schmitz, was involved.

I did what I could to mitigate the situation by asking Phil Cartwright, dean of arts and sciences, and chair of the faculty athletic committee, to call a meeting. The purpose was to conduct a general critique of the football program and identify those who were actually involved in corruption, no holds barred. Let us go where the facts take us no matter how high they go. I believed Harvey would be exonerated in the process.

I warned Harvey about what I planned to do. With a worried look on his face he asked for a private meeting. We met in my law school office on a Saturday afternoon. He begged me not to go forward with my plan. Harvey sat there, my good friend, whom I had always admired as a courageous guy, with tears in his eyes. I knew he was not thinking of himself or speaking from guilt when he asked me not to bring further notoriety to the school he loved.

I was convinced that Harvey had promised someone high up the food chain that he would resign. For one thing, he was vulnerable. He had high blood pressure. His wife was ill. In any case, he was close to a sensible retirement age. I was sure that there was a quid pro quo attached to Harvey's resignation that I never uncovered. My guess is that somebody on the board of regents, perhaps more than one person, guaranteed him a retirement stipend if he would keep quiet and take the deal.

I could not say no to Harvey. I asked Phil Cartwright to call off my request to convene a committee.

During my years teaching in higher education, I would find that scapegoatism was a familiar institutional strategy when something grossly embarrassing occurred. Find a scapegoat. Hang it on him or her. Buy silence with some kind of convenient and palatable financial arrangement.

I have no hard evidence that this was the deal here, but every instinct told me it was and the facts that I did have were consistent with that thesis. I believe from things Harvey said that Ed Guthman, a first class reporter in Seattle, knew the truth, but never published it.

George Briggs was named as Harvey Cassill's successor. He had been an assistant athletic director at UC Berkeley and he had a good reputation. However, he lacked Harvey's experience and his passion which drove his team to do their best.

FOOTBALL MADNESS

Harvey Cassill and Johnny Cherburg were not the only ones under attack. Torchy Torrance, a prominent citizen and an alumnus had been responsible for the successful recruitment of the university's star player, Hugh Mcelhenny. He had managed to steal the star player from under the nose of the University of Southern California and stash him at Compton Junior College so he could pull up his grades.

Torchy received some bad press because of his "contributions" to football over the years, but cast in another light he had also helped many hard-up players over the years. Torchy remained a prominent citizen in Seattle and a good friend of mine.

I had told the NCAA infractions committee back in Lexington Kentucky that we had learned our lesson. The NCAA fractions committee had asked me during our hearing if I thought we had control of our program. I gave the Committee a convincing, yes. I assured its members that Dr. Schmitz had directed me as his representative to make sure that this kind of thing never happened again, and so, I had promised him that it never would happen again. I made that same representation to the Pacific Coast Conference schools when we were on the grid for illegal financial aid to athletes, particularly football players. My intentions were good, if a bit naive.

I monitored the situation carefully. This included interviewing athletes to see if we were keeping our nose clean as we had promised the Conference and the NCAA. Then several athletes I interviewed mentioned that they had received money from the Bank of Commerce, which had a branch in the University District.

One of the athletes assured me, "It's all right, it's legal." I asked, "How do you know that?" One athlete answered, "Oh, I signed a promissory note." I responded, "You what! You signed a promissory note? To whom?" He said, "the Evergreen Educational Foundation."

I immediately called Briggs and asked him, "George, what the hell are you doing? You've got us right back into the honey pot for Christ's sake." George said, "Well, they all signed promissory notes. We did that at Berkeley." I said, "George, those notes are worthless. We'll go right now, we'll drive down to the University District to the National Bank of Commerce. We'll ask the bank to buy the notes and they will laugh us out of the room."

He said, "You're right." Then I said, "George, soon we're going another conference meeting. Do you expect me to defend this?" His answer was, "well maybe they won't find out." I said, "The faculty rep at the University of Oregon, Orlando Hollis, lives to stick it in my ear and he hates our guts because we voted against Oregon being in the Rose Bowl a few years ago. They have a hard-on. They are going to be after us and if they'll find out about this, we're done. We need a strategy to protect our athletes and the University." Then, I laid out my plan.

" Tell me how many guys got this illegal money and signed these phony promissory notes." He said, "I think, 27." I said, "Okay, at the start of the conference meeting in two weeks, which is going to be in Southern California at the Beverly Hills Hilton, I will announce: ' I regret to say I have discovered that 27 football players at the University of Washington are ineligible for competition' They'll want to know why. I'll refuse to tell them, just that it is my judgment that the players are not in compliance with the rules of the Conference nor the rules of the University and I am therefore exercising my authority and declaring them ineligible. Never excuse, never explain. Just tell them you are sorry.

"The predictable response will be that we will have no football team for the coming season. I will say, 'that's right. We'll have to cancel.' Do you think that USC or any of those California institutions are going to support cancellation of our football season? We've got the only stadium outside of California that's big enough to have a decent gate. The faculty will ask me to recant. Not for one or two players, they're not going to cherry pick. All 27 have to be forgiven. That's the position we've got to take. If we shut our mouths and do this right, this will work."

The strategy worked. Even Orlando Hollis bought into it.

As I said I would do, I refused to give details. I simply said, "You've got to trust me, guys. I'm asking you to respect my word. I assure you there is nothing criminal. I am a lawyer. I believe in the law. But those guys are ineligible to play ball unless the Conference chooses to pardon them, in which case, we'll reinstate them."

That is what happened. We had our season and our football players and that was the end of it.

The whole deal sounds more dramatic than it was. There was not that great a risk. I knew the University of Washington would never cancel its football season. Too much money was involved. Alumni, the Conference schools, and the community would not have allowed it. It was not going to happen.

If I had not taken action, the truth about student-athlete compensations would have come out in dribs and drabs. Too many people knew about the promissory notes and the media would have had a story with legs. I was sure that Victor Schmidt, the conference commissioner, would nose around to see if we were behaving ourselves and find ways that we were not. Somebody would say something and once again we would be in the middle of a widely publicized scandal. Even more innocent people would be hurt.

As it stood, everything broke our way. Thanks to my strategy, we received an unconditional pardon for unknown sins.

George Briggs was not implicated in any kind of improper activity, nor should he have been.

A few years later, George resigned as athletic director and became an officer of a major west coast bank. I thought, Jesus, this is the guy who tried to claim it was legal to have promissory notes executed by penniless football players to some phony organization.

I had a lawyerly knack for circumventing problems, but at times I would forget a cardinal rule for lawyers, which is do not take the client where he (or she) has not agreed to or is not ready to go.

Joe Kaplan, a renowned physicist, quit his position as UCLA's faculty representative. Brad Booth, a professor of English, replaced him. Brad and I took to each other at once. With a jaundiced eye, we agreed that major intercollegiate athletics was too dependent on underpaid professional entertainers. They were enrolled in universities as "students" but the vast majority of them had no hope of at least reasonable future earnings because of lack of support for their academic performance.

It was shameful how intercollegiate athletes earned so much money for their schools and received relatively small grants in aid, athletic scholarships, and illegal alumni gifts that carried risks for them in return. The whole deal was hypocritical.

We believed that reform was called for. The minimum change would be that the members of the Pacific Coast Conference pay the maximum permitted by the NCAA.

However, we did not think it was likely that Conference members would support such a reform. USC was the only interested school. Stanford was not. UC Berkeley was not. The smaller schools such as Washington State, Oregon State, and the University of Oregon were not either.

Brad and I decided that a dramatic event would shake things up. The tactic was to have the University of Washington publicly withdraw from the Conference without notice at its next meeting. I even convinced George Briggs that this was a viable strategy and the only course we could take. Nothing was going to happen otherwise.

I drafted a resolution which I called, "the bomb" for George to read at the upcoming Conference meeting in Spokane and told him to present it to the other athletic directors at the meeting.

George lost his nerve and the "bomb" stayed in his pocket. In retrospect, he was right and I was wrong. It is not that my strategy was not sound. While I had a lot of leeway, we had not cleared this radical position with the University of Washington president or with the Board of Regents. Without their support, it was drama without substance. We would have looked very foolish. I had over-stepped my client (the University) because I thought I knew what was best.

Ironically, while the University of Washington stayed put because we did not take action, UCLA made its move without us and withdrew from the Conference in a well-publicized event. Later we also left the Conference.

MORE MADNESS

My nemesis, Orlando Hollis, had been faculty representative for the University of Oregon during the same years that I had served that role at the University of Washington. Though we competed against each other and agreed on very little, I respected him. As a lawyer he was able and tough minded. As an educator, he had strong principles and the courage to adhere to them.

I also appreciated the fact that Orlando was a visionary. He wanted the University of Oregon law school to become the "Harvard of the West" – hard to get in and hard to stay in because of high standards of performance.

But football is its own force and it does not bring out the best in people. In an unguarded moment, Orlando somewhat shamefacedly shared a story with me.

He and Leo Harris, Oregon's athletic director, became convinced that their football coach, Jim Aikens, was running an illegal summer practice. In order to get firsthand proof they crawled on their bellies through an adjacent field to spy on him. They did catch the coach in the act, but I don't remember what they did about it.

I remember thinking to myself that here was a person who was an exemplar for the law and for the best in legal education. He had imposed strict decorum on his students, sometimes to an extreme. Orlando had rules for everything including dress and appearance. In fact, he admitted to me that he had sent a student from the classroom for not wearing a jacket the day before he decided to crawl through the grass. He lost it all to the madness of football.

Is football an invasive species with the capacity to permeated the brain matter of the most logical and brilliant faculty and administrators?

Why so many American colleges and universities, presumably educational institutions, remain in the entertainment business remains a puzzle to me. Robert Hutchins at the University of Chicago did not see the sense of it nor did Thorstein Veblen, the institutional economist who coined the term "conspicuous consumption." Surely, he was right when he said, "Football has about as much to do with education as bullfighting has to do with agriculture."

GPAs have improved for football and basketball players in recent years, but not enough. Even the NCAA's most stringent rules continue to be circumvented. The money is too big and subsidies of college football and basketball are basic economic facts.

At the end of his colorful and contentious career involving far more serious issues to do with university governance, Clark Kerr, president of the University of California and a beacon in industrial relations, said upon leaving the UC system, "the only problems that I could never deal with were faculty parking and…football."

STUDENT-ATHLETE RACISM

In 2009, a former student from my Harvard period, Derek Bok, published a book titled *Universities in the Marketplace: The Commercialization of Higher Education.* He observed that athletes remain advantaged in the admissions process and are more likely to be admitted at a given SAT level than other candidates. Division 111 players still sweep floors, but few will end up chairing a board.

In my days as faculty representative, blacks were a very small minority on football teams. In 2002, 56 percent of the players in major league football were black; 70 percent of the college basketball ball players were black. Few of these athletes would see a boardroom.

While the amount of money generated by these black entertainers grew exponentially, the clustering of easy pabulum courses at the University of Washington and elsewhere as a way for black football and basketball players to stay eligible deprived them of a future. This deprivation was to a great extent generational racism.

Racism is a theme that would return to me repeatedly. It was certainly present in universities, including the University of Washington.

On one occasion, Washington was scheduled to play Baylor at Waco, Texas in football. Harvey Cassill invited me to go as the University's guest. I accepted with enthusiasm thinking that it was nice of him to think of me. I thought that he wanted me along because he enjoyed my company. Maybe so, but as it turned out he wanted me with him because he anticipated trouble.

The year was 1950 and we had two black kids on our football team. Bob Herring, a backup halfback, and Fred Robinson, a superb lineman. When we arrived at Waco, the hotel that housed our players refused to allow Herring and Robinson to stay as guests. To this day, it is difficult to forget the words of the hotel manager. He said, "That will cost us business. We cannot have "niggers" running around the lobby and hanging around the restaurant."

Harvey replied, "Then I'm lodging a complaint with Baylor's faculty representative." He contacted the faculty representative and he told me the response was, "I can't do anything about it. It is beyond me… It's a level too high. You'll have to take it to the president of the school."

The president agreed to meet with Harvey face-to-face but refused to meet with both of us, so Harvey went to the meeting on his own.

I advised him beforehand, "Don't back down. We can't give in. Tell him that we're not playing if these kids don't get a hotel room." Harvey took that position and convinced the university president to put pressure on the hotel manager.

Following the meeting, the president called the manager and said, "if you don't let those two black kids stay there, we're canceling all our business with your hotel."

The kids were in. However, the manager of the hotel begged Harvey, "please don't have them hanging around too much in the lobby. Tell them to keep to their rooms as much as they can. We're not fighting a civil rights war. This is a football game. It is only a football game." Of course, it was "only a football game."

Sometimes I think of the losses caused by racism and the caliber of those who survived discrimination. I had two black students while teaching in the University of Washington law school. Both became judges and went on to stellar careers in law. Both broke color barriers.

Sponsored by Senator Scoop Jackson, Jack Tanner became a federal district judge and well-recognized civil rights activist. His father had been a longshoreman who fought for an integrated union. Jack followed in his footsteps. The quality I admired most in him was that he never shied away from a tough decision and often followed his own reasoning on the bench. He had a rare moral courage. He had also been a student-athlete.

Charles Z. Smith ended up on the Washington State Supreme Court and ultimately became its Chief Justice. He received quite a bit of acclaim over the course of his career. My friendship with these two men proved enduring.

I would be reminded repeatedly through the years that racism was more than a football game.

A FINAL NOTE ON THE OUTLAW FOUR

Not to nitpick, but the procedure followed by the Conference was *dog law*. We were not told what the charges were. There were no findings of fact. The penalties imposed unfairly affected our entire athletic program, not just those who were implicated in the violation of rules. In other words, the punishment did not fit the crime. I was reminded of the queen in *Alice in Wonderland* where she says: "first there is the sentencing, then there is the trial." Our strategy was to continue on without protest. A rule is a rule after all.

ARTHUR GARFIELD HAYS BELIEVED THAT THE AMERICAN COURT SYSTEM WAS AN UNTAPPED CLASSROOM THAT WAS POTENTIALLY RICH WITH EDUCATIONAL OPPORTUNITIES FOR LAWMAKERS AND THE PUBLIC. HIS HOPE WAS THAT THE WORK OF THE COURTS WOULD YIELD BROAD PHILOSOPHICAL STATEMENTS THAT WOULD SERVE AS A FOUNDATION FOR A STRONG LEGAL SYSTEM.

6

Exploring the constitution

I taught for eight years at the University of Washington and helped build a law school with a solid reputation. I had gained a reputation as one of the country's foremost labor law experts. I had a half-assed law business outside of academia that I could expand if I wanted.

I conducted an increasing number of labor arbitrations through the Federal Mediation and Conciliation Service (FMCS). I was also engaged in interesting work outside of academia.

During World War I, the government established a tripartite National War Labor Board (NWLB). The Board was empowered to impose final settlements on all labor disputes. My appointment to the temporary position of Chief Rulings Attorney for the Pacific Northwest gained me practical experience advising people on permissible or prohibited wage increases under NWLB rules and decisions.

It was particularly interesting work because the post-war era saw greater solidarity within unions, which contributed to unrest, including strikes against NWLB decisions. It struck me as humorous during these tense times that my greatest moment of physical danger while I held this controversial position came from a group of used car salesmen.

My family life was stable, too. Life was pretty good all things considered.

So, why would I want to be a politician?

I was urged to enter Washington State politics by two unexpected sources.

I had come to know Henry "Scoop" Jackson when I nominated him for the prestigious Order of the Coiff. I had also nominated William M. Allen, President of Boeing who was a graduate of the Harvard Law School.

Boeing's production had dropped severely at the end of WWII and Bill Allen was able to bring production up and lift the 747 off the ground. He was also an excellent lawyer and one of the most unpretentious individuals I have ever met.

Bill urged me to run for the State Senate. Scoop Jackson also thought I should chase a political career as far as it would take me. Whatever our ideological differences, he believed I had a good chance at a congressional seat.

Scoop had graduated from the University of Washington law school in 1936. His forte was politics. Scoop had never lost an election, other than a bid for the presidency. At 28 he was the youngest member in the U.S. Congress.

He was not the best of lawyers, but he was a brilliant orator. Perhaps my oratory skills convinced him that I was meant to be a politician. It is possible that I might have held my own against Scoop in a debate.

Scoop was an avid crusader against corruption, bootlegging, gambling, and so on. Scoop and I were tight down the line on such things, and on social welfare and labor issues. Nevertheless, as I became more liberal, the gap in our ideologies widened. I developed an extreme distaste for war, while the Washington State Senator became widely known as a "cold war" liberal and was later labeled a "neoconservative".

Scoop consistently supported military spending for a weapons system and he had strongly supported the Vietnam War. While he disapproved of the communist witch hunt taking place, he maintained a relentless stance on the idea that the Soviet Union was a serious threat to us. I believed he was preoccupied with a dead horse.

Since I had the promise of support for a political career from two highly respected individuals, I seriously considered the possibility of a political career. I might even have been successful in Washington State politics. After all, how much different could politics be from football shenanigans? But, after some thought, I decided that was not who I was.

Instead, I accepted an offer in February of 1958 to teach constitutional law and head the Arthur Garfield Hays Civil Liberties Program at New York University (NYU).

It would be years before I returned to the Seattle area to semi-retire and conduct grievance arbitrations.

THE ARTHUR GARFIELD HAYS PROGRAM

New York City law firms regarded NYU as a hometown law school similar to Brooklyn or St. John. NYU easily competed with the best New York City law schools partly because it had an excellent record for recruiting and mentoring the top academic talent at a prelaw college level.

Dean Russell Niles wanted to further elevate NYU's law school through programs such as the Root-Tilden Scholars program. Each year, two students were selected from the federal judicial circuits and carefully nurtured. These students were in high demand and their recruitment influenced the practice of law in New York City.

As the first director of the Arthur Garfield Hays Civil Liberties Program, I collaborated with top law students and we produced seminal reports on constitutional matters, including studies on the Louisiana State Legislature and the Fourteenth Amendment and on free speech versus fair trial.

As I saw it, the primary objective of the Hays Program was to

69

develop the capacity of law students to deal with constitutional matters.

This included building on research activities conducted by graduate law students to further cooperative efforts among organizations that were sensitive to governmental actions that threaten personal liberties, no matter at what level or in what form.

My effort to craft how this might come about is exemplified in a letter I wrote to Dean Russell Niles:

> I think that we should use our limited resources for utilitarian or "applied" rather than for "pure" research. I do not think that the program should be a service or briefing bureau for the American Civil Liberties Union. But I do think that good starting points might be provided by contacting the Union to find out what matters are of particular interest to it, reserving our right to reject suggestions that are not academically acceptable, e.g., geared to a particular piece of litigation.

A founding donor of the Hays Program, David Stern, agreed with this direction. He expressed his hope to me that the program would become both useful and authoritative, becoming a liaison, a clearing house for academic civil liberties concerns.

I believed that this approach would greatly benefit the law students. If Arthur Garfield Hays research fellows and students were able to emotionally and intellectually carry forward the tradition of the civil libertarian in their professional and academic lives, the Hays Program would have done something of an enormous importance.

The Hays Program was supported by personages such as Theodore W. Kheel, chairperson of the National Urban League; Francis Biddle, former United States attorney general; Patrick M. Malin, Executive Director of the ACLU, and not the least, Thurgood Marshall, counsel for the National Association for the Advancement of Colored People (NAACP).

I saw my position as stewarding a venerable history that had been crafted by strong and gifted legal personalities. This particularly included Arthur Garfield Hays. While many leading intellectuals and activists of the day participated in the program, the essence and the drive of the Hays program came from the personage of this jurist.

Some claim Hays was one of the greatest lawyers of the 20th century, not only because of association with high profile cases, for instance his co-counsel role with Clarence Darrow in the Tennessee Scopes trial (1925) (monkey business), but because of who he was. He was a corporate lawyer who hated poverty and inequality. As a lawyer he pursued truth and justice. Importantly, Hays had seen firsthand how fragile the rule of law could be.

Hays was a co-founder of the ACLU and had been a central figure in the organization during the 1920s and 30s while serving ACLU's general counsel. He maintained associations in a number of organizations and served as a ballast and peacemaker between organizations such as the ACLU and the NAACP.

This could be challenging because specific conflicts had emerged toward the end of the 1950s. Progressive organizations had to reconcile a focus on civil liberties with growing civil rights activities. There were also internal divisions experienced by organizations over how far left was left.

Hays passionately defended the American government and valued its institutions, yet he criticized both, however unpopular his perspective. It took a degree of courage to question sacred institutions such as the Daughters of the American Revolution. He equally criticized radical elements on the left who did not make use of existing American institutions to effect change.

Personally, he was witty, passionate, philosophical, pragmatic, and, not the least, theatrical. No constitutional transgression was too small for his performances or too large for his direct involvement in constitutional matters.

He peddled banned books on the Boston Commons in defiance of censorship laws. He defended the constitutional rights of a Nazi group as the American way. He denounced a New Jersey mayor's ban on public meetings with an attention-getting move where he argued for free speech on top of a car. As the attorney for the United Mine

Workers, he directly accused miner owners of owning company towns, including the churches and the post office, and therefore preventing free speech.

Like other intellectuals and activists during this time, his civil liberties activities were a magnet for unsubstantiated rumors and accusations that made him ready prey for the red hunt. Hays, Sterns, and others including some Program's sponsors, were at one time or another investigated for real or supposed communist associations or leftist tendencies.

By 1934 Hays had become increasingly concerned about how these kind of threats to democracy could too easily emerge whether from the Nazis, the Jewish people, or Americans.

Hays was a member of a commission of inquiry formed by The World Committee for the Relief of the Victims of German Fascism. The organization had branches in the United States and Europe. Its purpose was find the truth regarding the burning of the Reichstag. The Nazis had accused four communists of setting the fire, along with other fires.

Some called the resultant trial the trial of the century, as it was greatly responsible for setting Nazism on its course. The committee's findings were that of the four accused only one was involved. Its report received widespread coverage because of the reputation of the committee members.

As it turned out, this was a clever ploy on the part of the Nazi regimen. In later years, evidence emerged that the burning of the Reichstag was a setup. The acquittal of three of the defendants was inconsequential because the show staged by the Nazis had served its purpose in helping to establish the legitimacy of Hitler's new world order.

Despite the risks he faced because of his Jewish ancestry, Arthur Garfield Hays was not ready to return to America following his participation in the committee. He decided to stay and attend most of the Reichstag trial mainly because he wanted to know how Germany's legal system worked regarding such subjects as the role of hearsay, for example. He also wanted to understand the system itself in terms of the relatively minor role German lawyers played in court.

His objective was to understand how the German system was different than the American system in order to understand how something like Nazism might happen in the United States.

He came to understand the extent to which Nazism was encouraged by the complicity of jurists who either denied or actively contributed to the rise of Nazi Germany. He concluded that the lack of resistance on the part of the legal profession was a factor that allowed the Nazis to trampled what had been a viable legal system that had due process rights and other civil liberties.

A jurisprudence that had emulated the values of the Western legal system colluded to bring about the goals of the Third Reich. He believed the American jurisprudence was vulnerable to such a possibility.

He was idealistic about the Bill of Rights but he had become cynical regarding America's court system. He believed the American courts were removed from potentially rich educational possibilities that could inform both lawmakers and the public. He was convinced that at this stage in American legal history court proceedings needed to serve as a platform for broad philosophical statements.

I believed that I and my post doc fellows recognized the spirit and intentions of Arthur Garfield Hays in our pursuit of "middle-distance" investigations, that is, the examination of matters that had potential utility to persons and groups interested in advancing in protecting civil liberties. Unlike the ACLU, this pursuit was not tied to any particular litigation.

Free speech was an historic concern of both Hays and David Stern. Therefore, we initially focused on the issue of fair trial versus free speech which was contained in a the second Hays Program report.

Our work on this subject, *Free Press Versus Fair Trial* was disseminated during the academic year 1958-59. The study highlighted the extent to which the right to a fair trial was impaired by pretrial comments by the media and others. This was true whether the source of the comment was private, a newspaper, or public, e.g., a Congressional committee. Two illustrative cases in the study had black defendants.

In *Shepherd v. Florida*, 341 U.S. 50 (1951), Shepherd, an African American, had just returned from service in World War II when he was indicated along with three other black men for the rape of a 17-year-old white girl in Lake County, Florida. Shepherd was sentenced to death along with one other defendant. The sheriff in the case had said to the press that Shepherd had confessed. No written confession was entered into evidence at his trial. The media accounts inflamed the community toward violence. The Florida Supreme Court affirmed the conviction of the petitioners against the claim of denial of Fourteenth Amendment rights. The U.S. Supreme Court reversed the decision.

In a second case, *State of Maryland v. Baltimore Radio Show*, 338 U.S. 912 (1950), Eugene H. James, a 31-year-old Black man, was arrested by the police and charged with murder. Immediately following his arrest, several Baltimore radio stations announced that James had been arrested and charged. Unfortunately, they went further than that. The radio stations, following one particular radio commentator, effectively tried the case in its entirety on the air.

The media said that James had confessed to the crime, that he gone out to the scene with the officers, reenacted it, and during the reenactment he had dug up from somewhere down in the leaves the knife that he had used to murder the child.

This kind of explosive pretrial publicity inflamed the community. There was a strong likelihood of a chilling effect on witnesses that might have stepped forward with favorable evidence supporting James' case. The U.S. Supreme Court refused to hear the case.

Under my supervision, Fellows Edward Douglas Lanford, Jordon Derwin, and Kenneth Martin Greenfield completed a study entitled *Racial Integration and Academic Freedom in the state of Louisiana*. The focus was the constitutionality of Louisiana's legislative actions that undermined federal law in relation to desegregation. The study covered how procedural and remedial matters affected individuals. I prepared a section on federal judicial procedures and remedies. The report was published in two installments in the April and May issues of the *New York University Law Review*. Five hundred reprints were distributed to lawyers and organizations active on the civil liberties front.

Louisiana was a particularly interesting study because while other states found indirect ways to limit support for *Brown v. The Board of Education*, Louisiana was the only state that prohibited its school teachers from any actions that would advance integration. This was related to free speech.

If states enacted legislation prohibiting speech by public school teachers about *Brown v. The Topeka Board of Education*, then where and how was this education to occur, particularly given the sweeping statutory standards enacted in the Louisiana state legislature that sought to interdict constitutional protections such as free speech? How could this be addressed while keeping in mind the effects of imposing federal laws on legislative activities.

We had a number of questions associated with this case. For instance, was the judge who was up for re-election influenced by the press and subsequent public reactions to media accounts?

The topics we chose to research reflected issues that could not be solved by one organization alone. They required, at the least, broader discussion among a network of like-minded organizations, but how would this kind of cooperation be achieved?

In the spring of 1959 I participated in a symposium in Newark before the Essex County Bar Association on the subject. Our work on the topic of pretrial publicity under the Hays Program was also presented at the "First Annual Civil Liberties Conference" held at Vanderbilt Hall on Saturday, December 5, 1959.

My co-participants at the event were Gabe Pressman, a well-known newscaster, who had played an important role in pioneering TV news, and Tony Lewis, an investigative reporter on politics and social issues, and a powerful and knowledgeable voice speaking out for civil liberties. Lewis was probably the best of the *New York Times* columnists advancing progressive causes at the time. He was widely read throughout the country.

Noam Chomsky once described Lewis as, "far left of the spectrum," noting that Lewis had an unusual ability to discover the "tacit assumptions that underlie all mainstream discussion." As a leading authority on the First Amendment, Lewis reported on such oddities as the U.S. government's loyalty program and received a Pulitzer Prize for his efforts.

Besides effectively addressing critical topics concerning constitutional rights, I instituted interorganizational activities that would encourage active networking and collaborations on issues of concern.

David Stern envisioned the Hays Program as the most suitable choice to build relationships among organizations and, with his usual eagerness, he wanted this enacted quickly.

My primary interest was to focus on the students and seek student-related activities that would establish the authority of the Hays Program to eventually realize Stern's vision of the Hays Program as a liaison or clearinghouse for civil liberties concerns. These same activities also provided the best education for graduating law students.

Also, building trust takes time. I believed that a cooperative network supported by the Hays Program would require time because when it came to collaborative activities the organizations that advanced civil liberties tended to confine themselves to activities such as planning for the annual ACLU Conference with not much ongoing communication between them.

In any case, I initiated a development plan to encourage widespread participation and to cultivate sponsors. I established an advisory committee made up of members of the organizations involved in the ACLU conference. The initial committee members included the chairperson of the Bill of Rights Committee with the New York City Bar Association, the New York County Lawyers Association, the New York State Bar Association, the American Bar Association, and the Staff Counsel of the American Civil Liberties Union.

Paralleling this effort, I coordinated a joint research phase involving post-graduate students who researched the areas of interest expressed by the different organizations as a step toward bringing the groups together around common interests.

Toward this end, I instituted a seminar series.

Students worked with research fellows to generate intensive studies derived from insights provided by individuals and organizations that actively engaged in safeguarding civil liberties.

I also develop a plan to integrate students into a joint study of certain lower court practices and procedures in cooperation with one of NYU's Centers, the Institute of Judicial Administration.

The last conference I organized was based on our previous work, *Free Speech versus Fair Trial,* which resulted in a paper that was published in the *New York University Law Review* in 1958. Unfortunately, compared to a Hays conference I had organized earlier in New Jersey, the turnout was disappointing. This outcome was partially due to meager publicity. I also wondered about my strategy. Would a sexier, current, and narrower headline topic have attracted a bigger audience?

As another strategy, I explored potential alliances including a relationship with The Fund for the Republic, which had been founded in 1952. The Fund was a Ford Foundation program dealing with constitutional issues. It operated autonomously from the Foundation.

This brought me back in touch with Robert Maynard Hutchins from my student days at the University of Chicago. Hutchins had been appointed President of The Fund in 1957.

The Fund had remained under the scrutiny of the House of UnAmerican Activities since its inception. It became an even more serious target following its receipt of a $15,000,000 endowment.

The Fund could have played it safe in these circumstances with a safer, less passionate, and perhaps more diplomatic leader. Instead, its board selected the controversial and outspoken former University of Chicago president, Robert Hutchins. As the fund's president he easily weathered continual potshots from the right and had basically flipped off accusations of communism as he had done at the University of Chicago.

He had already been engaged in various programs under the auspices of the Ford Foundation when I renewed my acquaintance with him. Some of his activities and ideas had divided the Board.

Hutchins had made significant structural changes to the Fund. He had explored broader topics, many of them controversial, and he had moved beyond what had become the Board's allegiance to a narrow, defensive, and internalized position regarding the "communist menace" posture. He believed the Board's had unnecessarily polarized the organization, which limited his agenda which was to develop a useful understanding of the U.S. Constitution.

Hutchins' allegiance to the spirit of the Constitution carried the same depth and meaning as that exhibited by Arthur Garfield Hays when he defended a group of Nazi's. However, some board members could not discern the difference between what they perceived as his tacit approval of communism and his strong longstanding belief that every American, including communists and nonconformists, was entitled to equal protection under the Constitution.

In 1955, Erwin Griswold, with encouragement from the Ford Foundation, led a movement to fire Hutchins. Robert Hutchins retained his presidency, though the Board attempted to neuter him by taking control of all policy making.

Hutchins became frustrated and bored with his role. He continued to believe that the Fund acted in a circular, reactive, and incoherent manner without taking action on significant issues.

He was also frustrated because in his view the Board assumed that the general public understood constitutional issues and therefore required no education. He wanted to see clarification of basic issues as a first priority. Most fundamentally, Americans needed to understand the meaning of freedom.

He had hoped to use the Fund to establish a center toward that end supported by the country's foremost scholars. He made a presentation to the Board in 1957 and received minimal funding support along with the caveat that basic issues would be explored for one year.

Based on unexpected public support, the Board extended the basic issues program for three more years with the increased funding of $ 4 million. His goals were realized with the establishment of the Center for the Study of Democratic Institutions located in Santa Barbara California.

The Hays Program, in the spirit of Arthur Garfield Hays, wanted to educate potential lawyers and others broadly about constitutional matters. I believed there was a fit with the Fund.

I submitted two generic all-purpose proposals to the Fund respectively titled, *The Individual and the Trade Union* and *The Individual and the Common Defense*, that represented what I thought could be a common ground between the Hays Program and the Fund. I believe my proposals were in line with Robert Hutchins' interests. Unfortunately, the rigid guidelines associated with the Fund's Basic Issues Program did not appear to be a good fit with the Hays Program.

I do not know what happened to my proposals, whether they were shelved or assimilated into the Fund's Basic Issues Program because I left the Hays Program shortly afterward. My sense in later readings from the Basic Issues Program is that they might have been a contribution.

I encountered Robert Hutchins for the last time in 1969. His daughter was in one of my classes at the University of California Davis. When Hutchins was invited to serve as the 1969 commencement speaker, she arranged for us to sit together.

I had never doubted that Robert Hutchins was a genius. He also had a perhaps well-deserved reputation as a brusque individual. He had intimidated me when I was a student in his seminar. In later years I found him to be relaxing company and I enjoyed his Socratic way of relating and his impish humor.

We shot the breeze while we waited for the ceremony to begin. I reminded him that I had been in the graduating class at the University of Chicago when he had given the commencement speech. He looked at me with horror and said, "Oh my God, I was going to give the same speech today. Now, I don't know what to say."

I reminded him of our exchange when I had submitted my proposals to the Ford Foundation's Basic Issues Program. He had teased me, "Don, why do you worry so much about freedom of speech? The question for educator should be what good is freedom of speech if you have nothing to say."

As I recall, my reply was "protecting freedom for the thought we hate protects the good stuff." That never seemed to me to be a particularly wise thought on my part, more of an automatic response, but I realize now it was a good answer. It was what Robert Hutchins had always tried to sell along with the idea that what holds us back from positive change is the tight grasp we hold on the status quo. He said, once in a speech,

> One of the most pernicious doctrines these days is that what you seek is adjustment so you're stabilized and well-adjusted. If that were the end-goal of human kind there would not be any great paintings, any great poetry, adjustment is not the end game. Being perfectly right is not the end game.

The phrase, "being perfectly right...." stuck with me over the years. "Being perfectly right" guarantees a status quo. I wonder how we arrived at that point as a nation.

The ACLU was founded because a group of people believed that in practice the Bill of Rights was being implemented in a fragmented and sometimes abusive manner. They saw a threat to democracy-on the horizon. The solution was to *get* it right, not to *be* right.

Nevertheless, we think in gross categories; in black and white terms - Republicans and Democrats. When you think liberal, you do not think Republican. When you think ACLU, you think liberal and white. When you think of the Constitution, you think of the Courts, particularly the U.S. Supreme Court. We want perfection through predictability not in terms of getting the spirit of the Constitution right.

People have a fixed idea about our political parties with little sense of history. Looking at my files related to my directorship of the Hays Program, specifically my interactions with the ACLU, I found a letter dated January 6, 1959 from the organization to me.

The letter listed the names of its board of directors. I identified almost half the names as Republican, which fits my recollection.

Ernest Angell, a Republican, was chairman at the time.

As I read this list after so many decades, I thought about David Stern's vision for the Hays Program. There was a time when the Constitution was a shared document. Those interested in civil liberties were likely to have multiple memberships across groups, regardless of their partisanship. In this sense, the ACLU, the NAACP, and the Hays Program were intertwined.

I attributed the bipartisanship over the constitutional concerns of that era to those inspired leaders, regardless of political affiliations, that networked and pollinated key organizations serving as advocates for constitutional understanding.

There was the wisdom and experience of Roger Baldwin, ACLU's founder and principal organizer along with Crystal Eastman and Norman Thomas. Roger Baldwin was also a leading member of the committee that founded the Hays Arthur Garfield Hays Program. Norman Thomas was a six-time presidential candidate for the Socialist Party of America and a Presbyterian minster. Crystal Eastman was a lawyer and one of the earliest American writers on labor law.

Roger Baldwin remained executive director of the ACLU until 1950. The shared interest among these advocates for constitutional rights was frequently accompanied by enough wealth to make things happen. For example, like Arthur Garfield Hays, Roger Baldwin was well off. Both had wealthy Republican associations with the means to pursue civil liberty issues, including responding to immediate violations of civil liberties. This bipartisan power brought results.

The Goldmark case is illustrative of the bipartisanship that flourished. When the Goldmarks were accused of being communists, the long line of ACLU members testifying on behalf of John Goldmark and his wife, Sally, were as likely to be Republican as Democrat.

The Hays Program addressed both civil rights and civil liberties as a matter of course. This was not necessarily true of other organizations that had to more narrowly choose where to direct resources.

Roger Baldwin and the other ACLU founders had restricted ACLU activities to civil liberties. The organizational focus was on constitutional constraints on governmental action.

However, the ACLU and other civil liberty organizations were irrevocably drawn into the civil rights movement. As Roger Baldwin was increasingly exposed to civil rights trespasses, he began to envision a new direction for the ACLU that encompassed social issues beyond individual rights. Civil liberties issues became more informed by social unrest.

The ACLU began to address Fourteenth Amendment issues. This orientation introduced elements of class differences, which did not sit well with wealthier and powerful ACLU members. Their primary interest was First Amendment issues.

Many members, particularly Republicans, felt disenfranchised with the direction the ACLU was taking. One might surmise that Roger Baldwin's growing interest in social issues might have contradicted the interests of Republican members who were sincerely dedicated to the principles of civil liberties principles, yet had other economic interests at stake.

The Hays Program had the potential to adapt more readily to change without partisanship. I attribute part of this to the focus on educating students in both critical thinking on constitutional matters and real life experiences.

I had enacted a sensible development plan that would allow the program's potential to be realized according to the vision expressed by Dean Niles. David Stern, and myself. However, I was limited by the fact that the Hays Program itself had to more adeptly articulate its purpose in order to attract the needed participation and funding.

After working for months from the very early morning hours until around 8 or 9 p.m. at night, fractures began to appear at home. My wife, Mary, was diagnosed with postpartum psychosis. She and our daughter, Jenny, were clearly unhappy with our current life in New York City. I considered asking Dean Niles to adjust my load, but ultimately I accept the reality that someone else would have to continue the vision of the Arthur Garfield Hays Program.

David Stern wrote that he found my resignation a "deep disappointment."

Brown v. Topeka Board of Education was dosed with gasoline by controlling and greedy politicians speaking to university presidents, "poor white trash," white mothers, teenage thugs, and otherwise good people. All were manipulated by influential political bosses like Richard Rarick and Leander Perez.

7

THE FOURTEENTH AMENDMENT

Charlie Reynard, a professor of Constitutional Law at Louisiana State University at Baton Rouge, died unexpectedly and Paul Hebert, dean of the school, offered me a tenured position to take over his Labor Law and Constitutional Law classes. I accepted his offer and we moved south. I was wooed by visions of mint juleps, southern hospitality, and porch-sitting.

Instead of lazing on the porch, I learned in non-academic terms how the base treatment of people towards each other in the name of race comes to be sanctioned, whether in Nazi Germany or in our country. This life experience relating to oppressed and abused individuals as a class of people brought home the inseparability of social issues and individual rights.

Life in Baton Rouge began with promise. I managed to spend more time with my family. My wife, Mary, had her neurological symptoms under control. Mary was a common law lawyer. She received a civil degree so she could practice law in the state and found a good position as a law clerk for one of the Supreme Court justices.

My daughter, Jenny, adjusted well to her new school which was particularly important to us. I had a new flock of students to teach in a different culture. The law students generally were not of the caliber of the New York University students, but they were good.

I practiced law on the side and continued to do some arbitrations in Arkansas and Alabama through my affiliation with the Federal Mediation and Conciliation Service (FMCS). I remained with FMCS for almost 50 years.

Unfortunately, this peaceful existence was short-lived. My time with the Arthur Garfield Hays Civil Liberties Program as its director and my writings on the State's legislature had not prepare me for the firsthand raw reality of racial difference in Louisiana.

I was not licensed to practice law in Louisiana, but I became a legal advisor to anti-segregationists and I also represented those, regardless of their views on desegregation, who were afraid that the Louisiana State legislature would make good on its threat to close public schools.

WHITE MEETS BLACK

The crucible of race as a matter between individuals first happened to me on a rainy night when Mary and I drove to Baton Rouge after visiting New York City. A middle aged, nondescript black man person was hiking along the highway headed in the direction of Baton Rouge. It was raining hard and so I stopped and asked him if he would like a ride. He hesitated. Then he asked me warily, "Are you sure you want to do this?" I said, "Yes, yes, of course I'm sure." He was obviously cold and not equipped for a long walk. He wearily climbed in the back seat and said with some resignation, "I hope you know what you are doing." I told him that I was helping another human being get out of the rain on a dark, windy night.

He said, " I don't mean that."

I answered, "What else would I do? It's a long walk?"

We exchanged introductions and then he clarified his concern. It was not about his safety, but mine. He said, "What you're doing giving me a ride," as if I would understand.

On another occasion, I stopped in Tuscaloosa, Alabama to buy a bottle of whiskey. I stood in the shorter of two lines feeling lucky because there were only a couple of others waiting in line beside myself. I was not paying attention to skin color; I just wanted to get moving. I did not notice that the longer line was exclusively white men.

 I arrived at the counter with due speed and the person at the checkout stand asked, "You looking for trouble, sir?

I answered, "No sir, I'm looking for a bottle of booze."

He said, "Then, get in the right line."

I asked him, "You mean you have separate lines for white guys and black guys?"

INSANE LEGISLATION

All of the southern states had produced state laws supporting segregation despite the Fourteenth Amendment. However, the State of Louisiana lagged behind other states in implementing desegregation. Though several other states experienced more violence, Louisiana was the slowest to change primarily because no state legislature produced legislative acts as crazy as Louisiana's.

Its justification was simple. When the U.S. Supreme Court declared Louisiana's legislative acts regarding segregation to be without merit, the Louisiana legislature claimed there was no Fourteenth Amendment so they did not have to obey. Acts were expediently passed described as measures to protect the civil service system and to ensure public safety when in actuality these acts were to preserve a social order based on race and class.

 Class was used to stir up racism among white and blacks who lived in the same urban neighborhood. People should stay where they belonged. Rabble rousers told poor whites that they might live next to poor blacks but they did not have to go to school with them. Jobs were scarce and blacks had no right to jobs that rightfully belonged to whites.

Brown v. Topeka Board of Education was dosed with gasoline by controlling and greedy politicians speaking to university presidents, "poor white trash," white mothers, and teenage thugs alike. All were manipulated by influential political bosses like Richard Rarick and Leander Perez.

There were no limits to potential ways to divide people using dire pronouncements. If whites gave up their rights, said Perez as he stirred up crowds, their daughters would be raped by a Congolese male. Governor Jimmie Davis' man, Superintendent James Redmond said that, thanks to federal interference, classes in desegregated schools would now have to be divided by sex.

All this was a tantrum over the Fourteenth amendment following *Brown v. the Board of Education*.

THE INTREPID JUDGE

Brown v. the Board of Education were words spoken by the U. S. Supreme Court. The Court's decision did not come with a manual for local judges who had to implement the Fourteenth Amendment. Some judges did a token job. Others found themselves in a lonely position. Many judges were natives of their communities who had to implement a federal law against their neighbors.

Judge Skelly Wright's was among the latter. The New Orleans native had served as the Judge of the U.S. District Court for the Eastern District of Louisiana from 1949 until 1962. During that time, no matter how poor, anyone who came before him found a fair and honest judge.

His impeccable reputation, his longstanding history as a member of his community, and his long history with the Louisiana legislature as a federal district judge did not save him from condemnation.

HUMAN DIGNITY

Skelly Wright was steadfast in his decisions despite personal doubts about desegregation. His walk in the name of the Constitution was as long a walk as the person I had picked up that rainy night.

The day came when 137 black families attempted to enroll their children into all white public schools.

On October 27, New Orleans School Superintendent James F. Redmond announced that, after extensive "psychological and ability testing", five of 137 black applicants had been accepted and would attend first grade at two white schools. The selected schools were the poorest and the neediest schools in the system. Of the five, one potential student was disqualified.

On November 14, Ruby Bridges dressed up for school and entered the door of the white children's school. She made it through the door flanked by federal marshals. In response, many families withdrew their children and put them in parochial schools.

In late March 1960, black students attending Southern University, the largest college for black students in the country, planned a protest. They wanted to desegregate lunch counters in Baton Rouge. On March 28, 29, 30 sit-ins involving 16 students took place at Kress Drug store, the local bus station, and Sitman's Drug Store. Most of the students were political science majors. The leaders of the protest were Rev. T.J. Jemison and several of the students, including political science majors Major Johns and Marvin Robinson, the student body president, and Jannette Hoston, a psychology major.

The sit-ins were accompanied by public speeches, assemblies, and marches on the Southern University campus and around the state capital.

Felton Clark, President of Southern University, order the suspension of the sixteen students who were eventually expelled. Students struck on the Southern University campus in response to the suspension order.

The student protest at Southern University had mixed results. It would take three years before lunch counters were integrated. It is possible that if the students organizers had informed or included the black community they might have had more of an impact. On the other hand, the students' actions inspired the black community and contributed to eventual desegregation.

I served as a *de facto* legal adviser for the protesting students, At one point, Jim Foreman, head of the Congress on Racial Equality (CORE), asked me to find a white lawyer in the New Orleans area to defend the 16 students when they were arrested and charged with criminal trespass. He thought a white lawyer would play better.

I had a problem fulfilling Foreman's request because white lawyers were afraid to defend the students. Alvin Rubin, an adjunct member of the LSU faculty and a practicing Baton Rouge lawyer, was my first choice. I knew that he had the heart and the brains to win.

I thought I had Alvin persuaded to take these kids on, but then he informed me that while he had thought about it, his partners had told him that he could not represent the students and still stay with the firm. He was crying when he told me this. Such was the agony of the times.

Alvin Rubin later became an excellent justice on the Fifth Circuit. In a speech given at Loyala University in 2002 titled "Four Louisiana Giants in the Law," Ruth Ginsburg ranked him as one of the four best Louisiana judges in history along with Judge Skelly Wright. The accolade was well deserved. Over the years, Judge Rubin became widely loved and respected as a wise, honest, and compassionate jurist. I cannot help but think that some of his compassion came from his tears that day.

I finally found a white lawyer in New Orleans; I think it was either Bernie Marcus or Paul Barker, a union lawyer. I was about to finalize the deal when Foreman called me to let me know that they had found a black lawyer in New Orleans. He said that while they had wanted a white guy as part of their strategy, this guy needed the work. I was glad a black lawyer got the job, but I was also disappointed, because I had wanted to become more involved in the case.

The three sit-in cases were co-joined and went to the U.S. Supreme Court where Thurgood Marshall defended them against a disturbing the peace conviction. The lower court decision was overturned. The Court stated that the convictions violated the right to due process guaranteed by the Fourteenth Amendment. Chief Justice Earl Warren wrote the opinion,

The undisputed evidence was that the police who arrested

the petitioners had nothing to support their actions except their own opinions that it was a breach of the peace for the petitioners to sit peacefully in a place where custom decreed they should not sit. Such activity, in the circumstances of these cases, was not evidence of any crime and so could not be considered by the police or by the courts.

It would appear that the 16 protesting students, along with students in other states, had achieved a notable victory. Blacks could not be discriminated against in private facilities such as restaurants or bus stations.

Justice William O. Douglas wrote,

Restaurants, whether in a drugstore, department store, or bus terminal, are a part of the public life of most of our communities. Though they are private enterprises, they are public facilities in which the states may not enforce a policy of racial segregation.

Justice Douglas' opinion was the first statement against racial discrimination in places open to the public. That opinion led the way to a public accommodations law.

Meanwhile, The Louisiana Legislature refused to recognize this meaning of public. Following the sit-ins by the 16 students it amended its statutes to read,

No person shall without the authority of laws go into or upon any structure...which belongs to another...after having been forbidden to do so...by any owner, lessee, or custodian of the property or by any other authorized person.

The students paid a high price, including losing their educational opportunity at Southern University. The reason they were willing to pay that cost was expressed by Marvin Robinson, "What is more important, human dignity or the University? We felt it was human dignity."

In 2004, the 16 students received honorary degrees from Southern University. The Louisiana State legislature enacted a resolution honoring them. One student refused the accolade.

THE RIGHT TO A PUBLIC EDUCATION

When Ruby Bridges was escorted to the white school where a crowd waited, primed by leading segregationists, a defiant legislature ordered school closures.

I became legal advisor to a group called Save Our Schools (SOS) on constitutional issues related to the school closures. Its members, primarily parents, had diverse views on desegregation but they were dedicated to public education and believed in free choice.

SOS ran intensive campaigns designed to educate the public as to ramification of school closures including all the legal facts that were not made available to, or more likely not pursued, by the media. That is where I came in.

I developed arguments for the preservation of public education, which included the high costs of no public education. These costs included increased juvenile delinquency, loss of federal funding, a tarnished image of New Orleans, and a long list of lost benefits to children.

My past work with my post graduate cohorts while I was director of the Arthur Garfield Hays Program had included a research report on the Louisiana State Legislature that was presented in a fair and reasonable manner.

In this instance, I had carefully tracked legislative activity and provided careful interpretations of nonsensical legislative acts to lay audiences. Now I had worked on ways to appeal to the mindset of a legislature.

However, legal arguments require a competent audience. As Chicago columnist Jack Mabley said of the Legislature in 1961, "neither humor, ridicule, reason nor religion will reach them... .The Legislature earned an F in constitutional affairs mainly because its members never showed up to argue a viable position on the

Fourteenth Amendment or more specifically explain what their denial of the Amendment's existence had to do with school closures.

HEADING EAST.

I believe that I had mostly stayed away from political heat and adhered to reasoned legal advice and the academics of my classroom. However, offering an opinion proved irresistible when I was asked at an SOS meeting about the interposition doctrine Governor Davis planned to implement as "a last resort" to protect the sovereignty of Louisiana. This doctrine held that the a state had the authority to block or nullify an action by the federal government on the ground of constitutionality. My first reply to the audience was that interposition provided no legal basis for Governor Davis' sanction. As far as I knew, interposition was a bizarre position for sexual intercourse popular in France.

One would think that this was a minor throwaway line. Instead, the joke went viral and was one of several factors that cost Mary her job and forced us to leave Louisiana.

My family like other white families experienced consequences. Racism leaves no one untouched.

There was no physical retaliation against me or my family. Still, we had our share of repercussions. While I was supported in my department, I was under increasing pressure to curb my support for integration at the university and elsewhere. Paint was thrown at our house and I received nasty phone calls. My daughter, Jenny, faced serious threats at school.

The final straw for us was Mary's firing by a Superior Court Judge due to politics. She blamed herself for losing the job. She subsequently had a nervous breakdown and seemed to lose whatever stability she had gained following our move from New York. She never did grasp the depth of racism nor, perhaps, did I. She could not accept that the judge's action in firing her had nothing to do with the quality of her work.

No other state had exhibited such a virulent form of legally sanctioned discrimination. We decided to leave New Orleans and the South.

Ultimately, people grew sick and tired of the privatization of schools and other reactive schemes introduced by Louisiana's legislature and that matter ended.

Racism did not end. It continues to take on ugly forms. It remains a long road. Back then, for myself and my family the road took us back to New York City.

The decision of Armour, as a contractual obligation as defined by the Armour Automation Committee, and as a matter of management prerogative, taught me how a good working committee, a responsible employer, and a sensible union could voluntarily deal with an hourly employee's worst fear - "No work today."

8

THE AWAKENING

Bill Isaacson, former general counsel of the Amalgamated Clothing Workers, learned about my growing unhappiness in Louisiana from a mutual friend. He arranged for me to be interviewed by his partners at the management law firm of Kaye, Scholer, Fierman, Hays & Handler.

I flew to New York for an interview with the firm and was quickly offered an associateship with the promise of a full partnership once I received my New York license, which I did within a year.

The five lawyers in the labor department represented employers in all aspects of their relationships with unions.

During the next few months, with little hand-holding, I was thrown a discharge case, an ethics case, a mass picketing case, a breach of contract case, a tough strike issue, and finally the Armour Meatpacking case.

Kaye-Scholer brought me trials by fire. I learned how to effectively represent management and unions in collective bargaining.

A JEWISH LAW FIRM

As a Midwestern boy, I had been enamored by the diversity I experienced as a student at the University of Chicago. I believe a school is as good as its student body. The culture and intellect of the Jewish students I had encountered significantly elevated the student body at this university in my view.

I had the same experience as a partner at Kaye Scholer.

In the 19th century 60 percent of the nation's law firms were located in New York City. Most of them were gentile firms.

Jewish lawyers operated as sole practitioners. While the number of young Jewish lawyers graduates steadily increased, it was relatively rare for a Jewish lawyer to be hired by a gentile firm and most of the practicing lawyers were sole practitioners. The Jewish law firms that existed relied on smaller Jewish clients and Jews were restricted to Jewish firms and Jewish practice areas."

A few firms operating before the 1950s. Kaye Scholer was one of those firms. Other firms included Stroock & Stroock & Lavan; Weil, Gotshal; Proskauer, Rose; Fried, Frank; and the Rosenman firm.

In the 1950s, gentiles dominated downtown firms like Sullivan and Cromwell while Jewish firms like Kaye Scholer, (which at the end of the 1950s had added its new senior partners, Fierman, Hays & Handler) dominated midtown firms. This ethnic polarity remained until a few firms, notably Paul, Weiss, Rifkind, led the way with mixed firms.

The picture was different in the 1960s. The number of Jewish firms had grown exponentially. Gentile firms grew at 50 percent the rate of Jewish firms. Kaye Scholer on the other hand grew 375 percent. Gentile firms slowly adapted to a changing legal world, but they did not have the resources to stay competitive until they put discriminatory practices aside and hired more Jewish lawyers.

By 1980 four of New York City's largest law firms were Jewish. There were several reasons for this development. There was a post-war decline in antisemitism, an increased need for legal services by corporate clients, a growth in women-owned businesses, and, not the least, talented Jewish graduates who had been rejected by gentile firms. The diversity that distinguished New York City was also a factor.

One of the most important reasons for the growth of Jewish firms was the convergence of the Jewish culture that carried a particular kind of intellect that applied to training to become a rabbi with the changing legal picture defined by the growth of a corporate culture. Corporations needed firms that could handle diverse matters, including the rapid introduction of new regulations.

While gentile firms eschewed dirty kinds of law such as bankruptcies, litigation, hostile takeovers, and antitrust suits, etc. Jewish firms were more opportunistic and open to new possibilities. As a consequence, they gained greater reputations, often with large clients they had cultivated.

This represented a culture that presented a different ethos and values that were largely distinct from gentile firms. Jewish firms encompassed broader learning and a greater capacity for abstract reasoning. The firms tended to be distinguished by individuals who had left their mark in particular areas of law and engaged in broad-activities that strongly influenced the American legal system.

For example, Milton Handler, a senior partner at Kaye Scholer and a professor of law at Columbia University for 45 years, became the foremost expert on antitrust laws. He was one of the authors of the Federal Food, Drug, and Cosmetic Act of 1938, the National Labor Relations Act, and the GI Bill of Rights . He wrote the seminal text on trade regulation and served as general counsel to the National Labor Board.

As Jewish firms grew they were able to draw from a greater supply of Jewish graduates who were redirecting their intellect. Traditionally, Jewish families expected that one son in a household would become a rabbi. An increasing number of young Jewish men chose the alternative of a legal career. The qualities needed to be a good lawyer were not so different from the qualities required by a rabbi. These qualities included the ability to be adaptive, the ability to absorb new and diverse information quickly, and a capacity for abstract reasoning.

There was also a greater sensitivity regarding the sanctity of the Bill of Rights within many Jewish firms that again can be related to an ethnic heritage. I taught to an empty classroom on High Holy Days when I was a professor at New York University. Religious rituals and celebrations were equally present, though they remained in the background, in the lives of employees and partners associated with the Kaye Scholer firm. I sensed that the Bill of Rights held the same stature.

Due in great part to New York University's Root-Tilden Scholars Program, which was started in 1951, the caliber of recruits was going up. Both gentile and Jewish law firms that had previously ignored New York University as a recruiting ground competed for the "Roots" as they were called. It was a seller's market as there were no more than 60 students in the Root-Tilden Program at any given time.

I was a member of the Fifth Circuit Selection Committee for several years. Selecting students became a tougher job because of the greater numbers of high quality applicants that came out of the Program.

By the time I joined Kaye Scholer, the firm was actively attempting to recruit more Gentiles. However, it had yet to make a woman partner. Though larger numbers of females had entered law school, women struggled in their pursuit of a legal education.

Harvard had no females when I taught there in the early 50s. Women were still a rarity at Columbia University and at Yale. It is still a source of pride to me that I recruited a talented lawyer, Andrea Christensen, who became Kaye Scholer's first female partner.

My years as a senior partner at Kaye Scholer were rewarding. I worked with partners I highly respected and gained knowledge about labor and management. The culture of the firm was a good fit with my values which became even more highly honed. We were expected to work independently, yet overall a good deal of mentoring took place.

Perhaps more than anything, though, I recall the Jewish humor that pervaded the firm. I continue to value my stockpile of Jewish stories and jokes, including Leo Rosten's, *The Joys of Yiddish*. After listening to me deliver yet another Rosten joke, Robert Chanin, an associate at Kaye Scholer, subsequently informed me that a Jew telling a Jewish joke was funnier than my attempts would ever be. I do not know why this is true, but he was right.

MAKING DEALS

My first negotiation was with a business agent with the teamsters union. My client was a wholesale drug house owned and operated by Smith, Kline, and French (now Glasar, Kline, and French), a major pharmaceutical manufacturing house based in Philadelphia. The controversy was over wages and benefits.

Negotiations were failing. We tried mediation, which also failed. We went to impasse. That did not work either.

The union's business agent drew me aside during the impasse period and made an offer he thought I could not refuse.

Wollett, if you will be reasonable and come up with a proposal for X amount of money, we'll let you fire a couple of our guys who have been stealing for several years from the floor inventory. So far, they have successfully hidden their thefts from security.

Your client knows who they are. They fired them twice in the last two years. The employees grieved. We arbitrated. Each time the guys beat the rap and got their jobs back with back pay. They are shit disturbers, hard to get along with from the union's point of view. We know you'd like to get rid of them. If you can get your client to agree to that money figure, you can fire them. We're bound for image reasons to file grievances and go to arbitration, but we won't work very hard to win.

Everyone wins. Our people get a modest wage increase and

you get rid of two bad guys. Take this proposal to your client and see if he'll buy it."

I said, "No deal."

He asked, "Why not?"

I said, "He might can these guys with the understanding that he can do so with impunity if he gives you a break on a wage increase. I can't do that."

The teamster guy countered, "Under the canon of ethics you've got to take this offer to your client."

I responded, "My function as a lawyer is to protect him from a tempting choice that will get him in trouble."

The business agent threatened a strike. I laughed and he backed down. We compromised, That was the end of that, though it served as an ethics example for my students over the years.

Thus began my career as a management lawyer.

Next, I was assigned to go to Allentown, Pennsylvania for Mack Trucks, another of the firm's clients. The United Automobile Workers was picketing the company. There had been some rough stuff that resulted in the destruction of the employer's property. I was instructed to get an injunction in state court against UAW's picketing on the ground that it was hopelessly enmeshed with violence.

I needed an *omnibus order*. I convinced the judge that there was enough violence intermingled with picketing that this order was appropriate.

I was then sent to Michigan's upper peninsula to defend a small manufacturer that had shut down its plant and laid off all its former employees.

The employees were suing for breach of contract. They argued that the collective bargaining agreement was in effect a contract of employment. However, the employees could not ground their claim in solid legal theory. In fact, their presentation was absurd. I wanted a summary judgment.

Though the judge in that case was a federal district judge with a lifetime appointment and as such immune from local political pressures, he obviously sympathized with the terminated employees. He made it clear in a settlement exploration meeting that he would deny my motion for summary judgment and he would force me go to trial. The judge gave me an alternative. He provided a settlement figure that was far beyond anything that I had already presented or would present to my client back in New York City.

I told the judge that if we lost at this level, we would appeal. He laughed at my naivety and said, "For the amount of money involved it would cost your client more to appeal than it's worth. So, grow up, Mr. Wollett." We settled on his terms.

My first and perhaps most memorable experience with a strike involved production and maintenance workers at Cincinnati Galvanizing, a small metal fabricating company in Cincinnati, Ohio. The employees had hit the bricks complaining that the quality of materials provided to them by their boss was so poor that they could not make incentive.

Working out a settlement was difficult since Cincinnati Galvanizing stood firmly on the proposition that the selection of raw materials is a management prerogative and as such not subject to collective bargaining.

The dispute was settled but only because the workers were tired of being on strike. It was too expensive. Management was also tired. I sensed that both parties would be ripe for a deal.

I formulated a study committee. The proposal was more of face-saver than a real solution, or so I thought. As it turned out the committee became a fully functioning tool that eased labor/management relations and served to anticipate future problems. I learned something important from this form of cooperation that helped me in future dealings.

By now I was a senior partner with Kaye Scholer and a seasoned management lawyer. At least that's how I saw myself. However, my next case reminded me that I had something to learn about being a management lawyer.

I took on a corporate client that had recently purchased Nabors Trailers located in Mansfield, Louisiana (best known as the birthplace of Vida Blue, a superb pitcher for two or three years who played with the Oakland As).

Nabors Trailers had been a family business for generations. The company manufactured trailers for transporting sugar cane grown in Louisiana.

Our corporate client had recently acquired Nabors Trailers and entered into a three-year management contract with Claude Nabors who remained as the company's CEO. According to the agreement,- Claude would continue to guide the company.

Fresh-cut sugar cane is a specialty item that requires special care. The workforce was racially mixed with white guys having the best jobs. So racial tension surfaced when a newly organized union filed a petition with the NLRB for a representation election. The dimensions of the bargaining unit came under dispute.

It was obvious that the business agent for the union disliked me. I think the fact that I was a hotshot New York lawyer irritated him. He enjoyed demonstrating to the workers through various put-downs directed at me that he was not going to take any crap from a big city lawyer. His personal antipathy resulted in unnecessarily drawn out arguments over the dimensions of the bargaining unit, the workers' eligibility to vote, and other typical labor/management matters that needed to be settled.

Then the business agent threatened a strike. This worried me, but we had made a deal and we went to election.

Claude Nabors had predicted that his men would come around. He was wrong. I felt badly for him, particularly because we had become friends. Claude had never imagined that the workers would turn against him since the family operation had been good to its employees for many years. I explained to him that his employees did not see the issue as "pro company" or "anti-company," but as a new expression of worker independence. That did little to sooth his hurt.

It was an unpleasant experience, except for the hospitality of Claude Nabors who turned out to be a splendid fellow. Among his other qualities, he was a well-informed historian and had many stories. In fact, I violated the maxim, "do not get too close to your client." I became more involved with the Nabors family than I normally would because I liked them.

Anyhow, there was no strike. The union was certified. Nabors Trailers went on and I returned to New York. I was quite pleased that we had avoided a strike and I hoped that the upcoming negotiations would not be badly prejudiced because of the acrimony that had occurred before the election between myself and the union's agent. There is always the danger that things that are said and done during an election campaign will poison the environment and prejudice negotiations.

A few weeks later, I met in New York with the CEO of the corporation that now owned Nabors Trailers. During the course of our conversation, he said casually,

> Don, you know you never had to worry about a strike at Nabors Trailers. It didn't matter to me one way or the other. We acquired the company because we wanted a tax loss, not for operational purposes. We don't know anything about making sugar cane trailers. That is why we entered into a management contract with Claude Nabors. The fact is we expect the sugar business to be taken over by sugar beets. So, you didn't have to worry because we didn't give a damn whether Nabors Trailers operated or not. They are only a bookkeeping entry.

"Only a bookkeeping entry"....While he explained this to me, I thought of the generations of Nabors and the family pride they had held in their business. I thought, God, welcome to the real world.

I BECOME MORE THAN A LAWYER

I was assigned to Sioux City, Iowa to defend the Armour Meatpacking Company by my senior partner, Fred Livingston. The case involved a lawsuit brought by the packing house workers who had worked in a local plant.

Armour & Company was a large producer of quality meats with major production facilities throughout the United States and a nationwide network of distribution and food service marketing centers. It had closed its Omaha, Nebraska plant and acquired the non-union Iowa Meat Packers pork plant in nearby Sioux City.

The collective bargaining agreement between Armour and the United Packing House Workers stated that employees laid off in Omaha could exercise a company wide seniority to bid on jobs in the newly-acquired plant (Armour had unionized plants all over the country).

Laid-off union workers in Omaha were then pitted against nonunion workers who had been laid off in Sioux City.

I associated with an Iowa lawyer and moved for a *summary judgment* since no material facts were in dispute. The court proceedings involved primarily technical arguments involving a point of federal preemption and the Iowa right-to-work law.

During the arguments, the courtroom was packed with the attentive wives of the affected workers and their children. At one point, I glanced over at the audience and noticed how orderly and quiet everyone was, including the children. They seemed somber and still. I wondered why these women and children sat so patiently listening to drawn-out technical arguments involving esoteric legal theories they could not possibly understand.

Then I got it. This was more than a court case. It was their livelihood. If I win, and I had no doubt that I would win, many of these women will be married to unemployed workers in a depressed labor market. If their spouses are in the street, they will have no money coming in for themselves and their children. There goes the car. There goes foreclosure on their home mortgage.

The case went to the Iowa Supreme Court. I did not feel good about my win. This feeling was mitigated by a cooperative agreement between a willing management and labor that left me with a very good feeling.

Armour Meatpacking had been a party to Master Agreements with the United Packing House Workers (UPWA) and the Amalgamated Meat Cutters and Butcher Workmen of North America (The latter represented production and maintenance employees at Armour's 36 meat plants). The Master Agreements between Armour and UPWA and Armour and Amalgamated also covered 18 additional plants.

The agreements had no provisions requiring union membership as a condition of employment in states with a right-to-work law, e.g., Iowa and Nebraska. Accordingly, membership in UPWA (or any other union) was not required at Armour plants in West Point, and Omaha, Nebraska or Sioux City, Iowa.

The provisions in the Master Agreement, called for a six-month notice of plant closings to UPWA, which in this case was upon the permanent closing of the operations at its West Point and Omaha, Nebraska packing plants.

The notice said, "Slaughter ...will be discontinued as of today, and the remaining operations will cease as soon as work has been completed."

Approximately 100 employees at Armour's West Point plant, located 50 miles from Sioux City, were immediately laid off. Around 1,750 production and maintenance employees at Omaha, which was about a 100 miles from Sioux City, were subsequently laid off when the Omaha plant closed.

A month after announcing that its West Point and Omaha plants would be closed, Armour executed an agreement with Iowa Beef Packers, Inc. for the purchase of the Sioux City Dressed Pork plant. The plant (referred to as "Sioux City Plant ") was located about half a mile from Armour's now closed Sioux City Plant. The purchase agreement provided that Iowa Beef Packers would deliver possession of its Sioux City plant to Armour at the close of business and neither party would assume any of the obligations of the other party under the terms of "any labor agreements and/or contracts of employment." The seller, Iowa Beef Packers, also represented that it was not a party to any collective bargaining agreement covering any of its employees at the Sioux City Hog Plant" and that it had "fulfilled all its obligations to its employees at the Hog Plant up to and including the date of possession."

On that same day, October 28, 1967, even though there was no legal constraint, contractual or otherwise, to prevent Armour from terminating the entire workforce at the Sioux City plant, the company posted a notice announcing that the plant had been taken over and would be operated under "business as usual conditions." An announcement of the acquisition was released to the press the same day.

Three days later, A. S. Drain, the general manager of pork operations in Armour's meatpacking plants, made a more detailed announcement to Sioux City employees. He informed the employees that Armour was a party to master labor contracts with UPWA and Amalgamated under the terms of which is the Sioux City plant could be determined to be a replacement plant. The employees were told that if the Sioux City plant was found to be a replacement plant, job opportunities there "would be subject to the transfer and seniority provisions of the Master Agreements." Thus, from the beginning of its takeover of the Sioux City operation, Armour made clear to the employees of the former owner that pre-existing obligations might cause it to transfer displaced Armour employees possessing more seniority with Armour to the newly acquired Sioux City plant.

The idea that a newly acquired or established Armour facility might be treated as a "replacement plant" for a closed down Armour facility or facilities was set forth in the two provisions of the Master Agreements with UPWA and Amalgamated. The first provision was incorporated in the Master Agreements.

A second provision called for the formation of what was called the Armour Automation Committee to alleviate the adverse effects on Armour employees of loss of jobs and employment opportunities caused by changes in technology, plant shutdowns, plant relocations and the like. It was explicitly empowered to define a replacement plan.

I selected two neutral members to serve on the Automation Committee. Dr. Clark Kerr, former Chancellor of the University of California and former chairman of the meatpacking commission under the World War II War Labor Board co-chaired the Commit-with Dr. George Shultz, dean of the graduate school of business at the University of Chicago and later U.S. Secretary of State. The union representatives for Amalgamated were Russell Dresser, James

Wishart, Ralph Hellstein, and Jesse Prostein for the UPWA. The members representing the company were Harold Brooks, Clifton Cox, my senior partner, Frederick Livingston, and Walter Clark.

On November 10, 1967, Kerr and Schultz, applied experience they had already gained in handling prior Armour plant shutdowns to the following decision:

> Based on the contracts and precedent set in earlier cases and after hearing the presentations of the parties, it is our decision that the Sioux City Dressed Pork Plant is a replacement plant for Omaha and West Point.

That decision from the joint labor/management committee triggered rights for the Omaha workers. Altogether, the Automation Committee issued six binding decisions defining the rights of workers.

On November 22, 1967, Armour and an UPWA executed a letter of agreement, which formally recognized Sioux City as a replacement plant for West Point and Omaha, amended the coverage of the Master Agreement by deleting the West Point and Omaha plants, and committed Armour to give preference in selecting its workforce at Sioux City to employees based on Armour seniority. Armour said:

Independent of this decision of the Automation Committee or its contract with the UPWA, sound management policy in the exercise of company prerogatives would obligate it to give preference to old Armour employees who were losing their jobs at West Point and Omaha and to offer them an opportunity for continued employment at the Sioux City plant."

The statement reflected the shared concern of labor and management as each party assumed responsibility for the workers.

THE CONVERSION OF THE NATIONAL EDUCATION ASSOCIATION (NEA) INVOLVED CREATING A HYBRID UNION THAT CALLED FOR MULTIPLE STRATEGIES TO SUPPORT THE NEA'S LEGISLATIVE MEANS AS A TRADITIONAL WAY OF DOING BUSINESS WHILE DEPLOYING RESOURCES TOWARD AN UNTRIED COLLECTIVE BARGAINING SCHEME WHERE, DESPITE ASSURANCES TO NEA MEMBERS, THERE WAS BOUND TO BE TROUBLE.

9

TEACHING NEA

In 1962, Fred Livingston, my partner at Kaye Scholer, Fierman, Hays & Handler, and I met with Allan West with the National Education Association (NEA) to assess whether we wanted to take a union on as a client. I knew nothing about NEA.

As Robert Chanin reported in his book, *More Than a Lawyer*, I wrote a proposal following our meeting with the NEA representative arguing that there was no conflict for Kaye Scholer since NEA was more of an association than a union. Nevertheless, the firm's decision to take on the NEA as a client was unprecedented.

I was a full partner in Kaye Scholer and de facto head of the labor department. I had a background in higher education as a teacher. I also had experience representing unions. Therefore, I was considered to be the most qualified to pull together a team to transform NEA into a union throughout the Northeast. The "association" would have to learn how to successfully engage in collective bargaining activities and how to recruit local membership in competition with the American Federation of teachers (AFT).

I had grown accustomed to being a management lawyer. Now I had to transform the largest employee association in the country even though its key leaders and members did not want to be a "union."

I and my associates understood from a management perspective that the NEA would have to walk a line between fostering a union mentality that allowed organizing on the ground, feared by some NEA members, while maintaining some of its association identity in terms of membership benefits and its relations with state legislatures.

While it proved necessary to repeatedly assure NEA leaders that the organization would not be reduced to a rabble, the reality was that there was no middle ground. Teachers were on the move. They were asking for more professional respect and economic compensation. We had to act quickly before the more aggressive and experienced AFT acquired resources for further expansion.

Easing the concerns of its leading members required presenting a well-crafted proposal for what one might call a hybrid union. This called for introducing multiple strategies. It was important to support the NEA's legislative means, which was its traditional way of doing business, while deploying resources toward an untried collective bargaining scheme where, despite assurances to NEA members, there was bound to be some rough spots.

I put together a team of bright and eager associates who had worked with me on other accounts including Mack Trucks and Armour Meats. Of these young associates, Robert Chanin was a natural for organizational work. He played a critical role in implementing our strategic plan. He also had a good sense of humor. Teachers not only liked him, they trusted and believed in him.

The other associates serving on the team were equally talented. They were Cy Goldstein, Bob Schanzer, Peter Fishbein, and Bob Sands. I tried to recruit Peter Nussbaum, a graduate of Cornell University and Harvard Law School to the NEA team as another superior young mind, but he turned me down to accept a Fulbright Scholarship at the London School of Economics. That was the caliber of the associates assigned to NEA. I had put together a tireless and formidable team.

William Carr, NEA's CEO, continued to be unhappy about engaging in collective bargaining, as was Allan West, Special Assistant for Urban Affairs and later Assistant Executive Secretary for Field Services.

Carr was caught between two worlds. He believed that strikes were actions against the Constitution and engaging in collective bargaining opened the door to that possibility. However, these NEA leaders also knew that the conversion was unavoidable and that the transition would not be easy. There would be esoteric questions that NEA had never faced such as the composition of the bargaining unit, what subjects should be negotiable, who should be the spokesman for an organization that represented teachers, how should dispute between negotiators be resolved, how should election issues be handled, and so on.

In terms of wooing the membership, a critical factor in the relationship between Kaye Scholer and NEA was that the latter trusted Fred Livingston, my senior partner, and with good reason.

Fred had created Kaye Scholer's labor department in 1947. He was highly respected as a labor arbitrator by fellow labor law academics including Benjamin Aaron, David Feller, a former partner of Arthur Goldberg who was appointed as the Secretary of Labor and served on the U.S. Supreme Court during the Kennedy Administration, and William Willard Wirtz, who served as Secretary of Labor during the Johnson Administration.

He had played a vital role in leading labor and management toward a cooperative agreement in the Armour Meatpacking case. He had a well-deserved reputation for sincerely caring about the real problems of working men and women. Even better he came up with workable solutions.

Fred genuinely wanted collective bargaining to work for everyone's benefit. Fred often said that law was all about relationships and along those lines his favorite saying was, "there is always tomorrow." The lawyers would be gone from the scene, but those left behind had to live and work together.

Bob Chanin once said in an interview that I had been his mentor. Fred Livingston was mine.

BUILDING STRATEGIES

Wisconsin was the only state in the country that recognized the legitimacy of collective bargaining for public employees. Therefore, we required extralegal mechanisms to set up representation elections there and help us structure our negotiations.

Luckily, Fred was well acquainted with American Arbitration Association (AAA) officers and staff, so we used its services. AAA performed all the essential services, including the smallest details, at cost. Its staff provided hand-holding. AAA helped us to organize and monitor elections, and appointed a neutral party to supervise elections.

Finding the right neutral was critical when an election in Newark ended up 1373 to 1373. AAA took the vote in stride and worked it out.

I contacted the best labor experts in the country to help refine a strategy for the Northeast. I met with Dean George Schulz, of the Graduate School of Business at the University of Chicago. George had been the contract arbitrator who dealt with disputes associated with the Armour Automation Committee that had been set up between Armour Meats and the Packing House Workers and the Butcher's Union. He had some ideas as to how we might adapt what NEA preferred to call "professional negotiations" and how we might articulate differences in its new approach from its previous approach based on "consultations."

I introduced my hybrid model to NEA delegates at a meeting held in Miami. I had done a good job, but my section-by-section presentation of a model bill for "professional negotiations" did not go over well. Teachers supported what was a proposed bill to a degree, but it became clear from reactions in the audience that NEA delegates and administrators were not going to accept any proposal that hinted at the possibility of adversarial relationships with school administrators and school boards. NEA's staff people were appalled at the thought of a possible combative relationship with superintendents because they were traditionally considered essential to NEA's membership recruitment.

The idea of exclusivity contained in my bill did not go over well either. Some members complained that it was too close to the private sector industrial-style collective bargaining. You create a bargaining unit and this defines who gets to vote. The winner is the exclusive bargaining representative. Minority units are not involved in the actual collective bargaining process.

NEA staff and members who were strongly opposed to this idea wondered, why goes this route when NEA had three or four times the membership of AFT. They believed that if NEA operated on this basis it would lose elections, card checks, and so on. They saw it as too big a risk.

The bottom line was that few members wanted to divert resources to collective bargaining based on what was fundamentally a philosophical issue. My proposed bill, no matter how tempered, was antithetical to how many NEA delegates perceived its representative democratic structure.

As Allan West later described it, "the fireworks began" as soon as I finished. My model bill was "marked 'for discussion only' and "buried in a well-secured file" deep in the catacombs of time - in the second basement of the NEA's Washington D.C. headquarters.

The proposal might have bombed at the time, but whatever its perceived demerits, most of its elements saw the light of day in practice as they were adopted by affiliates in different parts of the country along with the members' growing understanding of collective bargaining practices.

At the time, chastened, I stepped back and reassessed how to win this crowd. The questions I had were, who exactly were NEA members? What did this membership want to achieve? What price was the membership willing to pay for what it wanted to achieve? Effectively answering these questions proved to be an educational process for Fred Livingston and for myself. It was for NEA, as well. Its membership was large, but its local understanding of its members in organizing terms was almost non-existent.

As it turned out, shortly after my presentation NEA was forced to deal with the issue of exclusivity in a localized face-off with AFT in

Philadelphia. It was an election that NEA had never expected to lose. The local AFT was small, but it won the election 3 to 2, some say with a little help from a visit by Martin Luther King, or so the story goes.

This defeat did not go down well with NEA's leaders, particularly since the United Federation of Teachers (UFT) had already taken a huge chunk out of NEA's base in New York City.

But the experience had benefits. Members began to recognize the social and political reality of the times. NEA had lost ground in Philadelphia because it had ignored exclusivity. There were instances where its comparatively larger membership held little value.

It was time for a second strategy meeting with experts. Allan West and I met with George Schultz again and John Dunlop, a distinguished professor of economics in the Harvard Business School, at Washington D.C.'s Shoreham hotel. Their combined knowledge of unionization and collective bargaining helped us articulate critical topics such as the question of the permissibility of strike activity, which was a touchy subject with NEA that could not be avoided in practice.

Allan and I then drafted a preemptive strategy. I would use my young lawyers in a geographical head-to-head battle with AFT. Hopefully, this aggressive move by NEA would surprise our competition. At the same time we would shore up NEA's strength by reaching out to its affiliates and to state legislatures.

The former plan involving union organizing tactics was a particular challenge since NEA did not have much control over the autonomous actions of its affiliates. For his part, Allan West attempted to attract the interest of these affiliates by initiating a program for school reform called the "Urban Project."

Backed by the resources of the Industrial Union Department (IUD) of the AFL-CIO, AFT was already poised to hit the Northeast hard so I rapidly deployed my NEA team. We went to work in New York, Massachusetts, Michigan, and Connecticut.

I sent Bob Chanin to several districts in Massachusetts and Michigan to seek professional negotiation status recognition, and bargaining rights for local NEA affiliates. We also went after Saginaw, Midland, Holland, and Flint, Michigan, not to mention Union Beach, New Jersey, and Newark, among other locations. I did the same activity in Connecticut where I relied a great deal on my associates. I covered most of New York myself and paid special attention to potential flagships that would demonstrate we knew what we were doing when it came to collective bargaining.

To give some idea of the reasoning behind this showpiece strategy, NEA was the largest association of its kind in the US. It had around 900,000 members; 64 state affiliates and 8,100 local affiliates consisting of around 1.5 million teachers. There were 33 departments, 14 divisions, 26 commissions and committees, and six special projects dealing with subjects such as research into curriculum, methodologies in teacher education, academic freedom and tenure, dropout statistics, the advent of technological teaching aids (automation), and lobbying activities.

In other words, its organizational focus had not been on local affiliates, which it now depended on, rather on selected issues and joint projects at a state level, which had allowed it to maintain revenue sources. For other revenues, the NEA had relied on around 4 percent to 4.5 percent federal aid per annum over the past 30 years and on the continued and varied support of state legislatures.

Because of this structure, NEA members at local levels did not have the capacity to organize resources in support of NEA's new direction.

The only way to effectively get the local affiliates on board was to target school districts that were "ripe" with the goal of achieving as many felicitous collective bargaining agreements between local teachers associations and school boards as we could. We could then showcased successful outcomes to demonstrate that "collective negotiations" by affiliates could be achieved and benefit teachers.

We could only hope this strategy would work. It was a different approach than that used by the AFT. Its organizing approach was analogous to industrial workers in the 1930s. Also, the Industrial Union Department (IUD), the de facto organizing arm of the AFL-CIO, was highly motivated because it needed a white-collar breakthrough in order to gain entrée into the public sector. The union was having a successful run at achieving that goal. AFT had hit New York City in 1961, Detroit and Cleveland in 1964, then Philadelphia in 1965, along with Boston, St. Louis, Washington DC, Minneapolis, and Los Angeles.

Unlike NEA, AFT was opportunistic. It understood social movement in a way that NEA did not. It was able to use growing teachers' grievances on the dock, especially in larger cities, to introduce the kind of militancy that was needed.

Teachers' strikes had occurred in New York City, Gary, East St. Louis, Hoboken, Jersey City, Louisville, New Orleans, Oklahoma, date County Florida, Catoosa County, Georgia, Pawtucket, Rhode Island, and Utah. These small wins had created larger expectations among k-12 teachers, including NEA members.

In the face of rising expectations, NEA was not prepared to deal with questions about teachers' motivation and the fact that many of them were novices when it came to organizing.

The majority of affiliate members did not have a strong desire to organize. They did not want to risk the basic benefits and the amenities offered by a professional association. Local affiliates had mostly organized around social events and workshops and had not involved themselves in policymaking. Rather, when NEA itself negotiated or "consulted" it had generally relied on a white cane approach or what was called "organized supplication."

NEA had an abiding faith that its comparatively larger membership would carry the day. However, the real question was not how many members NEA had, rather how would its teachers vote? Since NEA's local affiliations were largely autonomous, leaderless, and inexperienced in collective bargaining, there was little information on which to predict election outcomes.

Without an understanding of what unionizing would give them, many teachers had habitually accepted patriarchal relationships with school administrations and school boards. The introduction of possibly greater militancy required finding the right local leadership. This proved to be more difficult than anticipated.

In addition, there was no identifiable legal forum to support teachers. With the exception of Wisconsin, there were no statutes in the various states that applied to public employees at a legislative level.

We tackled this problem as part of our strategic plan by working closely with state legislatures. With more or less specificity, states were moving towards statutes and laws on how elections would be conducted and how unit determination was to be defined. We tracked this progress.

All of our team members took a turn at testifying before the different state legislative committees in order to get legislation passed that would give NEA a reliable vehicle to achieve a collective bargaining status. I must have testified before at least 15 legislative committees about the virtues of collective bargaining statutes for public employees.

Our NEA team worked tirelessly around the country on all fronts. We conducted numerous negotiations. We strengthened linkages and ties to affiliates in large urban areas such as Chicago and Los Angeles. We gain recognition for bargaining rights in places like Seattle and Denver. We successfully pushed through legislation in New Jersey, Connecticut, Rhode Island, Massachusetts, and Michigan. We developed election procedures in Rochester, Newark, and Philadelphia. The team planned election campaigns in Milwaukee, and achieved negotiating agreements in Denver, Milwaukee, New Rochelle, and Rochester. We engaged in disputes over who was going to represent the teachers, the eligibility to vote, and so on. We reached political settlements in Utah.

While these activities took place, internal divisions within NEA existed over its direction. This tension directly affected NEA's organization and staffing considerations.

How was our hybrid union model doing? In 1965 AFT's membership numbers in urban areas exceeded ours almost 6 to 1.

In the past, NEA's recognition had come without elections, however, because of AFT's successful elections, we had to keep trying. We persisted in our geographic strategy to deal with elections before the union could gain sufficient strength. We had some successes, for instance in Rochester, New York. Despite our efforts, AFT remained on our back.

By 1966, NEA and its affiliates had competed in about 30 representation elections. We had won big in cities such as Milwaukee, Rochester, and Newark, but generally speaking our track record with elections was lousy. Our advantages were (1) collective bargaining had not spread enough yet to undermine NEA's over 700 professional agreements as a way of doing business and (2) we were still way ahead of the AFT in total membership.

Newark's Fed-up teachers

We won an election in Newark in 1964, but that didn't mean much and AFT knew it. The issue wasn't whether New Jersey was ripe for organizing. Places like Newark were over-ripe and life was tough for teachers, students, and for their advocates.

Newark, New Jersey was one of the worst black marks against the nation's k-12 educational system. Increasing numbers of teachers were fed up. The situation was particularly dire for teachers working in impoverished areas.

I remember driving home late one night and losing my way. For some reason, perhaps because I was exhausted, I completely blanked out. I did not know where I was for about 20 minutes. I entered the east side tunnel and told myself to keep going because sooner or later I would recognize something familiar. I finally wound up in Manhattan. I think my blackout or whatever it was was not just exhaustion from not enough sleep, but a consequence of the stress I had felt throughout my Newark dealings.

I had dealt with blatant crooks in government, observed the relentlessness of racial discrimination, and observed the high levels of anxiety and physical fear that defined the educational environment.

Newark's teachers worked under untold barriers to education and taught in the middle of violence and in the face of persisting poverty. Almost all the teachers were white and female while their students were mostly black.

The grievances of Newark teachers represented a long list. The hopelessness of many teachers was palpable. Teachers could not see a way out of their students not failing. For many, this was not what they had signed up for. Some teachers could not live with that any longer. They could quit or fight. I met many teachers who chose to fight.

I remember standing in front of a large meeting of well over 1500 teachers who were almost exclusively white and female. They described their teaching experience as spending more time with the effects of intergenerational poverty and poor school management than teaching. The teachers wanted to strike. On behalf of NEA I urged them not to strike. I reminded them that there was a court order and they would be held in contempt.

One teacher responded to my counsel, "How can we get anybody to pay attention to us? I'm an English teacher and I've got 46 students, mostly black, in my class. What can I do about that? When and where am I going to get help?"

Another teacher in the audience cried out, "Enough is enough, Goddammit. Fifth grade students should not have to stand in a disgustingly obsolete bathroom in front of a broken commode to study English."

Still another teacher yelled, "Let's clean up the facilities, now!"

This was not unionization. This was a social movement. These teachers taught under the worst conditions and they wanted more qualified teachers. They were going to do whatever it took to get the attention of the school board and the city administration. The teachers voted to strike.

A horrified William Carr blamed Kaye Scholer for encouraging the teachers adopt this course and threatened to fire the firm. The New Jersey Teacher's Association (NJEA) said in that case the affiliate would withdraw from NEA and hire Kaye Scholer directly.

The AFT and NEA competed in Newark. Though it was a drop in the bucket, both organizations developed some programs and reforms, and found areas of agreement that benefited the teachers.

This support served the respective agendas of NEA and AFT. For example, the United Automobile Workers (UAW) under Walter Reuther set up a special teachers organizing task force with the hope that it would serve as a model for other white collar workers. It was the first of its kind.

An election facilitated by the American Arbitration Association was held in December of 1964. In this instance, NEA and the Newark Teachers Union (NTU) reached agreement on important matters, e.g., that bargaining units should be communities of interest that excluded principals, superintendents, and others who held decision-making positions.

The main disagreement between the AFT affiliate and the NEA was a somewhat silly symbolic dispute over where to hold an election. NEA wanted the election held on school district grounds. NTU wanted it off the school grounds in order to avoid undue influence from school administrators. The AAA moderator went with NTU.

Since time was short, (a hearing was held in November and the election was planned for December) both sides agreed to follow National Labor Relations Board (NLRB) guidelines, though it was understood by the parties that this was not to assume that the private sector and the public sector had the same requirements.

NEA's LOSS OF VIRGINITY

AFT had strikes. NEA had sanctions. One NEA New Jersey delegate said the term "economic sanction" was simply NEA's term for a strike. In reality, there was a difference.

NEA sanctions were in the form of publicity campaigns, withholding of professional services or refusing to sign a contract. Sanctions were a limited strategy because they did not call for an interruption of work when a contract was in force.

On June 9, 1967 we imposed sanctions at Union Beach, a small shoreline community 45 minutes from Newark. Sanctioning in this instance relied on a American Association of University Professor's (AAUP) blacklisting technique which might be accomplished through word-of-mouth, by picketing, newspaper ads, and so on.

The technique called for publicizing the Union Beach School District as below standard. In other words, it is a lousy place to be so do not take jobs there, do not hire from there, and do not teach there.

We had another sanction going in Florida at the same time. In this case we sent out circulars to different industries telling them not to accept Florida jobs until the Governor and the Florida State Legislature came up with additional financial support for education.

The teachers' issues at Union Beach, New Jersey were declining educational conditions and the school board's" arrogance, ineptitude, neglect, and arbitrary reprisals against teachers.

If teachers were blocked from taking action or could not afford to run ads at least they could picket. And that's what teachers did at Union Beach. In return, the school board quickly obtained a temporary injunction, which was granted in August by the New Jersey Superior Court. The injunction prohibited the teachers association from publicly or privately airing any grievances. The reasoning of the court was teachers were public employees and therefore they had no collective bargaining rights.

The Court also held that teachers' affiliated association tactics were "coercive" and that the NEA's tactic of sanctions were designed for the sole purpose of compelling the Union Beach Board of Education to act. Well, yes. That was true.

NEA already had sanctions in place in Fort Wayne, Indiana, Chicopee, Massachusetts, Jersey City, and in Florida. However, it wanted to avoid permanent injunctions.

On October 8, 1968, we appealed to the Supreme Court of New Jersey regarding the Union Beach case. [1]The "clean hands" doctrine was invoked by the Court and we lost.

There is no doubt that I should have won that case. By picketing

A rule of law that a person coming to court with a lawsuit or petition for a court order must be free from unfair conduct (have "clean hands" or not have done anything wrong) in regard to the subject matter of his/her claim.

the teachers were clearly exercising their right to free speech. Therefore, their motivations were not relevant because the sanctions were implemented by speech. In other words, criticizing a sub-standard school district for poor teaching standards was permissible under any notion of academic freedom as a species of civil liberties covered by the First Amendment. That should have settled the matter.

The Chief Justice, however, found this argument ridiculous. His questions forced me to defend unnecessarily and uselessly what was inherently defensible.

All of us at Kaye Scholer had understood, or thought we had when we accepted NEA's retainer, how new and startling, and even repugnant, the idea of the schoolteacher on the march was for many people. Still, using my knowledge of constitutional law, I had presented my case well. I never imagined that a chief justice would consider squirming out of the First Amendment.

The question of speech did not end there. The New Jersey Superior Court "permanently" restrained and enjoined the Union Beach Teachers Association, the New Jersey Education Association, and the NEA from any distribution of press releases, notices, or statements that "sanctions" have been or are being applied in the Borough of Union Beach, New Jersey. Because the imposition of such "sanctions" was illegal, the Court directed New Jersey Education Association and the NEA to publish and distribute this notice of the Court's determination upon as wide a basis as the "Notice of Professional Sanctions" was originally distributed.

The teachers' inexperience allowed judges to deny them constitutional protections based on reasons to do with supposed motives or property rights. These kinds of things, a picket line that is too long and enjoining the distribution of literature, even though there was no evidence of any intent to violate property rights, might seem silly given the broad protection that we assume under the First Amendment, but that was the letter of the law as defined by a particular judge. The decision was not constitutional but at that point, nobody wanted to take it further.

Judges are not immune to biases. The New Jersey courts were

beleaguered and perhaps even increasingly angry by the protests happening around them. Many jurists were favorably biased toward management prerogatives when it came to teachers who were considered out of line. They belonged in the classrooms

It was tough to get the media, the courts, or local school management to take our sanctions seriously in this climate. The media mostly called for containment as a solution to the unrest and decried the fate of business interests if teachers won. This was a typical media response in other states as well.

There was little in-depth reporting of the complex causes behind the teachers' rebellion. Instead, the media focused on bread and butter issues such as salary demands, though teachers repeatedly publicized the fact that their grievances were to a great extent the consequence of a seriously dysfunctional educational system.

NEA had no sanctions in Newark, New Jersey, but the city had its own story of teachers' protesting against teaching conditions and the response of one otherwise good judge who delivered an unreasonable decision.

On February 2, 1966, members of the Newark Teachers Association (NTA), headed by Ruth Buehrer, a first grade teacher who was the NTA president, voted overwhelmingly to strike.

On February 9 Superior Court Judge Nelson K. Mintz, Chancery Division, Essex County, issued an interim restraint enjoining the New Jersey Education Association, its affiliate the Newark Teachers' Association (NTA), and its members and officers, from striking against the Newark school system.

More than 1,700 determined teachers disobeyed the order and were absent the next day. This constituted more than half of the entire Newark teaching force. On February 11, a hundred more teachers also ignored the judge's order and joined their fellow teachers. Thirty-five NTA members were also in direct violation of Judge Mintz' injunction. The teachers had struck. When the strike ended a few days later the president of NTA president said, "The purpose of the strike has been served."

Judge Mintz was extremely unhappy with the teachers' disobedience. Thanks to the media coverage of an inadvertent and innocent action (as was true in the case with Union Beach with the long picket line), he was about to become unhappier.

Just before the Newark strike action, the head picketer called me at home and said, "They're serving copies of a restraining order on us, Mr. Wollett, what should we do?"

I said, "accept it, take it, put it in your pocket, and go home." I thought I was quite clear with my instructions, but perhaps I was misunderstood because the teachers did not go home and instead milled around in the rain. Then, (and I believe this was an innocent happening) the judge's restraining order slipped out of someone's hands or pocket and fell unnoticed into the mud. The newspapers showed photographs of some of the picketers apparently deliberately trampling Judge Mintz's order. The headlines read, "Teachers Defy Judge Mintz" and "Teachers Show Contempt for Judge Mintz's Order. "

A FURIOUS JUDGE

Thirty NTA members were cited for contempt and the five members on the negotiating team were ordered to appear in Judge Mintz's court on a Tuesday morning. I defended the defendants in the proceeding against charges of criminal contempt of court because of failing to obey his order, and even more with his ire because they had dropped his order in the mud and walked on it.

Needless to say, he gave the negotiating committee hell from the bench. He said, "You ought to be ashamed of yourselves. Here you are, schoolteachers. Newark children look up to you as role models. You should be teaching law and order, not contemptuous behavior."

The four male members of the negotiating team were almost reduced almost to tears following his law and order sermon.

Diminutive Ruth Buehrer remained calm with no hint of tears during the proceeding. She had originally pleaded with the teachers not to strike because she was in the middle of sensitive negotiations.

However, she came to realize that the negotiations were going nowhere in the current climate.

Ordinarily your former school marm is adept at reducing you to size. Ruth was no exception. She drew herself up to her full height in front of the judge. She said, "Excuse me Judge Mintz, do not lecture me about law and order. Recall that 40 years ago you were my first grade student and your behavior was dreadful. You were up and down. You wouldn't be quiet. You demonstrated no respect for law and order. So don't lecture us on law and order. I know what it is."

Judge Mintz was in no mood to listen to his former teacher.

Instead, he turned to me and said, "You're here on sufferance, Mr. Wollett. You're part of this proceeding because your client needs a lawyer, but you're laughing at your client, Ms. Buehrer, and that's not very good behavior on your part."

He was right, but it was one of the funniest courtroom scenes I had run across.

As far as the judge was concerned the teachers needed "rehabilitation." On March 7th, Judge Mintz entered orders directing the 35 NTA members to show cause why they should not be held in contempt of court, noting that state law forbids public employees to strike. On March 9th, he placed the 30 persons who received jail terms on probation for a year and ordered them to report to a probation officer once a week for that period. Fines against three NTA officers were $1,000 each. Thirty-one others were fined $500.00.

Contempt of court exists in some legal wasteland. The teachers were not exactly criminals, yet they had received less rights than most criminals.

The strike was depicted in the media as primarily in support of salary requests, but as the teachers had expressed many times, a list of genuine and pressing grievances related to the gross failings of the school system was their greatest concern.

I was personally proud of Ruth and the teachers. I held little hope that they would be "rehabilitated."

On September 25, 1967, we appealed Judge Mintz' contempt of

court decision before the Supreme Court of New Jersey and lost. The Court fundamentally reasoned that the teachers were not remorseful enough and fines had done no good.

This attitude regarding the rehabilitation of teachers carried through for the next few years in New Jersey with some tragic outcomes. I thought at the time that Judge Mintz was a good judge, but in later history the role he played against teachers indicated that he had never stopped being angry over the teachers' actions and lack of remorse.

The teachers were right to strike. They were neglected, the schools were neglected, and the students were neglected. Ruth had the guts to stand up and tell it to the judge. Like so many k-12 teachers I had met who ended up leading a fight, she was an amazing woman.

Aside from losing in the courts, Ruth was up against politicians. While the above court appearances were taking place, NTA and the school board were at impasse in their negotiations. The school board refused to bargain and there was no statute to make it bargain.

A CROOKED MAYOR

It did not help that Newark had become known as one of the most dysfunctional cities in the country because of graft, corruption, and race riots, and a crooked mayor.

Following the judge's last order, the school board and its lawyer, Jack Fox, its general counsel, Norman Shiff, and Hugh Joseph Addonizio, Newark's mayor, finally, after repeated tries, agreed to meet with us and negotiate. However, they were not serious. There was no negotiation.

Rather, Mayor Addonizio asked Ruth in a patronizing tone, "What do you want, dear?" She answered, "Don't patronize me. I submitted our salary proposals. You have read them. You have them right there in front of you and that's what we want."

The Newark mayor responded, "Ruth, if I did that, I'd be voted out of office at the next election, which is only a few months away. A taxpayer revolt? I like this job and I intend to keep it."

Ruth assured him, "Well, the teachers will support you if you give them this package of wage and benefit increases that they're seeking. And we also want to hire some new teachers."

He repeated in a kindly voice, "Ruth if I did that, I would be voted out of office."

She again attempted to persuade him, "The teachers will support you." Mayor Addonizio dismissed this. "Ruth we've done a demographic study and discovered that only 30 percent of the teachers even live in the city and are eligible to vote. So that's not going to do me any good. What else?"

When it came to percentages, it turned out that the mayor was a criminal. About 1 percent of the money Addonizio collected for the city went to the mob. He was later convicted and served time.

So, we stayed at impasse and once again the teachers talked strike. I was trying to figure out how we were going to get out of this when my senior partner, Fred Livingston, saved the day thanks to his close friendship with John Dunlop, one of our early advisors.

Fred persuaded John to mediate the dispute and perhaps arbitrate. John agreed and with relative speed presented his proposal and reached a settlement between the school board, the city, and the union.

Jack Fox, the school board lawyer called me and said, "Don, I smell a fix; that's the odor in the air. I'm not fooled by what you guys are pulling off." I played dumb, but Jack had a good nose. The fix was John Dunlop's best guess as to what the terms of a settlement would be if the parties had continued to negotiate and there was no strike. This procedure is easily criticized, but the schools resumed operation.

That did not seem like such a big deal. There was not much of the school year left, and the Newark school system was a shabby affair. The kids didn't pay attention anyway. So, one might ask what is the point of keeping schools open in Newark, New Jersey?

Maybe those few weeks did make a difference. The students were not on the street. They were not loitering. They were not playing hooky – they were in classrooms. The parents were happy because they had their babysitter (the schools). The taxpayers were happy. The teachers were reasonably happy. I suppose that the only ones who were not happy were the students, but at least they weren't being shortchanged.

I did not like fixes, but I held my nose and went along. I would make the same choice today. Sometimes a strike is the only path, but the cost of a strike would have been enormous and it would have performed no useful function in this particular situation. Despite any sense of self-righteousness on my part, the fix was a righteous act.

Unfortunately, the events I participated in were not the final chapter in the Newark story. The problems were there and they continued to fester cumulating in the 1971 strike.

AFT and NEA might claim credit for some successes during that period and they did institute some programs along with their respective agendas, but any wins really belonged to the courageous teachers. The truth is that the organizations could have offered the teachers more support. When it came down to the wire, the teachers were the ones who demonstrated the most informed concern about the plight of schools and the fate of their students. They made many sacrifices to convince others that there was a serious problem.

MY KINGDOM FOR A LAWYER

We operated around the country and lent support to NEA's local and state affiliates. However, we desperately needed good local lawyers. We had recruited local lawyers like Ted Swift and Erwin Elmann in Michigan, Cass Ruhlman in New Jersey, and Larry Trygstead in California, but it was increasingly difficult to find competent local lawyers willing to risk being labeled radical by taking on a local school union as a client, especially when there was serious talk of strikes, sanctions, work to rule, etc.

Then, Bob Chanin came up with an imaginative strategy in Florida. The NEA affiliate there was talking strike, and again we ran into the problem of finding local counsel.

Bob created a pool or network of competent local lawyers that we could draw upon when needed. That required organization and Bob with his organizing skill set it up. Initially, the pool of lawyers was called the National Association of Teacher Attorneys (NATA). The organization grew like crazy. Lawyers were finally realizing that unionization and collective bargaining for public school teachers was a growing market for any gutsy lawyer who wanted to build a business. Bob saw this and he was right. A couple of years after Florida we had lawyers from 40 states answering the call.

As for myself, I moved around the country representing Allan West's Urban Project, representing teachers, and troubleshooting. On one occasion Allan West asked me to go to Utah (his home state) and make a deal with Governor George Clyde who was in conflict with the executive secretary of the Utah Educational Association (UEA) over state aid. While representing the Urban Project, I ran into problems with the executive of the NEA Commission on Professional Rights and Responsibilities, a guy named Dick Kennan. It was bad timing. While Allan West was pushing teacher rights, Dick Kennan was in Utah preaching teacher responsibilities. Judging from his rhetoric, Kennan seem to have no clue as to NEA's strategies or its shifting mindset. Consequently, he hurt my credibility with Governor Clyde who was already a tough challenge.

I attempted to resolve the problem when I returned to the NEA headquarters in Washington. D. C. by calling Dick to let him know that he was blocking my way in the Utah negotiation so would he please cease and desist until I finished the job. Following the call, we had a schoolyard scrape in the anteroom to Dr. Carr's office. I finally said, "This is unseemly for you and me as two presumed adults arguing loudly out here within earshot of secretaries and other staff outside Dr. Carr's office. Why don't we just go into Carr's office and settle once and for all who's in charge in Utah?" Dick refused. I asked him why. He said, "Because Carr will sustain you." At this juncture I knew that Allan West had already dealt with the matter and that I had won this internal skirmish.

While Allan West did not like strike actions, he remained generally open to whatever would advance teachers' interests. He was a great client, mainly because he followed my advice. Louisville, Kentucky was a notable exception where it was good that he didn't heed my advice. The districts in Jefferson County, Kentucky (Louisville), believed they were being discriminated against in the state aid formula and they wanted to sue. Case law was against us so I advised Allen not to spend NEA money on a lawsuit.

However, the pressures from unhappy Kentucky teachers were irresistible so Allen decided to go ahead with an action against the Commonwealth of Kentucky. A former associate on my NEA team, Pete Fishbein, was now my senior partner. Pete engaged the services of a Kentucky lawyer, Rucker Todd, and, by God, Rucker won. It was a fragile victory. It was not worth the taking, but, in the bigger picture, it was another example of NEA's growing assertiveness in its transformation into a union.

After six years I knew the NEA could not afford our services much longer, though it always paid promptly. There were internal jealousies and a lot of staff bitching within the organization about our legal bills regarding how much of NEA resources were going into the promotion and development of professional negotiations versus how much was being directed into the coffers of an expensive law firm.

We had successfully brought NEA into the world of collective bargaining. The question was could NEA afford us or rather did they need to afford us? I could see that NEA was going to have to move from retaining a very expensive New York City law firm to obtaining counsel through salaried staff lawyers.

Allan had asked me if I had a successor in mind. I recommended Bob Chanin. Allan agreed and Bob then became NEA's staff lawyer. He served as NEA's general counsel until his retirement in 2010.

Bob and I kept our connection with each other over the years. I continued to represent NEA on a contract basis as one of my activities and I occasionally did work for him.

On one occasion Bob sent me to Hawaii to deal with a statewide teacher's strike by an NEA affiliate. Hawaii was one of the first states to allow state and local government employees the right to strike.

It was a strange strike. A walk-out was scheduled to coincide with a one-week Easter vacation. Maybe NEA was still partly in a place where it did not find the strike that strange since it did not involve any lost time which made it appear more like a sanction. So, technically there was a strike that brought a lot of media attention, but no actual shutdown of schools.

Still, teachers picketed and I got the usual feeling where my heart swelled, kind of like listening to an oncoming train or the sound of a newspaper press, or a social movement for a good cause.

Following the Easter parade, we worked out a good deal for the Hawaii State Teachers Association (HSTA).

Bob and I had an interesting, somewhat competitive relationship. It is fair to say that we had become the two foremost experts on teacher negotiations in the country, so it was natural that we put a book together to help teachers deal with collective bargaining. Our co-authored book, *The Law and Practice of Teacher Negotiations* (1970), published by the BNA press, received good reviews and became a commonly used reference on the subject.

Bob and I might have been excellent negotiators, however, whose name should be first on the book was a tough one. Our flipping a coin was a funny scene until I finally got sick of coin flipping over who should go first and stood my ground. I was the senior one here with the most experience. There was no way I was going to be second author. I said to Bob, "Either I'm first or there's no book"

Bob said mildly, "Okay."

As it turned out, perhaps Bob really was unhappy with my being first author. When the president of the California Teachers Association (CTA), affiliated with the NEA, submitted a letter to the CTA board calling me "the nation's top expert on collective bargaining for teachers," Bob returned the copy of the letter he had received to CTA with a signed note scrawled at the bottom that said, "I find this impossible to accept!"

THE COURAGEOUS HUNTINGTON TEACHERS BROKE NEW YORK STATE'S NO STRIKE LAW AND ACHIEVED ONE OF THE NATION'S FIRST "REFORM CONTRACTS" FOR TEACHERS WORKING IN THE PUBLIC SECTOR.

10

INNOCENTS ABROAD

Our team at Kaye Scholer implemented demonstration projects to show what NEA could achieve through collective bargaining. Our showcases (flagships) included two districts in Connecticut following passage of a collective bargaining law, two showcases in Michigan where a collective bargaining bill had passed, and other selected districts across the Northeast.

Huntington, Long Island was first in this string of showcases. I had arranged the selection of Huntington because Huntington had educated teachers. It was an affluent community that had commuting parents with young children. Many of the parents preferred to work without interruptions, such as making sudden arrangements for childcare. These parents also had high expectations for their children and wanted them to have a good education. Based on these reasons, I believed that using this community as an example for NEA members and others would demonstrate that collective bargaining could be viable and orderly.

I miscalculated.

Mark Twain once said, "God made the Idiot for practice, and then He made the School Board." I had not factored the possibility that a highly resistant school board might drive teachers in the affluent Huntington suburb to strike.

The strike of 400 elementary and high school teachers in the suburban setting of Huntington, Long Island did not compare in numbers to the walkouts of 50,000 New York City teachers that had occurred the previous September, nor did it have the motivations and complexity of racial and decentralization issues involving the Ocean-Hill Brownsville community in the City.

However, the Huntington teachers' strike did have the distinction of being the first illegal strike outside of New York City following the enactment of Article 14 of the Public Employees Fair Employment Act of the New York State Civil Service Law in 1967, otherwise known as the Taylor Law. The teachers themselves were not initially aware of this distinction because for the most part they had never imagined participating in a strike or breaking the law.

Though I had dutifully cautioned the teachers not to strike, I was generally accused by the school administration, the school board, and the media of being a troublemaker and an outside agitator. When they chose not to follow my advice. I had no choice but to go along for the ride and negotiate as best I could.

A RECALCITRANT SCHOOL BOARD

There is rarely a single reason why a strike occurs at a particular time and place. Low salaries were one reason why the teachers decided to strike, but certainly not the most important reason. They struck because they wanted to be seen as professionals and be paid as such. They also wanted an improved school system.

The confluence of unpredictable public services budgets, school boards that were poorly qualified to make budgetary decisions, the public's negative view of public sector strikes, along with distressing signs of a trend toward economic austerity in New York City, worked against k-12 teachers having much voice.

It is safe to say that the teachers' strike happened primarily as a response to the school board's attitude. The Huntington school board's arrogance and dismissive attitude during the collective bargaining negotiations shut the door on reason and fairness. Consequently, whatever NEA's dislike of strikes, the teachers of Huntington, New York became a force in their own right.

The Huntington school board for District 3 was no different than thousands of others operating in independent school districts across the country. Despite scattered efforts to limit some of their power legally and politically, many school boards held broad powers, but were ignorant as to how to manage those powers. School boards not only controlled who would teach what, but the level of teachers' salaries for indefinite periods. There were no legal measures that could force the Huntington school board to plan for teachers' salaries in an equitable fashion.

From the school board's perspective the idea of teachers making demands was unconscionable. Gordon Campbell, a member of the negotiating team for the Associated Teachers of Huntington (ATH) believed that the chance of having an enlightened Board willing to consider increasing teachers' salaries to significantly to attract the very best teachers was remote. He recalled in a letter to me,

In spite of clear warnings, the administration, the superintendent, and Board members did not seem to realize the consequences of their inaction and resistance. ... It was almost as if the first year of New York's Taylor Law, establishing collective bargaining as a cooperative effort to reach a mutually agreeable contract, had just the opposite affect than conceived of by the New York State legislature. The Board of Education did not accept the fact that it was supposed to negotiate as equals with the teachers' association. The Board seemed determined to handle salaries and benefits exactly as they had in the past; that is to say, that it would determine what a fair and equitable settlement was for the teachers.

The teachers

AN ILLEGAL STRIKE

I believe the Huntington school board created an adversarial environment primarily because they had never been forced to deal with teachers as a collective interest. Therefore, the board members had no experience with bilateral problem solving nor did its lawyers.

The new Taylor Law was not useful to negotiations. The school board primarily saw the Taylor Law in black and white moral terms, i.e., a strike action against the law is wrong. The school board did not have the capacity to see the strike action as an indicator of employer-employee relations or possibly legitimate concerns about the condition of the local school system. The Taylor Law legitimized any action the school board chose to take without repercussions.

Whatever the language of the law, few people were clear as to how the Taylor Law was supposed to work. The advent of the Taylor Law made it easier for an uninformed media to depict the teachers as breaking a new high-profile law rather than then their *reasons* for breaking the law.

Ignorance of the new law was pervasive. The school board received little help from the school system. Even pleas from the school board to the Commissioner of Education met with a wait and see response. The Commissioner claimed that in the event the situation ended up in the courts, he might be able to play a more definitive role.

Rather than engaging cooperatively in collective bargaining processes under the Taylor Law, which included arbitration and fact-finding, the school board hired "experts", not to learn how to manage its employer/employee relationship, but to become more expert at controlling the ATH and NEA.

These experts did not assess the teachers' demands or the value of their services, or guide the school board through the steps required by the Taylor Law. Instead the school board and the acting superintendent, Christopher Vagts used the experts to teach more adversarial skills such as "ferreting out" "hidden" items in the union's contract proposal. While the issue of seniority and other issues were presented in a manner common to most collective bargaining agreements, the inclusion of these issues were viewed as "sneaky" efforts by the union to slip items past school board members.

Accusations that the teacher's were manipulated by outside agitators, were reinforced by hired experts who had no stake in the process. This contributed to misinformation and misdirection away from opportunities for positive interactions between the parties.

THE AUTHORITY TO BARGAIN

The school board's behavior was the primary reason for stalled collective bargaining processes. The lack of an effective bargaining authority also prevented processes from moving forward.

My work as NEA's counsel had included associations with Ralph Flynn in San Francisco, Don Behr in Los Angeles, and John Donaldson, head of collective bargaining with the California Teachers Association (CTA). When I sat down with these representatives we shared an understanding that even as we negotiated with a school superintendent, whatever happen at the table was meaningless unless it was confirmed by the unseen authority behind the representatives. We had to know who or what this authority was.

There were many unanswered questions which had to be answered by a knowledgeable authority as a prelude to the Huntington agreement. Only this authority could answer critical questions such as, what exactly was the school board's authority as part of District 3 in Huntington, Long Island, which was a fiscally independent system? Would both the district and the school board confirm or reject our proposal? Would one or the other aim for particular items and let go of others based on respectively some lesser known agenda?

Any seasoned negotiator clearly identifies the authority and the desire that lies behind the negotiations and finds the means to drop enough clues to these authorities as to the progress of the collective bargaining process in order to move the negotiating process along. That critical piece was non-existent during the Huntington negotiations.

The school board usurped or mis-used other kinds of authority.

The superintendent, Christopher Vagts was irrelevant to negotiations. This had been established when the Board over-rode his predecessor's ability to make decisions by becoming the dominant force in establishing and enforcing policy, making educational decisions, and confronting teachers at the negotiation table.

Vagts allowed this usurped authority to continue and for the most part followed whatever the school board wanted. (In 1969, he co-authored a primer for handling future teacher strikes with a sexy and elongated title, *Anatomy of a Teachers' Strike: case history of teacher militancy and how a board of education coped with it.*

In any case, I had no effective counterpart representing the school board who was familiar with public sector collective bargaining. The school board's young lawyer, William Gould, from New York City, had potential as a good attorney however he had no understanding of either negotiations generally or foundational precepts that drove public sector collective bargaining (admittedly public sector collective bargaining under the Taylor Law was still a new area of law).

In their book, Stone and Vagts gave their impression of the school board's attorney.

> William Gould, right, able, and knowledgeable in labor relations, was young and rather inexperienced in dealing with teacher organizations and burdened with many other clients. His lack of familiarity with the workings of schools was an obstacle throughout the proceedings, and built into the situation a strain on communications with his client.

From my perspective, the authors were wrong in their assessment of his ability, primarily because they had no expertise in labor relations and they refused to look at their own communication problems.

William Gould's lack of familiarity with "the working of schools" was not an obstacle, his inexperience with labor negotiations was. As happens with novice labor lawyers, his client intimidated him and consequently he did not act to move the process forward. Instead, he let his client take the lead without much guidance on his part. Consequently, he had no credibility with either the teachers or the school board.

His inaction hurt my credibility. As the bargaining processes continued to remain at impasse, the teachers' feelings intensified and their impatience grew. I told Gould that he was going to have to do something, anything, to bring us closer together on his end. I suppose I should not have been quite so literal when I said "anything."

Gould promised me that a "big change was going to happen" by the next day. I shared his promise with the teachers.

His "big change" involved a few minor corrections in punctuation that had no substantive relationship to the contents of the school board's proposal.

Dorothy Day, an English teacher to the core, had been patient up until now. When she saw the "big change" William Gould presented to the teachers, she lost her cool and walked out of the meeting.

By now it was clear that the board would hold out until it got its way and that its attorney had no idea what to do.

In my negotiations, I typically made a point of educating all parties on the state of public sector collective bargaining and when particular items in a proposal needed a basic understanding. I did this because I firmly believed that there are better outcomes when both sides come away looking good to their constituencies. Most of the time this is possible to achieve.

So, I paid a visit to the young lawyer from New York City to see how I might clean him up and give him a little more stature in dealing with his clients. Unfortunately, despite a productive visit, my counsel did not help much. This was not Gould's fault. The school board remained stubborn in terms of teachers having any voice and the polarization between the parties was too great. The bargaining process had extended too long. It was clear that without some effective third-party intervention, the gap between the parties would grow larger, which is never good.

THE LONG TIMELINE

At the beginning of the 1966 school year, 1967-68 contract negotiations appeared to be underway. However, by December 1966, the school board and the ATH were at impasse.

In November, the Huntington teachers submitted a lengthy proposal to the school board that contained reasonable demands, but overall the proposal contents were more ideal than doable. Vagts and Stone recalled in their book, "The proposal, dated November 27, 1967 [was] received without comment by two board members - representatives responsible for personnel matters."

The school board then submitted a short, terse, boilerplate counter proposal that ignored most of the items listed in ATH's proposal. Its nonresponse left me no foothold for negotiations. Based on this response and from future communications it seemed clear that the school board would most likely to reject any subsequent proposal presented by ATH.

Further negotiations took place in the Village Green elementary school cafeteria following New Year's Day in 1968. Little was accomplished toward resolution and the District 3 teachers were even more frustrated by the "glacial" negotiation processes. I recall thinking at the time that this meeting and meetings that followed were similar to most of the faculty meetings I had attended during my academic career - filled with petty concerns and no closure. The meetings certainly did not resemble negotiating sessions with solid reference points.

Negotiations had been going on since November and it was now January 30. The school board distributed a letter to parents, teachers, and the media absolving itself of any responsibility for the impasse. The school board claimed in the letter that it had been willing to agree to collective negotiations with ATH almost two years, before the Taylor Law went into effect, "because we believe in teacher participation."

The board presented itself to constituents as calm, reasonable, and long-suffering, saying "enough was enough."

The letter characterized president, Dorothy Day, as an over-emotional female. The ATH president was described as volatile in contrast to the board's professional and reasonable demeanor. She was "obviously a rogue troublemaker" who had "made a series of emotional charges to the newspapers in response to the board's economic proposal." The school board stated further, "We accept the collective-bargaining proposal and counter proposal -- not charges and counter charges."

Dorothy was an extraordinary leader. She had been diagnosed with late stage cancer during the negotiations between the teachers and the school board, but chose not to receive treatment until the there was a settlement. I had found her leadership to be active, steady, effective, intelligent, and inspirational.

Following procedures outlined under the new Taylor Law, the negotiator for the school board sent a telegram to New York's Public Employees Relations Board (PERB) on February 1968 declaring an impasse between the school board and ATH. A month later PERB ruled that an impasse existed.

Thomas Christenson of New York University was appointed mediator by PERB. He was unable to resolve the majority of the issues brought before PERB by the parties. His mediation sessions with ATH and the school board ended acrimoniously the first week in April.

Following the Taylor Law's prescribed process, the board's negotiator then requested a fact-finder. Bertram Wilcox, professor of law at Cornell University, was appointed. While waiting the arrival of Wilcox, nominal negotiations took place with no forward movement. At this point, the ATH said it would accept in total the findings of the fact-finder.

Bertram Wilcox presided over six days of hearings and gathered evidence. The parties agreed to Wilcox' request for a joint submission representing their positions which would then be reviewed by the fact-finder.

The parties received the fact-finder's report on May 5th. Wilcox gave the teachers a 13 percent salary increase. He had ruled in favor of the teachers on all but five issues, saying"… [I]… make

145

recommendations which fall short, in my opinion, to a full justice to the teachers."

Needless to say the school board was unhappy and refused Wilcox' recommendations, including the salary increase. \It quickly issued a statement to the public saying that the fact-finder's recommendations represented "blatant inequities."

The board wrote its own version of a teachers' contract with the belief that they would have no problem compelling the teachers' acceptance. It offered teachers a 10 percent salary increase and dismissed almost all of the fact finder's recommendations.

The ATH rejected the school board's revised proposal.

It was clear that yet another neutral party was needed. With the help of Gordon Campbell, I arranged through PERB to have Thomas Fitzgerald, a conciliator from New York City, conduct an on-site review of the parties' proposals. After reading the proposals, Fitzgerald facilitated extensive talks and caucuses between the parties.

The dialogue did not change the parties' positions. At this point, the ATH held a membership meeting and called on teachers to withhold their services until a fair settlement could be reached. It was apparent that the frustrated teachers did not believe withholding services was enough. There was an agreement that a strike was the only way to get the school board's attention.

I SAY "STRIKES HAVE CONSEQUENCES"

I reminded the teachers that strikes were illegal under the new Taylor Law and asked them to reconsider their decision. I warned them of the dangers. A strike is a potential juggernaut that can bring further resistance. If the Huntington k-12 teachers called off the strike before they achieved a reasonable agreement, they would lose all their leverage and we would be back where we started - with nothing. When you deal with an adamant employer and take away the leverage of strike action, you are not likely to get anything but leavings of no great consequence. I did not believe that the Taylor Law's arbitral processes in lieu of a strike action would help much in that instance.

There are other negative effects of a strike. Sometimes a strike leaves damaging residual effects in that relationships might heal slowly.

THE FINAL SOLUTION

Given the extent of the school board's resistance, I had no alternative to offer the teachers. They were right to strike. The process had gone through the proper steps under the Taylor Law. It had dragged on too long with no closure, and no signs of agreement over important concerns.

ATH authorized a strike on May 7, 1968. Over half of the union's 516 members in District 3 voted to strike. Picketers arrived early in the morning the next day before school started. The strike lasted for eight days.

JUDICIAL INTERVENTION

The school board quickly filed for a court injunction, which was granted. Under the Taylor Law, the courts would now decide whether the teachers were in technical violation of New York's legal ban on strikes by public employees. The injunction was issued and both sides were ordered to appear on May 14 before Supreme Court Justice Jack Stanislaw presiding in a Riverhead court.

Judge Stanislaw ordered a lock-down, instructing the parties to remain in the room (he joked half seriously, other than to possibly visit the jail house across the street) until they negotiate a settlement.

I remember thinking, well, at least we're finally all in the same room. Maybe the court's authority will finally move negotiations forward. As a minus, I was frustrated by the fact that the judge did not put greater pressure on a clearly intransigent school board that had demonstrated no desire to negotiate in good faith.

Fortuitously, Justice Stanislaw's law clerk, a very competent and astute young lady, who I hope received her own judgeship at some point, took the initiative. She knew enough about the Taylor Law to provide the stick. She privately warned the school board president of the consequences if the Board continued to resist negotiations with

ATH. Thanks to the judge's lock down and his law clerk's initiative and insight, a memorandum of agreement was signed at 5 a.m. the next morning. It is possible that neither side would have given in if the astute law clerk had not intervened, The teachers simply didn't care whether the strike was legal or not. They would have gone to jail. On its side, the school board truly believed it could act with impunity no matter what.

The Taylor Law's progressive steps, which had involved hard work from both the mediator and fact-finder appointed by PERB, did not work particularly well overall. The ultimatum by Judge Stanislaus as the final step did work, however. It was a little like a sewer pipe breaking in front of your house. You can't get coffee. You can't sleep. You can't go home. Your husband or wife is mad at you and you are going to miss your favorite TV show - unless you make a deal.

MOTIVE POWER FOR AGREEMENT

As proscribed under the Taylor Law, the matter ended in the courts. Judge Stanislaus' order to the parties was to reach some agreement then and there with concrete and immediate consequences if they did not. This created a motive power for agreement. But, it was the strike action, not the Taylor Law, that forced a judicial forum, which then demanded a deal on the spot.

The actions of a single judge cannot replace the collective action of a strike, the uncertainties surrounding a strike, and the resultant costs of a strike as a motive power for agreement. The uncertainty of a strike threat helps mitigate disparities between labor and management. If the right to strike is denied, there had better have something that works equally well. George Taylor, creator of the Taylor Law, was not a fan of strike actions, but he recognized that the Taylor Law was flawed in the sense that it had not produced an adequate substitute for a strike action.

Ultimately, the best outcome is achieved through the most optimal structure for skilled, voluntary, and informed bilateral negotiations. This has to start with each party possessing some motive power for agreement.

The subject of a motive power of agreement was introduced by me to my law students over the years. I believe it should be a central law topic in any negotiations seminar for senior law students. Unfortunately, it is not. The subject is tough to structure and, if it is done right, it is time consuming. Then there is the question of how to grade it, which can be a challenge for some teachers. As I tracked the careers of former students over the years, I found that those students who successfully grasped the concept turned out to be the best labor lawyers.

BREAKING BARRIERS

A rough agreement was drafted. This agreement then became a more formal memorandum of agreement. Following long hours in the offices of the school board's attorney, the memorandum of agreement was put into contract language. I and two other NEA lawyers were exhausted when we met with the Huntington teachers to announce that a settlement had been reached.

The long conflict between the parties appeared to be over. The teachers overwhelmingly ratified the agreement. As part of the settlement, I insisted on a no reprisals agreement to remove the possibility that the school board could take any punitive action against the striking teachers.

Although my Kaye Scholer partners and NEA had become understandably nervous from the day the strike was called, the first teachers' strike outside of New York City under the new Taylor Law, achieved one of the nation's first "reform contracts" for teachers working in the public sector. The contract demonstrated that NEA was an effective and knowledgeable player in the collective bargaining process.

A policy for the best quality education had been an over-riding theme of the teachers and this was fulfilled to a great extent. Additionally, due process rights for the teachers were firmly established.

The agreement covered the basics of collective bargaining negotiations such as salary, benefits, and teachers' time, etc. But, the agreement was outstanding primarily because it went beyond the basics to achieve a bilateral relationship between teachers and their employer in effective ways: (1) The distinction between union and management was blurred. (2) The product of the negotiations spanned diverse views of educational policy. (3) The contract set the stage for future negotiations that would effectively depend on a process based on labor/management cooperation in such a way that teachers had a greater voice in educational decisions than they had before.

The agreement called for teacher involvement in every major decision involving recruitment, promotion, and retention in support of standards of quality. In terms of recruitment, two elementary school teachers, a subject matter supervisor and one teacher selected by the teachers of that subject matter would review candidates. Secondary teachers would be interviewed by the department chairman or the appropriate district Subject Matter Supervisor and an elected teacher.

Any peer evaluation of teachers' performance, including monitoring and observation, would be conducted with the full knowledge of the teacher. Teachers of primary or intermediate levels at elementary schools would serve as observers, along with the principal, at the elementary school level and at the secondary school level, the department chairman. Following that, the observer would meet with the teacher in a timely manner to review the observed lesson.

Establishing committees

The formation of the Educational Development Committee was a significant reform in the contract in terms of involving teachers in efforts to improve the quality of education.

The purpose of the committee was to establish major goals in the district, set priorities, and make recommendations to the super-intendent. It supported the coordination of studies, project, and other activities, and evaluation of existing programs. Findings by the committee would be used to devise, test, and to introduce new programs and to conduct research in pertinent pedagogical and subject matter educational areas.

150

The committee consisted of eight teachers, four designated by the union, four by the superintendent. Labor and management would designate at least one representative from each of the three school levels.

Teachers were also to be involved in curriculum by serving on Subject Matter Councils, which would evaluate and considered all proposals regarding what is taught, how it was taught, the use of aids and materials, text, and equipment.

Council members included a secondary school department chairman, a teacher elected by the senior high school faculty, a teacher elected by the junior high school faculty, and a teacher elected by the primary elementary school faculty.

Committees would also be formed in each department or elementary school to determine curricula practice and textbook selection. Secondary schools would developed their own committees depending upon the subject matter or grade level. This task in secondary schools had previously been the responsibility of the school district's Subject Matter Council.

AN AGREEMENT THAT LASTED

I do not know the overall impact of what we achieved. I do know that Huntington's successive agreements after 1968 retained significant elements of the Huntington collective bargaining agreement related to shared policy decisions.

In 2008, Jim Finley, a retired Huntington teacher, sent me the ATH's presidential announcement celebrating the anniversary of the union which stated,

On May 7, 1968, 40 years ago, the Associated Teachers of Huntington went on strike. An agreement between the ATH and the Board of Education was finally reached after lengthy negotiations, unsuccessful mediation, fact-finding, a 7-day strike, and the intervention of State Supreme Court Judge, Jack Stanislaw. This agreement has stood the test of time. Our current contract contains virtually the same language and terms of conditions and employment.

In a personal correspondence to me in 2009, Gordon Campbell also recalled that the agreement became a prototype for collective bargaining agreements in Hicksville, Sosset, and other suburban communities throughout Long Island.

So we at Kaye Scholer achieved our showpiece with surprises along the way. As a product of the process, the Huntington teachers won unprecedented rights beyond bread and butter issues.

This does not end the story. Moving the public past the perception that all teachers want are wages and benefits remains a difficult task.

THE LEGAL QUESTION

On May 15, 1968, the chief legal officer for the school district filed a charge against the ATH for conducting an illegal strike in violation of the Taylor Law. The case was tried by George H. Fowler, a hearing officer appointed by PERB. Fowler conducted hearings from July 10 to July 15. He submitted a report on August 9. He found the union guilty. The ATH appealed. The court of appeals found for ATH on the ground that there was extreme provocation by the board.

.... Contrary to the mistaken view of the hearing officer, 'extreme provocation' does not require proof of a design to thwart or prevent negotiation of an agreement. It is enough to show, as the record in this case clearly does, a totality of conduct – a pattern of behavior – which causes statutory procedures to collapse and substitutes ... the power of the employer to impose its will on the employees.

The school board raised the issue of its legal authority to enter into agreements on certain matters on September 1969. The Board claimed it lacked the power to bind itself to provisions set forth in the collective bargaining agreement with ATH. The U.S. Supreme Court in earlier decisions had upheld the supremacy of a contractual obligation in common law and under states' statutory schemes.

Since New York's new Taylor Law was vague on the permissible scope of bargaining, the door was open for the school board to contest certain contract provisions in the collective bargaining agreement as matters that intruded on the over-riding concerns of the State.

In the Huntington situation this involved matters such as teachers' compensations, retirement, sabbatical leaves, and arbitral authority.

In 1972 the Board of Education and ATH/NEA submitted briefs to the New York State Court of Appeals. At my request, Bob Chanin and Bernard Ashe wrote a brief for NEA.

The issue before the Court was to decide the authority of the school board within New York State's statutory theme. Specifically (1) whether a school board had the authority to enter into a collective bargaining agreement granting economic benefits to schoolteachers absent specific statutory authorization to do so, and (2) whether the board lacked the power to enter into a collective bargaining agreement containing a clause which provides for the arbitration of disputes concerning and compensations.

The Court supports ATH

In its decision rendered on March 16, 1972, the court found for the NEA. It said the Board's premise was "fallacious" since under the Taylor Law the obligation to bargain on all terms and conditions of employment is a broad and unqualified one. The court stated:

> "It is of more than passing significance that the Taylor Law explicitly vests employee organizations with the right to represent public employees not only in connection with negotiations as to the terms and conditions of employment but also as to the administration of grievances arising thereunder."

In a second case in 1973, ATH appealed a court decision over an arbitration award involving revocations of sabbatical leaves under a 1971 New York State moratorium. The Board of Education again argued that the State had an over-riding interest.

The court found for the ATH on December 27, 1973 saying that a contract was in effect at the time the moratorium was in place. The court upheld the power of the contractual right versus the state's statutory interest. It said in its decision:

> Only a small number of problems have been recognized as so interlaced with strong public policy considerations that they have been placed beyond the reach of the arbitrators' discretion.

The court's decisions in regard to the Huntington case, in lieu of the right to strike, effectively lent greater authority to collective bargaining processes.

THE VALUE OF A STRIKE

In collective bargaining, strikes hold their own value. Strikes or serious strike threats expand the rights of a party, especially when a party reaches a realization that it has been withheld rights in the past that it fairly it should have had.

People learn things they would never learn otherwise. When the Huntington teachers began their rebellion due to a number of causes they were mostly concerned with bread and butter issues even though other issues were more important to them. They were able to act on these most important issues because they fully engaged in the process of negotiations. The teachers made the tough decision to strike for the right reasons.

The Huntington experience showed that, at least in this instance, a strike was the only way to get attention, not because the two parties were poles apart, but because the school board obtusely refused to provide some reasonable initial ground for negotiations at the beginning of negotiations.

They found unexpected rewards as they experienced a strike action in the face of condemnations. Their collective experience raised the teachers' consciousness. They were able to see the value of their potential professional role in the educational system more clearly on an individual level. There is no substitute for this empowering experience either in the courts or through statutory schemes.

As the collective bargaining process progressed, they demonstrated not only to themselves but to others that they deeply cared about the quality of education. As a result, the teachers ended up with a collective bargaining agreement that moved in significant ways beyond where they had previously imagined they could go. The agreement and the means they took to reach the agreement given the circumstance of a non-cooperative board effectively increased the power of the Huntington teachers to participate in policy decisions.

These benefits conceivably might have come about through the legalities of fact-finding, or a process sans a strike threat, but in the absence of self-expression, including protest, by people and groups of people, it is too easy to cover up or normalize cumulative injustices.

Strikes can be messy because democracy is messy. As long as people work for others labor will be messy. However, do we really want to live without the freedom to strike as part of a democratic society and as a human right? Do we want to give up free assembly and due process rights under states' no strike statutes?

OVER THE YEARS I ADVOCATED FOR TEACHERS IN COURT AND IN COLLECTIVE BARGAINING PROCESSES. I BELIEVE MY MOST IMPORTANT LEGACY WAS TO ENCOURAGE SELF-HELP METHODS.

11

TEACHER ADVOCATE

In the summer of 1970, I accepted the position of chief collective bargaining consultant for the California Teachers Association (CTA) for a monthly retainer of $2000. Per our agreement, I devoted my entire private counseling service to the organization.

Reaganomics and the inequities of Nixon's tax benefit program in 1972 and 1973 were hard on both California consumers and public sector workers.

K-12 teachers in California had experienced hard times during 1970 and 1971 partly because of the seasonal nature of their work and they had been hit harder by wage freezes compared to other public sector employees.

A hostile political environment and poor fiscal decisions by the State of California had resulted in increased teacher workloads, more classes, more students, more office hours, and substandard supervisory systems that interfered with the job of teaching.

Department heads and principals became the academic analogue of shop foremen and plant superintendents.

There were attempts to erode the tenure system by ridding it of tenured teachers since experienced teachers cost more than inexperienced ones. Experienced teachers were pushed into early retirements, though not with higher annuities. These teachers had no alternative work protection.

It was a buyer's market. There were more workers than jobs.

Teachers who remained in the classroom faced uncertainties. They had an unpredictable product in a job that had no predictable future or safety net. Many teachers wondered, why teach?

The union role

Under these circumstances, teachers needed to learn what CTA could do for them. They needed to know how to ask or demand help from their union. Teachers also needed to learn how to rely on self-help.

The CTA had to establish a strong identity based on defining teachers' rights in the contexts of teaching, administration, and policy formulation. For instance, teachers had a right to resent having their real income demands ignored. They had a right to demand fringe benefits, absolutely and comparatively. They had a right to a voice in items that affected how and what they taught. This included a voice in the selection of colleagues and in decisions about student teacher and student-teacher specialist ratios. They had a right to a voice in how facilities were managed, and in curricular planning.

After 28 years as a teacher and an advocate- lawyer for teachers, I knew that more than anything teachers wanted a union that worried about them. Teachers wanted an organization that asks, What is education? Is it arbitrary school orders, the domination of curriculum or teachers' time by school boards or parents? Is it extrinsic standards of appearance or behavior as conditions of employment?

A large question was the administration of teachers' time. Teachers had a number of concerns including squandered time spent policing playgrounds monitoring buses, and guarding study halls.

In the case of the Huntington collective bargaining experience in chapter 10, the school board's proposal gave an account of duties teachers should assume as part of their job aside from teaching. Toward that end, the Board's proposal contained a count of the minutes it would take a teacher to get from one room to another. There was no reference to the unpaid hours teachers clocked in their attempts to reach students.

Teachers as public employees

Self-help starts as an unvarnished picture. Public sector work has always been an attractive choice because it is perceived as more secure employment compared to the private sector. Hard times show that is not necessarily true.

Compared to k-12 teachers, I had a great deal of autonomy as a tenured professor teaching in higher education in a prestigious school. But, like them, I was reminded every single day that I was a state of California employee. Even I, working in higher education, was not really exempt from lay-offs and other actions that could derail or even end my career.

Self-help requires identifying with others. Many teachers had never left the classroom to engage in collective actions on their own behalf. It was important to get the message across that teachers were workers, like other workers, with the same rights.

I told stories of miners and pipe fitters to bring a sense of solidarity. Teachers were not uniformed firemen or policemen, which grabs public attention and brings better dividends because these public employees keep us safe, but teachers needed to know that they had something important to sell. The risk of not having enough qualified and empowered teachers meant a substantially compromised and unsafe future for the nation's children.

I sincerely believed in the power of collective bargaining because the United States was built on group work and cooperation between groups. There were school board groups, taxpayer groups, student groups, union groups, civil rights groups, political groups, and professional groups. Groups survive on meeting the special needs of their members.

In my consultations with the teachers, I asked them what does their group, the CTA, give them? What do they want from the CTA? Judicial reform? Direction and support in daily life? Do they want to learn how to maximize their income? Do they want summaries of new laws and decisions or, perhaps, tax-sheltered pension plans? Do they want a code of ethics for their profession? How does an organization give their membership these things and yet also survive and prosper along with other groups that also must meet special needs?

SELF HELP

Over the years that I had advocated for teachers in court and in collective bargaining processes, I believe my most important legacy was to encourage self-help methods.

A reporter asked George Meany, after a wage freeze – "when the day comes along [where] the workers do not get deferred increases which they have been promised under contract, are you saying at that point the action of the president has nullified their contract and therefore they are not under contract?"

George Meany replied, "that's right... I don't think he (the president) has the power to abrogate or nullify a legal contract."

The reporter asked, "Would they then be free to strike...?"

George Meany replied, "in my book they would. Whether they take action or not, that is another thing."

Self-help requires foresight. There were cases in California holding that public employees did not have a legal right to strike. However, California law did not say that participation in a strike by public employees was illegal in the sense that such action exposes the strikers to criminal or civil liability. The principal difficulty was when a court issued an injunction prohibiting participation in strike activity.

I challenged CTA members given this scenario, what are you going to ask of the court? How far would you be willing to go if the court issued an injunction, which effectively obligated teachers to perform under a contract of employment even though the school board had dishonored the heart of the contract – for instance, its salary commitment? Would you sue your employer?

The process of looking at scenarios such as these was meant to illustrate how important self help was. Self-help is the core of successful unionism. This required revitalizing a spirit of self-reliance in the CTA teachers. For CTA as a union, it meant self-renewal. This a capacity to deliver actions of service and loyalty to teachers. This had to be a transcending and controlling principle for every officer, staff member, and local chapter president.

In my last year with CTA, California's k-12 teachers finally won the right to collective bargaining. That same year the CTA successfully sponsored the Educational Employment Relations Act, known as the Rodda Act, signed into law by Governor Jerry Brown. Within 18 months, following the new law, 600 of the 1000 CTA/NEA locals gained statewide secured bargaining rights in their school districts.

As of 2012, education employs more unionized staff than any other profession, according to the Bureau of Labor Statistics. The nation's largest teachers unions, the National Education Association and American Federation of Teachers, have approximately 4.6 million members. How well are the teachers being represented? This is a question many teachers are asking in this decade. Too much money taken from NEA's membership ends up subsidizing political messages to its members.

The NEA and AFT both lobby elected officials in order to maintain a $600 billion monopoly. In 2008 alone, New York's United Federation of Teachers and its parent, the New York State United Teachers, spent $6.6 million on political activities (Scott 2009). I am not sure how this benefits the need to better address local negotiations, which is really the heart of unionism. A former Wallingford Town Councilor provides an insightful description of a typical local public sector negotiation that illustrates this point.

Today, negotiations are like this: The two sides meet. The town says 'We're $4 million short. We can't raise taxes. The state is cutting our funds. We need to talk.' The union responds 'You always say that. We have a contract.' The town says 'But really, something has to give.' The union responds 'We feel your pain, but we have a contract and we aren't touching it.' The town says 'But people will lose their jobs.' The union responds 'If we reopen the contract once, we'll be doing it forever. No can do.' In other words, they have no idea of how to surmount this obstacle, and even their legal advisers are telling them: better to throw forty teachers under the bus than to risk setting a precedent you will have to live with in the future. It seems counterintuitive to the stated goals of unionism, but that is the reality.

As teachers are laid off in unprecedented numbers or are coerced out of the classroom through policies detached from classroom realities, one might ask the unions about hard choices, should unions depend on political means at state levels or should they invest more time closer to the ground strategizing and negotiating shoulder to shoulder where the teachers live and work?

What I said in the early '60s and what I would say now in my response to this question is that in the absence of fair enabling legislation, agreements are moral commitments. Ideally, their written obligations are effectively compelled by the force of community opinion. This is true no matter whether the document involved is a collective bargaining agreement in New York City or a professional negotiation agreement in Denver, Colorado. Without this decisional authority, the antithesis is powerlessness. This condition has serious consequences to future generations, particularly in poorer areas.

In the 1960s, teachers left the profession in droves because they were frustrated and demoralized by adverse working conditions. In 2009, 18,000 teachers in California left the profession. According to NEA figures (2006) half the teachers in the US public school system left within five years because of low salaries and working conditions.

Studies indicate that the least qualified teachers leave the profession within the first year or two so counter to the mandates for performance that are handed down there is a natural attrition of "bad" teachers.

On the other hand, researchers examining separation rates for public schools in a longitudinal study found that teachers with higher test scores and better college records leave the profession at higher rates.

Performance objectives imposed outside of the local setting

also penalize teachers who are willing to take on the problem of problematic schools. Teacher salaries are not equitable. Teachers in poorer schools generally make less money than teachers in wealthier schools.

These objectives do not address the most fundamental problems. Rigid wage structures in public schools work against teacher retention. Wage scales are backwards in terms of retaining and keeping good teachers. In the last 40 years, pay compression rewards mostly female teachers with less aptitude and penalizes teachers with higher aptitudes.

Jay Edgar Benton, a Denver lawyer I knew, was a member of a school board. He was one of the few school board members that I respected. He said once,

> I think the miracle is that we have extracted from the teacher corps. in the United States the quality of performance that we have given the conditions that we have subjected them to – a condition of general servitude, I will describe it. They have lived in a condition where they were told what to do, when to do it, how to do it, and then excoriated for not having done the when, where, and how as indicated. This is calculated, it seems to me, to squeeze the vitality out of almost anyone except the vegetable – the guy who comes into teaching because he was a vegetable and stays in it effectively because, in fact, he is.

Another study showed that pay compression increased the share of the lowest aptitude female college graduates who became teachers by about 9 percentage points and decreased the share of the highest-aptitude female college graduates who become teachers by about 12 percentage points. Teachers are blamed for this impoverished system and though research has yielded models for redistribution, little changes on the political or policy scenes.

The bottom line is wage and benefit distribution is largely based on our values , how we value education, our young, our teachers, and how we value our society.

In 2010, there were unprecedented layoffs of teachers around the country. Federal mandates demanded more paperwork and instituted more rules and regulations, which meant less time teaching. The rationale for this was laid at the feet of the teacher as incompetent. The competency of policy mandates such as "No Child Left Behind." "Turnaround Schools," and "Race to the Top" was apparently not an issue.

Valuing teachers

There is nothing like a teacher dealing with a subject he or she is familiar with where the teacher has tried out various plans and has adapted one which he or she prefers and which produces better results. What's the objective of the course? Why this course instead of some other?

Other skilled employees have the option of rejecting the raw materials that are given them on the ground that they are not adequate to produce the kind of work that will survive inspection. It is foredoomed to failure because of its quality or lack thereof, to not getting by the inspection process, to being cast aside and spoiled, or to be required to be reworked, or some such thing. This is not true of public school teachers. They don't pick their raw materials, or in many cases even their tools.

As a lawyer, I was one tool. A plaque from the Huntington teachers hangs in my home office. The teachers thank me for supporting them "with the impeccable logic of a great lawyer...with clear and persuasive arguments."

In 1971, the CTA honored me with a plaque for serving them as a "teacher advocate. That is what CTA members decided to call me. That is what a lawyer should always be.

As far as I know, the departure from the University of California, Davis law school of 10 tenured professors in protest was a first in the country.

12

MARCH OF THE TENURED PROFESSORS

I accepted a position at the University of California, Davis in 1969. The law school had been established in 1965 and was about to graduate its first class of law students.

Dean Edward L. Barrett, Jr., a noted constitutional scholar who had previously taught at the University of California, Berkeley, described the opportunity as participating in "a very exciting enterprise to build a high quality law school that would successfully compete with Berkeley, UCLA, Stanford, and the University of Chicago."

The offer was appealing. The UC Davis law school was young and not a captive of history. I could design a labor law curriculum from scratch, which I always found exciting.

There were other attractive attributes associated with the position. Class sizes were small and there was a reasonable teacher-student ratio. Additionally, UC Davis was close to Sacramento, the state capitol so there were viable job prospects for law school graduates. The proximity of Sacramento also held promise in terms of training law students. The fact that my students would be exposed to one of the most important legislatures and executive offices in the country was a definite plus.

A QUESTION OF GOVERNANCE

As far as I know, the exodus of 10 tenured professors, was the first in the country. I am sure there was more than one reason for each individual's departure, nevertheless the departing faculty shared strong concerns about the climate of the law school which included the law school's development practices, its affirmative action policy, and a breakdown of collegial relations which is an aspect of university governance.

The problem of development was so serious that high caliber faculty who visited the law school usually decided not to teach there. In one instance, three people were hired for three permanent appointments from a group of six candidates when there should have been at least 20 candidates. None of the hired candidates had achieved much distinction.

The law school was off the beaten track and yet it ignored obvious strategies to compensate for this, e.g., generating lecture series to attract distinguished judges and lawyers.

Little effort was made to find jobs for graduating law students. The dean of the law school had approached alumni, but the law school was new, so there were few alumnus. Those who were solicited had limited power and influence because the school had yet to build a reputation.

Complaints also included a lack of structure in the law curriculum which was related to the extent of student participation in curriculum decisions. Students held unprecedented positions on what should have been faculty or administrative committees. Without guidance or balance, courses proliferated according to a combination of student caucuses and ego trips on the part of individual faculty members.

ADMITTED TODAY, GONE TOMORROW

Perhaps the largest governance issue was the law school's admission policies. In 1970, a law faculty group, working with the Office of the Dean of the law school decided that the school had a special mission to open its doors to minority students who could not access the state's other three publicly-funded law schools.

Charles (Chuck) Davenport and I sat on a student admissions committee. Chuck served as chair. We were against this policy. While ideally everyone should have access to education, the law school had sent out a mixed message that was harmful to the law school, its faculty, the law profession, and most of all to the students.

The UC Davis bulletin claimed that admission to the Davis law school required an LSAT of 600 or better and a GPA of 3.3 or better. My review of statistics for the class of 1973 showed that over half the people admitted to the law school were below 600 and below 3.3.

There was no way to measure the quality of applicants using the basic mechanisms such as aptitude test scores and grade-point averages. Instead, the university relied on subjective criteria in order to evaluate the "whole person," e.g. letters of recommendation, and essays on why an applicant wanted to become a lawyer. Unfortunately, interpretations of these subjective materials were done by a inexperienced joint student/faculty admissions committee.

Its members reviewed applicant files, then for the most part voted who should be admitted and who should not without much in the way of standards. This meant that there was little relationship between who was to be admitted and who would be rejected at the end of their first year.

The percentage of African American, Chicano, Native American, and Asian students admitted to the law school in 1973 and 1974 ranged between 35 and 40 percent. This was the highest rate of minority admittance into what was being advertised as one of the best law schools in the country. Many substandard Caucasian applicants were also admitted which defeated any argument that minorities were granted admission to the law school as a matter of race.

Poorly thought out affirmative action policies and a lack of lack of clear guidelines for admissions resulted in the exclusion of male Caucasians who, on the basis of objective criteria, were better qualified than other white males and minority applicants.

After we reviewed the files of people who were turned down, Chuck distributed a study backed by extensive data to demonstrate to the rest of the faculty that no admission standards existed in the law school. The study noted a pattern of reverse discrimination in the name of affirmative action.

Following its distribution, Chuck was removed as Committee chair.

The law school was not the only school with admission problems related to a vague policy called "diversity in the classroom."

The UC Davis medical school received national attention over *Regents of the University of California v. Bakke, 438 U.S. 265* which was settled in 1978.

The U.S. Supreme Court decided that by maintaining a 16 percent minority quota, the UC Davis, medical school had discriminated against the plaintiff Bakke, who was white.

This was a landmark decision by a fragmented U.S. Supreme Court that handed down six different opinions on the permissible scope of weighing factors in an admissions program, though agreed in its decision on the improper use of strict racial quotas.

Factors to be weighed should only be for the purpose of achieving diversity to benefit the learning environment, and in accordance with the university's constitutionally protected First Amendment right to academic freedom. Within this meaning, achieving diversity might involve race as *a* factor, but not as *the* factor. That decision became a generally accepted standard.

In his dissent, Justice Brennan said that a well put together affirmative action program could have dealt with these issues.

In 1974, the law school had not receive the same attention as the medical school, but its admission policies were as bad or in worse shape than the medical school.

The law school's entire procedure was fundamentally a denial of due process and the Fourteenth Amendment. This understanding could have informed a policy to ensure that minorities and whites alike were accepted into the law school on equal terms given particular standards.

Instead, the law school's version of affirmative action resulted in not only a lower quality class on average than its predecessor classes, despite a few excellent students. It was a set-up for failure for minorities and whites who did not belong in law school. They had lost opportunity costs, high student loans, a sense of failure, and little hope of a rewarding future in law.

Even if students made it passed the first year without being rejected, a significant portion of the students admitted each year never passed the bar examination. Some made seven or eight tries.

The study Chuck and I conducted contained reviews of student files. Based on this data, it was obvious that a number of students would have faced a struggle simply because they did not have what it took to successfully complete law school and pass the bar. When or if they did finally pass, the student would inherit a huge debt without the salary to pay it off.

An experienced committee with the right guidelines would have seen this immediately and avoided trouble down the road. Once a student is admitted, it is difficult to be the one to face a seriously troubled student and eventually find a way to redirect him or her.

It would have been more honest to establish a two-track system in such a way that due process could be dealt with. This was one of several options of the kind Justice Brennan had pointed out in the case of the medical school that was not considered. As Chuck Davenport said, "we're so afraid of taxing ourselves, we put the educational debts on individuals. This does not just involve monetary costs."

ACCOUNTABLE GOVERNANCE

During my years at UC Davis, I delivered widely distributed presentations and papers on the subject of governance in universities. I referred to different university systems, including large multi-camps systems such as the State University of New York (SUNY) and the City University of New York (CUNY) along with the University of California apparatus.

The central concern expressed in these presentations was not the soundness or morality of affirmative action per se, but the question of accountability in terms of access to a meaningful education. The question I invariably asked about university systems, which characteristically have complex mixed governance situations, was how are we going to assure that publicly funded universities are accountable for the scope and quality of what they promise or offer students. How does this relate to the public which might or might not benefit from the education students receive?

I sent a letter to UC President David Saxon recommending the appointment of a board to review these issues as impediments to the development of the UC Davis law school. I received no response. Upon his death President Saxon was heavily eulogized as caring about the public benefits of a university education. Yet, what are those "public benefits. We do not know. At UC Davis and in schools across the country, public accountability is still a serious issue.

COLLEGIALITY AND POWER

The autonomy collegiality brings is one reason why the role of collective bargaining among faculty members in higher education continues to be debated. This autonomy can support free expression. On the other hand, one might say that since tenured professors have more access to collegiality they have relatively more power. Collective bargaining could harm that.

Tenure was initially meant to protect free expression, but that meaning has become elusive. Meanwhile, the tenure system does not address the question of the power as unpredictable, subjective, and ultimately unaccountable.

This kind of power might even curtail the free expression tenure was meant to protect since those with tenure frequently hold power over less endowed peers.

I served on the tenure committee while on the UC Davis faculty. As one example, we denied tenure to an art historian because of the nature of her expertise. She was considered to be less valuable to the art department. For this reason only, her educational investment and special expertise were not considered.

At first, I was undecided, but I knew she was unusually well qualified and she was an excellent teacher who would be an asset to the department. I believed she had earned her tenure (Subsequently, I was an expert, unpaid witness in lawsuit she brought against the University).

During the time I taught at UC Davis collegiality had become seriously eroded as divisions widened between those faculty members who wanted change and those who wanted to keep the status quo.

The divisiveness among the law faculty reached a critical stage during a recruitment process for a new law school dean. I was chair of the search committee. While I personally hoped for a dramatic change in leadership, I attempted to remain neutral and seek a ground for consensus.

The current dean, Dean Edward Barrett Jr., was a talented scholar and he had administrated well enough so that a measure of students did reasonably well in bar exams and, for the most part, his administration ran smoothly. However, his only notable action related to the development of the law school was the erection of Martin Luther King Hall (King Hall).

The school had a worthy aim which was to provide a public law school, but it had stagnated. It needed new policies, vision, and direction, none of which were Dean Barrett's strong point.

There was a consensus among the search committee members that one candidate for the position of dean was obviously superior. The law school faculty unanimously agreed to vote for James O. Freedman. His background demonstrated that he would be innovative and yet focused in directing the law school.

However, when it came time for a formal vote, the majority of the faculty reversed their vote, resulting in 13 nays against Freedman and 12 yays. Consequently, James Freedman was taken off the list of candidates to be submitted to the administration.

There was a good deal of anger and frustration from myself and others directed to the faculty members who had reneged on the initial consensus. We believed they had tainted the entire process of consensus which in the spirit of collegiality was primarily how faculty decisions were made.

Chuck Davenport attempted to give them the benefit of the doubt by surmising that those faculty who changed their minds probably did not understand the process. A positive faculty vote did not necessarily mean a candidate would be dean, but it would keep the chosen candidate in the running.

Several senior faculty members, including myself, asked the Chancellor to renew or at least review the process. However, he refused their request.

By the end of the 1974-75 year, dissatisfaction among the faculty members had grown over issues such as the ones I have presented. Out of 25 law school faculty members, ten members left the following fall. In other words, the law school lost over 40 percent of its faculty. A woman who was an nontenured faculty member also resigned. Despite her lack of tenure, she was one of the most significant losses to the law school.

Five professors directly stated their reasons as associated with the way the law school and the university was run and the policies of both. John Whalen, Chuck Davenport, Mead Emory, Dov Grunslage, and I believed the law school process was hopelessly corrupted.

Five professors made no statement but given the timing and some of their comments it is safe to assume that they had some similar reasons for leaving.

The faculty left quietly and went on to other jobs without making a public statement. Chuck Davenport went to Rutgers to teach tax law. Emory went to the University of Washington to put up a tax institute. Dov Grunslage went into practice in San Francisco. John Whalen joined the faculty at Hastings. I eventually ended up in Albany, New York working for Governor Hugh Carey.

For a time, I was the only one of the ten professors still living in Davis, California.

Perhaps unwisely, I decided to occupy myself during the interim by writing a long letter to the University of California president, Dr. Charles J. Hitch, to explain why the mass resignation of tenured faculty occurred. I sent copies of the letter to the law school's faculty members and released a copy to Norman Brand, who had been my student assistant. I did not intend to make the situation public, however, someone on the faculty anonymously sent my letter to the two main newspapers, the *Davis Enterprise* and the *Davis Democrat*.

Davis, California was still a small town in those days so my letter was big news. To say that the surviving law school faculty members were angry because of my published letter is an understatement. I was cast as the perceived leader of the mass exodus, which was not the case.

The enmity was even greater because Chancellor Jim Meyer had appointed me chairman of the committee to find the new dean (Our second choice had been Dan Bykstar and he did become dean for a couple years).

CAN TWO SYSTEMS CO-EXIST?

Chuck Davenport wisely said once that without strong leadership, faculties tend to replicate themselves. I have found this to be true. In the beginning of my academic career, I had been a strong advocate of the tenure system simply because I associated tenure with academic freedom. Perhaps tenure gives the time and space to produce leadership and good practices. But over time I have come to believe that tenure represents a survivalist mentality where faculties regenerated as clones.

Collegiality on the other hand potentially helps promote a functioning decisional structure that ideally allows management and faculty to work together.

Accountability is an issue that collective bargaining might be able to address, at least partially. I do not have all the answers regarding collective bargaining and collegiality as part of a governance system, but it is worth considering if collective bargaining could embody a contractual arrangement that provides a better balance to arrangements between faculty, administration, and other university employees, as well as more transparency for the public.

Although the rule of law governs their daily existence, most people see "the law" as a disembodied entity.

Gordon Schaber saw the law as a broad engagement. He extended law school resources to engage youth in the community in order to cultivate skills such as critical thinking, research , collaborative thinking skills, and citizenship skills through establishing moot courts and mock trials with the help of volunteer judges for high school participation involving hundreds of students at a time early in life. Some even went on to law.

13

A MEMORABLE LEADER

After working for the Hugh Carey Administration in Albany, New York following the UC Davis experience, I took a position teaching at the McGeorge School of law in Sacramento California. This is where I ended my academic career.

As a private school, McGeorge could not compete with the University of California system's relatively low tuition. Still, it held a respectable place among law schools and McGeorge law students consistently did well on their bar exams.

Gordon Schaber's leadership as Dean of the law school was largely responsible for this success. As the youngest dean of a law school in the country, he had turned an unaccredited night school, using whatever surroundings were available, into a renown law school that produced some of the country's most prestigious judges, lawyers, and politicians.

I had come to know Gordon when I moonlighted as a guest lecturer at McGeorge while teaching at UC Davis. I had tried to be circumspect about my moonlighting activities at McGeorge because of the strong competition between the two schools.

I was still burned out from my last professorship at UC Davis when I returned to academic life and asked Gordon for a job. Nevertheless, I needed steady work now that I was back on the West Coast. I told Gordon I would take anything he had to offer on a part-time or full-time basis as long as I did not have to attend faculty committee meetings. He agreed to these terms. I stayed at McGeorge until I retired from teaching in 1991.

Gordon was not only the youngest dean in the country at age 29, after 34 years in the position, he became the longest tenured dean in the country.

Gordon shared some of the same qualities held by Robert Hutchins, the youngest president in history at the University of Chicago. Like Hutchins, he valued inclusiveness in higher education and the capacity to make that happen. Like Hutchins, he was unfettered by bureaucratic thinking. Many saw him as an educational leader ahead of his time.

Gordon did whatever he promised to do with relative speed. For instance, when I joined the faculty, he asked me to create a labor law library. It would have taken weeks, perhaps many months, to wade through the red tape and finalize this kind of project in most universities. When I went to Gordon with my plan for the library. He simply said, "fine" and gave me whatever I needed. A few days later, the labor law library was underway.

Gordon ran the law school based on meritocracy. His perspectives on inclusiveness and the development of the young brought greater yields than affirmative action mandates.

He mentored the more famous, including U.S. Supreme Court Justice Anthony Kennedy who then taught Constitutional Law at McGeorge for more than 23 years. He gave equal time to unknown quantities of prospective lawyers, including single working mothers.

Thanks to Gordon, students in the community received an opportunity to learn about court systems early in life. Some even went on to law.

Gordon extended law school resources to engage hundreds of youths. His purpose was to cultivate skills such as critical thinking, research, collaborative skill bulding, and citizenship skills. He established moot courts and mock trials with the help of volunteer high school students and he convinced judges to become involved in these events.

As for myself, I had the latitude to innovate new methods for teaching law. I experimented with classroom techniques that were still unknown to law schools such as an extensive use of simulation exercises, using whatever technologies were at hand.

One reason why I valued teaching at UC Davis and McGeorge was my students' proximity to job possibilities and also internships. I strongly promoted apprenticeships with seasoned firms. This was not a widespread practice at the time.

While completing this book, I received a welcomed visit from a former student, Norman Brand. Norman had been one of my best and brightest students. During our visit, I asked Norman to tell me about his best experience as a law student. He answered without hesitation that it was his 10-week apprenticeship with labor lawyer Duane Beeson. Norman went on to a highly successful career as a labor lawyer and arbitrator in the San Francisco and was awarded the "super lawyer" status.

After teaching at McGeorge for ten years, I received the Order of Pacific, the school's highest teaching award. Today, younger colleagues teaching law, such as Laura Cooper, a member of the Labor Law Group, use some of the same methods I had introduced at McGeorge.

My time at McGeorge was one of the most fruitful periods of my academic career. I completed my third book, co-authored with Joe Grodin, *Collective Bargaining in Public Employment* (West Publishing Company, 1993). I served another term as Secretary of the Section of Labor and Employment Law with the American Bar Association. I was on the executive board of the Industrial Relations Research Association and president of the Industrial Relations Association of Northern California. I served on numerous arbitration and mediation panels in California and Washington State.

I continued to deliver speeches on governance in higher education. This subject was becoming increasingly complex, partly thanks to *National Labor Relations Board v. Yeshiva University*, 444 U.S. 672 (1980).

Faculty members working in private institutions were now considered to be managerial employees. The implication was that they were excluded from NLRA coverage which eviscerated their right to organize. With this decision, the NLRB encouraged bureaucratized administrations with less impetus to address faculty concerns.

Though Yeshiva was directed to the private sector, it had a substantial affect on the public sector at a time when collective bargaining in higher education was becoming more frequent. In 1985, only 61 private colleges and university had faculty agreements. This represented 4.8 percent of faculty members at private institutions. In the public sector, faculty agreements had risen to 36 percent.

I and other labor law professors published an open letter in the AAUP publication citing the harm that NLRB had brought with the Yeshiva decision.

Justice Brennan had aptly said in his dissent, "the notion that a faculty member's professional competence could depend on his undivided loyalty to management is antithetical to the whole concept of academic freedom."

The day came when Gordon became fatally ill. I had hoped that John Ryan, the associate dean and a good friend of mine, would be offered the position. However, Gordon's position as dean was filled by Gerald Caplan. His background was in criminal justice. This was a significant shift in leadership at McGeorge.

I decided that this was a good time to retire. I had always insisted on being called "Mr. Wollett" in the classroom, not "Don." Upon my retirement, I was now "Don" to many of my former students.

Over the years, some of these students became close friends and colleagues. These included Marty Geiger, Scott Boras, and several other students who saw me as their mentor.

Marty had been my intern on a number of arbitration cases. It was good to see her grow and evolve professionally.

I worked with Scott Boras for several years on salary arbitrations. Scott had a legendary impact on major league baseball. He was also a good lawyer who had a fierce loyalty to his clients. I was honored when he named one of his conference rooms after me.

While teaching at UC. Davis I had seen the dangers of allowing a politicized and inexperienced student body to engage in critical decision making processes that belonged to administration or in cases faculty.

Gordon Schaber had the unique ability to run an egalitarian and collegial organization that was sensitive to the needs and concerns of students and yet respectful of authority.

As dean, Gordon Schaber imparted a sense of ownership in the future of the law school to students and faculty alike. He listened carefully.

A EULOGY FOR GORDON SCHABER

Andrea, a gifted former non-traditional law student, relates below how Gordon Schaber put a vision of education as a community of interest into action using his own brand of "affirmative action."

> I have two comments on Dean Gordon Schaber: one relating to his support of the evening school and one regarding his inclusion of families in campus activities. However, it occurs to me that this is really one subject -or at least the discussion of the two topics combines into one seamless whole. The final topic is his insistence that the students and the faculty develop a true collegial relationship.

> We (the students) all knew that the dean was absolutely committed to getting McGeorge accredited by the American Bar Association. I'm not sure how many of us realized how difficult that task was rendered by the fact that McGeorge had an evening division. It was, according to conversations I had with him, a major obstacle because it made the school look somewhat pedestrian and suggested that it might employ more than one academic standard for the two classes of students it

served.

I was an evening student, both by choice and, to a degree, by necessity. When I entered McGeorge, in 1975, I had two children who were 7 and 9 years old, a husband who was principal of Dixon High School which required me to act as "hostess" on many occasions, and {I held] a part-time job to help subsidize my educational costs, which [was] not inconsequential.

I had applied to and been admitted to UC Berkeley, Boalt Hall, and UC Davis Martin Luther King (although I'm not sure it was named that at the time) School of Law, while I was still living in Southern California and wasn't sure whether we were moving to the Bay area or to Sacramento. When I realized that neither of those institutions had a night school, or part-time academic program, I felt stymied. Then an Assistant District Attorney in Los Angeles, who knew Edie Deutch rather well, suggested that I visit McGeorge and consider attending there since it did have an evening program. I'd never heard of it, so I was somewhat skeptical. On our next trip to Sacramento, however, I nonetheless found it and visited the campus. That was it for me! Here I was with little kids, this was an enclosed campus with some recreational facilities, and I could conceivably bring them with me to school if I had to be there during the daylight hours. It was close to Dixon where I now knew I'd be living. It seemed to offer everything I needed.

I did not know precisely how perfect it would be. Not only were the amenities I mentioned above everything I expected them to be, I discovered we had a a law school dean on that campus who was absolutely committed to the night school concept and to keeping the kinds of students who would typically become involved in night school and committed and engaged in the McGeorge educational process.

As did almost everyone else, I became personally acquainted with the Dean quite early in my student career. He learned everything about me -and all the other students he met -so he knew I had a husband who was a high school principal, that I had two children and their ages, and what kinds of activities I was juggling to manage these various aspects of my life. This was very nice, but it was the actions that followed that were most impressive.

Whenever the dean became aware my children were on campus, which they were a great deal after I became Editor in Chief of the *Pacific Law Journal,* he would invite them over to the dean's house for strawberries, which they had made clear to him they absolutely loved. (He had those great big old strawberries and would serve them with whipped cream, powdered sugar and sour cream dips). He talked to them about their schoolwork, about their swim team, about anything they were currently enthusiastic about. They have never forgotten him and, when I took my son to a reunion dinner the year before the dean died, he recognized him (at 30+ years old) and greeted him by name. My son again thanked him profusely for one of the great experiences in his yet young life and for remembering him.

The other thing the Dean did to assure the comfort and commitment of night students was to always include and praise spouses. If I had to attend a dinner for Journal directors, the first iteration of the Inn of Court, etc., he would always ask me, and all other married students who were participating, to bring their spouses. He would always introduce spouses and comment on the commitment they were making to the education of their husband or wife and the contribution they made to the atmosphere of the school. He made them feel very special.

I found this especially remarkable from a man who had not had a family of his own. I think it was a critical element to the participation he got from night students in working toward his various goals. I think it was also critical, in the long run, to accreditation, because when we were interviewed in the process all of us were able to paint a picture of a school that required the same of us as was required of full-time day students only it provided us with extraneous assistance to allow us to meet those requirements. Further, we were able to demonstrate that the dean's approach resulted in night students participating in the academic activities of the school that occurred outside the classroom at a record level.

From the moment I began attending McGeorge it became apparent to me that there was an emphasis on the development of personal, collegial, relationships between students and faculty. The dean talked about it a lot. He explained to new students in orientation that the law was a lifestyle as well as a discipline and that we could become top notch lawyers only if we learned how to be lawyers, not just how to do what lawyers do. He told us that the faculty at McGeorge was committed to our individual development as lawyers, not just our education in the law. He encouraged us to take advantage of the opportunities available to us to get know our professors and to interact with them outside the classroom.

Almost immediately, I found that the faculty was very open to this stuff -in other words the Dean's words again translated into action. They would announce gatherings where we could "socialize" with them at their behest, which gatherings, of course, always turned into discussions of the law, how it works, what it's like to be a "real lawyer."

There was also a little bar nearby where they would gather at the end of the academic day -different ones at different times -and they let everyone know about it so we could drop in. The name of the bar was Lee Joes and it was on Franklin just about 5 blocks from school. You could stop there about 5:30 and there would be professors and students gathered in the "back room" talking law". You could stop there at 9:30 after the night school sessions and there would be professors and students there, as well.

In, I think it was, 1976, there was an armed robbery at Lee Joe's and several people were either injured or killed when a shotgun was fired. One of them was a McGeorge student. That pretty much ended the "gathering" practice. But the dean was not about to let it go. Within weeks he announced the plan for the student center, complete with a downstairs pub. From the point that place opened until now, as far as I know, there were always some professors there available to schmooze with students about whatever was on their minds. What a boon!

What did we get from this? An understanding that to be a true practitioner of the law is to be immersed in the law. That you will be successful or unsuccessful to the degree that you remain accessible and giving of your mind and your compassion. That your responsibilities go beyond just "learning" into the area of sharing, teaching, and mentoring. Fabulous!

Over the years, I had disagreements with the dean, but he was a great man who almost single-handedly build a wonderful institution. As to any disagreements, if a situation developed, as long as I worked at a solution, he ultimately supported my decisions and he praised me for those solutions. So, I thought I'd better add that - it is important.

I hope that those who are following Gordon Schaber can measure up to his "whole student" approach and continue to turn out great lawyers.

When I was a training mentor at Kronick, Moskovitz, Tiedemann & Girard and at Bartel, Eng, Miller & Torngren, I really began to recognize what an overall great job they do at McGeorge. I would rather, to this day, train a McGeorge graduate than one from Georgetown, Boalt, or one of the other wholly academic law schools. That's because it is easy to train on the legal standards and procedures. It is hard to train on balance, ethics, service, and compassion! McGeorge gave me those things and it continued to give those things to other students long after I was gone. I hope it still does and will maintain that standard of creating the "whole lawyer." Andrea

As for myself as a teacher, I can only say that I was fortunate enough to wrap up my years as a law professor under an exemplary leader who through his compassion and keen interest in his students produced "whole" lawyers.

On August 1, 1990, my colleagues and students celebrated my final moments as an academic and teacher. My most touching eulogy, along with a fine roast by former students turned friends over the years, Robert Chanin, General Counsel of NEA and Norman Brand, was given by my former student, Nancy Peck. She captured what I had hoped to achieve in my leadership, perhaps most of all not only instilling lawyerly ethics, but finding jobs for my students.

Bob Chanin roasts me from the podium

MY DAUGHTER, PENNY, WAS A FREQUENT VISITOR TO THE OFFICE OF EMPLOYEE RELATIONS.

14

New York, New York

In 1975, I was hired by Gov. Hugh Carey as Chief Negotiator and Director of the Office of Employee Relations (OER) in the middle of one of New York's most severe fiscal crises.

Some thought I was an unlikely choice because I was an "outsider" with no New York political connections. Nevertheless, the Governor did not typically hire top administrators out of political expediency. He chose those whose skills fit the task at hand, and who could think and act independently.

Melvin Osterman, my predecessor, had been on the ground floor of changes in New York State's labor law, which now dictated public sector collective bargaining in the State. Mel had an intimate knowledge of the regimen in New York brought about by the advent of The Public Employees Fair Employment Act which was Article 14 of the New York State Civil Service Law, known as the Taylor Law.

As a newcomer to New York State's public sector labor relations, my hiring was an adjustment for some staff members and union leaders.

Luckily the staff I inherited proved to be good teachers. Yolanda "Yonnie" Brower, OER's secretary, knew almost all of the union leaders who walked through OER's door. Jim Northrup, OER's Deputy Director, had encyclopedic knowledge of New York's gubernatorial history and public management. He ultimately served five administrations.

Then there was Jake Kelliher, OER's assistant general counsel, a former priest, and a radical guy, and perhaps most importantly in terms of my continuing sanity, a humorist of the first order. Jake, the most political savvy person I've ever met, kept stressing to me, " In the private sector, the capital you deal with is money that is going to be spent or earned. In the public sector, the most valuable capital is political capital."

Howard Rubenstein served as my first general counsel. When he left the position, I replaced him with Joesph Bress. He was a novice in labor relations and fairly new to law, but he was talented and willing to learn. Joe later became general counsel for Amtrak. Gov. Andrew Cuomo, son of New York's former Gov., Mario Cuomo, called on him in 2010 as an expert consultant on labor negotiations issues in New York when the State entered into yet another fiscal crisis.

The OER accomplished a great deal prior to my tenure including cleaning up many collective bargaining contracts from the prior Administration. However, its most difficult task lay ahead.

The Taylor Law was a rudimentary structure for collective bargaining in lieu of strikes. It was not a blueprint for the future. That was where I came in. I was not a politician but I was a builder by nature. I wanted to create a sustainable and viable collective bargaining structure for the State.

I had some experience devising such a structure thanks to my membership on a previous task force in California that had been chaired by Benjamin Aaron. Our job had been to come up with a proposed bill to submit to the California State Legislature.

Unlike the Taylor Law, the California proposal allowed strikes given certain circumstances. Our task force had proposed well-thought out steps that could possibly lead to a strike, but would be more likely to lead to an agreement.

I was now a bureaucrat, however personally I did not believe trading a strike threat for interest arbitration served the sustainable development of public sector labor relations. If I followed that belief in my new position I would have to work toward some significant reforms to the existing law.

BIRTH OF THE TAYLOR LAW

As background, Congress passed the National Labor Relations Act of 1935, also known as the Wagner Act, in response to labor unrest happening throughout the U.S. The statute excluded two major categories of employees: farm workers and public-sector workers. These exclusions opened the door to state regulation of public sector labor relations.

Because there was no federal law that addressed civil service unions or personnel policies, legislation varied widely between states.

Different states borrowed and, to varying degrees, modified large parts of the Wagner Act as a public sector structure for collective bargaining. However, the Wagner Act was inappropriate to the public sector because bargaining involved fiscal priorities related to running a government.

The rapid growth of public sector unionism contributed to fears regarding public workers engaging in collective actions. This climate did not leave much room for the development of a suitable democratic model for public sector workers.

In *Railway Mail Association v. Murphy,* (1943), New York's lower court represented a prevailing view that challenged the right to freedom of association,

> To tolerate or recognize a combination of civil-service employees of the government as a labor organization is not only incompatible with the spirit of democracy, [it is] inconsistent with every principle upon which our government was founded...

The U. S. Supreme Court followed this view for the private and public sectors until in *J. I. Case Co. V. NLRB* (1944), the Court decided that democracy was served by the collective interest.

> ... The workman is free, and he values his own bargaining position more than that of the group, to vote against representation; but the majority rules ...individual advantages or favors will generally in practice go in as a contribution to the collective result.

This decision recognized majority rule within the federal system. However, fears of an unstable public sector system pushed demands for labor peace. This included protection against strike activities. This was particularly true when it came to uniformed employees responsible for safety.

With the Taft-Hartley Act of 1947, the U.S. Congress prohibited public sector strikes and established strict penalties (immediate dismissal and a three-year bar to reemployment) for striking public sector employees.

New York State passed the Condon-Wadlin Act in the same year following a strike by public school teachers in Buffalo New York. The 1947 act called for automatic terminations for striking public sector employees. If an employee was reinstated, he or she was barred from pay increases for three years and placed on probation without tenure for five years. The act was deemed constitutional, but it was too draconian to enforce.

Public sector union membership in New York State rose exponentially in the late 1950s and throughout the 1960s compared to private sector union membership. One year after the passage of the Taylor Law in 1967, 360,000 state and local-government employees obtained bargaining rights for the first time.

States adopted statutes that extended various bargaining rights to public employees. Twenty-one states enacted fairly comprehensive statutes. For instance, 15 states passed separate laws dealing specifically with teachers, 10 states dealt specifically with firemen, policemen, or both.

Most states went no further other than to grant unions the right to "meet and confer" with employers. Consequently, as public sector collective bargaining became more pervasive, its concepts remained fuzzy and applications were uneven. A reliance on private sector precepts continued to prevent the development of models to address unique labor relations challenges in the public sector.

Given the problem of enforcement and the negative effects the Law had on collective bargaining, New York State amended the Condon-Wadlin Act to a gentler form in 1963. The amendment lessened the severity of the penalties for individual strikers, but the law remained draconian. Employees faced a sanction of the loss of two days' pay for each day an employee was on strike. The amended act was also enforced uneasily, unevenly, infrequently, and unwillingly. Its severity made it impractical in terms of worker replacement costs and the value of good labor relations. Furthermore, it did not fulfill its primary purpose, which was to deter strikes.

While Gov. Rockefeller approved the 1963 revision of the Condon-Wadlin Act, he also recognized its effect on successful negotiations. He said in a memorandum: "[there is a] need to consider possible improvements in the overall relationship between state and local employees and their employers." This was the first acknowledgment from a government of the need for more bilateral public sector labor relations.

The amended act expired after two years and four bills were introduced to the legislature. The Rosetti-Lentol bill, the most radical of the proposed bills, provided for less punitive and more labor friendly measures and it called for decentralization. It passed the legislature, but was vetoed by Gov. Rockefeller because he believed the bill would not deter public sector strikes.

Jerome Lefkowitz, then Deputy Industrial Commissioner of the State Labor Department, proposed measures for collective bargaining and a guarantee of public sector employees' right to organize. This proposed bill was also defeated.

Gov. Rockefeller introduced the "Rockefeller Plan" which was put before the legislature along with a revival of the Lentol-Rossetti Bill. Both bills were defeated at the end of the 1966 legislature.

No strikes in New York State

A strike by employees of the New York City Transit Authority occurred in January 1966 with serious consequences for New York City and the State coffers. This event highlighted a pressing need to produce a viable structure for labor/management relations that warded off strikes and gave unions something in return.

At the behest of Gov. Rockefeller, a five-member committee spent three months drafting a report on how to manage public sector collective bargaining. The bill proposed by the committee would enact an experimental law called the Taylor Law, named for George Taylor who led the committee. It was submitted to the New York legislature on March 31, 1966. The Law passed the legislature in April 1967 after contentious debate and became Sections 200- 212 of the Civil Service Law, effective September 1, 1967.

All public sector employees now had a lawful right to organize and the right to representation.

The Taylor Law empowered state, local, and other governments and political subdivisions to recognize, negotiate with, and enter into written agreements with employee organizations representing their employees. With its enactment, New York State became the seventh state in the nation to grant collective bargaining rights to public employees. In 1967, one year after passage of the Taylor Law, 360,000 state and local government employees became unionized. By 1971, approximately 900,000 of New York State's public sector employees belonged to a union.

The new statute spurred a burst of union organizing outside of New York City, including teachers in dozens of smaller school districts upstate. Smaller unions were able to get into the game for the first time. This broadened union representation across the state. The Taylor Law and its associated political processes brought permanent victories to many unions.

Public management also benefited. This was the first time that concessions were sought from the unions in the bargaining process.

Management had to engage in the collective bargaining process and take a tougher management role.

NEW ORGANIZATIONS

Perb

The Taylor Law included the creation of new state entities to manage labor relations and collective bargaining. These were the Public Employee Relations Board (PERB), the Office of Employee Relations (OER), which was my office, and New York City's Office of Collective Bargaining (OCB).

The Public Employee Relations Board (PERB) was a three-member panel with broad statewide jurisdiction. PERB had mediation, legal, and administrative duties under the Taylor Law related to the right to organize and the right to good faith negotiations. PERB also had the authority to make unit determinations and to initiate processes to resolve an impasse. Either party could invoke the assistance of PERB in the event of an impasse.

"Mini-PERBs" could be created under Sections 206 and 212 of the Taylor Law. Governments, other than the State or State public authorities, could form a legal entity through the legislature to implement procedures that were consistent with PERB's provisions. These entities performed the same function0s as PERB except for determinations of impasse involving uniformed law enforcement and firemen.

The mini-PERB's were not particularly effective almost all the counties opted to use the State PERB. By 2011 only four of the original 35 mini-PERB's remained in existence. The exception was New York City.

Contractual agreements reached by the parties through the collective bargaining process were outside of PERB's authority. The contracts were managed by New York City's OCB, and by OER.

Office of Collective Bargaining

The Office of Collective Bargaining was created under New York

City's administrative code. It was a counterpart of sorts to the state-wide PERB. One of its primary challenges was to develop a manageable bargaining environment specific to New York City. Its functions related to unit determinations were similar to the statewide PERB. This involved working with New York City's sophisticated and powerful larger municipal unions.

These unions had gained their authority when labor law pioneer, Ida Klaus, drafted the Little Wagner Act in 1954 and collective bargaining was sanctioned in New York City for the first time.

I had the privilege of working closely with Ida. She served as my mentor when she and I formed the Committee on Public Sector Bargaining of the ABA Section on Labor Law in 1959. At that time, unionization and collective bargaining in the public sector were still a whisper. In fact, I dedicated my book, *Collective Bargaining in Public Employment*, fourth edition (1993), co-authored with Joseph Grodin and June Weisberger, to Ida with the words, "who pointed the way."

New York City had a fragmented bargaining process following the Little Wagner Act years. From 1968 through 1973, the number of bargaining units in New York City decreased 36 percent, but around 250 separate units still remained, which created a chaotic bargaining environment between public management and the different units.

Office of Employee Relations

OER managed contractual relations statewide with unions including the Police Benevolent Association (PBA), Council 82 of the American Federation of State County and Municipal Employees (AFSCME), and the Civil Service Employees Association (CSEA), the largest union. These statewide unions represented a total of 180,000 state employees with memberships in ten bargaining units. Five were broad horizontal units that crossed department and agency lines. OER bargained with the respective unions regarding matters common to all units, such as financial and retirement issues.

OER personnel put in long nights on an annual and bi-annual basis, with minimal breaks between rounds, negotiating contractual agreements with these unions. Our state office also worked routinely with unions and public management on grievance arbitrations and other matters including proposed legislation related to labor/management affairs.

The Taylor Law empowered public employers to enter into written agreements with recognized or certified employee organizations, Part of OER's role was to send labor and public management to bootcamp in relation to basic collective bargaining knowledge and how to apply the Taylor Law.

The advent of the Taylor Law led to a massive restructuring of existing agencies and the introduction of new ones. Political and administrative processes were reformulated which affected labor/management relations. Broad issues began to emerge that would somehow have to be resolved in new forums and different levels of New York's complex governance system. OER helped both unions and government agencies adjust to these new realities.

Since New York State shared tax revenues with local governments, OER also acted as a silent partner in negotiations between local governments and the unions representing their employees. The State's numerous smaller governments had no background in formal collective bargaining and now had to address the effects of the new opportunities that had opened up for their employees.

1974-1976 FISCAL CRISIS

The 1973-1975 fiscal crisis was considered the most severe since WWII as the country went from an economic boom to a severe economic slowdown. The recession spread from coast to coast and throughout the western world. A large part of the cause was perceived to be a result of union demands. By November 1975, it was obvious that union demands would tip New York State far into the red.

Even as economic growth slowed, New York State's public sector labor force grew exponetially. All eyes were on New York City because the city had the best paid public sector workers in the country and the highest consumer demand. The City of New York led the nation in terms of reforms in education and welfare. The cost was a public budget second only to the federal government's and the highest in the country.

THE CITY AND UPSTATE BUMPKINS

"There are no mirrors, no rollovers, no fiscal gimmicks to postpone reality." Ella Grasso, governor of Connecticut.

Gov. Rockefeller's contributions to building the State University of New York (SUNY) system and other capital projects are legendary. He initiated new ways to spend money in areas such as transit, education, and welfare.

However, the New York Gov. overspent when it came to the City of New York. The state of New York funneled money into the city through grants and funding functions that had been funded locally in the past. This weakened both the city's resiliency and its autonomy. Federal aid had been generous but this aid provided incentives to spend more. When the federal cutbacks inevitably came and the city sought help, [1]*The Daily News* ran the dramatic headline, "Ford to City: Drop Dead."

Per capita costs for public services rose exponentially during the 1960s and early 1970s. By 1973 state aid contributions of $2.5 billion almost equaled the entire expense budget of the previous decade. By the spring of 1975, the city's municipal government had an operating deficit of $2 billion and faced the task of refinancing $6 billion of outstanding short-term debt. The city's tax base could not cover the city's public sector costs.

When the fiscal crisis blossomed fully, municipal unions ultimately came to the rescue. Among the larger municipal unions there was membership money. There were pensions. There was generally greater union wealth compared to the rest of the state.

In order to save the city from bankruptcy, the United Federation of Teachers (UFT), District Council 37 of AFSCME and other unions

---

1   This was not a verbatim statement from President Gerald Ford.

deferred pay increases. Under the leadership of Victor Gotbaum and his predecessor, District Council 37 of AFSCME had gained good benefits and salary increases for its members, and a viable pension scheme therefore it could defer all or a portion of its expected 6 percent wage increase.

The unions agreed to divert $2.5 billion from pension funds into Municipal Assistance Bonds (MAC). Mayor Abe Beame then borrowed from these funds in the face of the banks' refusal to lend the city any more money.

For the most part strike actions were put in abeyance during the worse of the crisis. Al Shanker, president of the United Federation of teachers (UFT) called off a teachers' strike after five days saying, "A strike is a weapon you use against a boss who has money. This boss has no money." He asked the Teachers' Retirement System to invest $150 million in MAC.

New York City's default deadline was met and there was relative labor calm in New York City. The cost was a political coup in which the largest municipal unions in New York City achieved unprecedented leverage at the polls. These unions had acted collectively as the primary creditor of the municipality and this created a situation in which the strongest unions sat on both sides of the table (The United Federation of Teachers (UFT) and the Transit Union remained outside the purview of the OCB and made special deals).

One manifestation of a special deal occurred in the 1970s when the unions and the mayor made common cause against the Emergency Financial Control Board in order to gain approval of labor contracts, which were substantially funded by the State. The Board had been created by the State to save the In city from insolvency and to make its paper marketable.

In a speech I delivered to a New York City audience I said "… in the private sector where I used to work, we used to say, if only we owned the company, this is what we would do." Then I looked directly at Victor Gotbaum sitting in the audience and said, "You own the company."

In reviewing this history, one wonders if it is ever possible for the elected heads of a city that is heavily organized due to the trade union movement, to act like managers and still survive politically. The threat of a union to mobilize its members to vote against a mayor when he stands again at the polls will not be disregarded when public employees constitute a substantial part of his constituency.

The State is not New York City

In terms of my job as director of the statewide OER, it was clear, that the state of New York was not the city. New York City's more militant and experienced municipal unions had something public management needed, e.g. pension funds. Austerity was managed by richly textured political deal making, common cause, new entities, and coalitional arrangements.

The state's public sector challenges were different. We had to deal with PERB's unwieldy unit determinations and negotiate with the state's largest union, the Civil Service Employees Association (CSEA) as the union metamorphosed from an association into a serious union without much leadership.

OER also had to work with legislators who were reluctant to give up the advantages they had achieved by dealing directly with the unions on state and local levels.

There was also the matter of persistent attitudes. Upstate New York was a wasteland of secondary considerations. Jake Kelliher had a favorite story about Stanley Fink, majority leader and speaker of the Assembly at the time:

So, I went over to his office to deal with him and his staff about why they should not support the continuation of interest arbitration. At some point I asked him, 'Listen, what are you going to do with the Association of Towns, the Association of Counties, the School Board Associations - They are all opposed to this continuation [of interest arbitration]. Stanley's chief of staff stared at me and then finally said, 'Bumpkins, kid, they're all bumpkins.'

NEGOTIATING WITH EMPTY POCKETS

Fiscal 1975-76 showed a large budgetary gap between income and expenditures. Inflation had sent the costs of government up; recession had impaired the growth of revenues; the tax base had shrunk, and the fiscal crisis was revealing serious past mismanagement.

I had not been on the job long when I was called into the Governor's office, along with Peter Goldmark, State Budget Director, to discuss austerity measures to present to statewide unions. The Governor's directive was simple, "Don, give me two years of salary increases. Give them nothing. But for God's sake don't have a strike."

A freeze was the only way to respond to unions' salary and fringe benefit demands without drastically curtailing services to the public or seeking major increases in a severely burdened tax structure. The governor was not prepared to do either. In his famous "the days of wine and roses are over" speech, Gov. Carey announced an across-the-board salary freeze across the state, including municipal and county governments.

The OER office signed a memorandum of agreement with the PBA on February 9 1976 agreeing to no increases in salary and benefits. Sixty three percent of the 4000 PBA membership ratified the agreement. The same terms were then offered to CSEA which in return delivered a warning that we had better come up with concrete benefits for its members in exchange. The PBA representing the State Troopers was not going to control the agreement with CSEA and its 147,000 members.

I was convinced that I had to thump my shoe on the table as the unproven director of OER. I had to put CSEA on notice that things were different. There would be no more of the patronage the union had enjoyed during Gov. Rockefeller's Administration, no more end runs and discrete political deals. Collective bargaining through OER would be the only watering hole in the wilds of New York's labor relations.

A plan for austerity bargaining

I set out four cornerstones for negotiating with CSEA with the understanding that fiscal modifications are not likely to happen

203

unless the following were in place:

(a) Demonstrable evidence that the status quo has proven unworkable or mischievous.

(b) External evidence establishing obviously "changed circumstances" which impel modification.

(c) A perceptible trade-off in which the party seeking change has "bought" an agreement.

(d) A presentation of productivity as a shared concern for the good of the industry.

Under my directorship, OER began its 1975 contract negotiations with CSEA. In terms of the first two precepts, my challenge to all of New York State's statewide public sector unions was for them to consider the relationship between more money and the rising number of unemployed members.

As I began negotiations, New York State employees already ranked at or near the top of compensation levels for state employees in the United States across occupational groups. Ten thousand workers had been laid off in New York State at a time when the State's base salaries, already the highest in the country, increased 50 percent for most civil service employees, and even more for law enforcement personnel. Local and state public sector workers were paid 46 percent above the national average.

Public sector employees deserved timely wage increases, but labor costs had to be managed. In 1975, the $10.4 billion state budget was $50 million in the red and CSEA wanted a $69 million or a 15.5 percent wage increase over the terms of the proposed contract. That was not going to happen.

I had been in office for about a month when I first sat down with about 50 CSEA leaders and members who had gathered at the opening session for the next contract negotiation.

I lobbed my first symbolic act when I entered the meeting room before the other arrivals and observed tables loaded with coffee and an abundance of food. This impressive spread had been billed to the State per usual.

I looked at all the food and asked with feigned puzzlement "What is all this food? We're in a fiscal crisis… There must be hungry people somewhere… Take it away, leave the coffee." The union representatives arrived anticipating the usual good food and there was only coffee.

Unlike more aggressive unions with a history of organizing, CSEA had happily accepted the Taylor Law's no strike provision because the union was already favored by former Gov. Rockefeller to win big on unit determinations. My implementation of small and large acts, symbolic or otherwise, helped to transform the patronage system that had allowed this expectation under Gov. Rockefeller. Uncertainties are key to successful collective bargaining. These acts moved collusive understandings off center and brought a measure of uncertainty toward an acceptance that the state could no longer pay public sector unions to organize as it had been doing.

AT THE TABLE

New York State went from around 5 percent unemployment to 8.56 percent in the period of a year. CSEA threatened to strike in December 1975 in the middle of the fiscal crisis. I did not take the threat seriously. CSEA was not in a position to mobilize its members. It had no viable structure to accommodate a new and diverse membership. Its units largely lacked a strong community of interest, and its local units had typically operated on their own with little central support.

In addition, CSEA's past showed half-baked, badly planned strike activity, which reflected the belief of CSEA's leadership, Theodore Wenzl. He believed CSEA was all powerful and could comfortably survive without negotiating with the State or building relationships with other public sector unions.

As a consequence of this attitude from the union's leadership, CSEA had little capacity to work through difficult negotiations with the State. Instead, CSEA chose to strike for the first time in its history, four years after enactment of the Taylor Law. The union's plan was to mobilize 150,000 members in order to save the jobs of 8,250 state

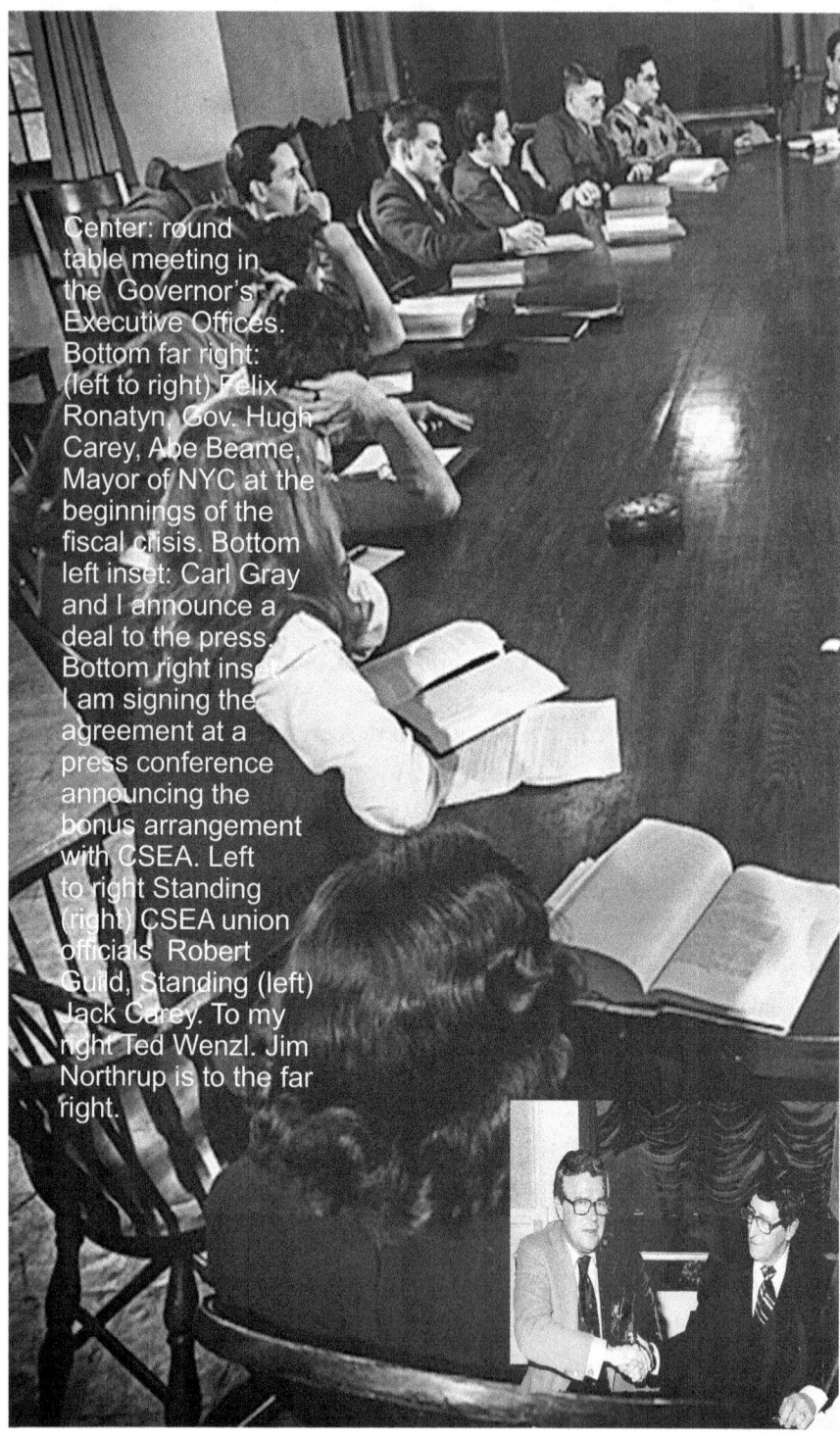

Center: round table meeting in the Governor's Executive Offices. Bottom far right: (left to right) Felix Ronatyn, Gov. Hugh Carey, Abe Beame, Mayor of NYC at the beginnings of the fiscal crisis. Bottom left inset: Carl Gray and I announce a deal to the press. Bottom right inset: I am signing the agreement at a press conference announcing the bonus arrangement with CSEA. Left to right Standing (right) CSEA union officials Robert Guild, Standing (left) Jack Carey. To my right Ted Wenzl. Jim Northrup is to the far right.

Fiscal challenges and negotiations

employees slated to be eliminated because of budget cuts. The strike was aborted the day it was to begin.

One CSEA representative recalled:

Ted, having no relationship at all with the Gov. [Carey] decided the only answer to that difficult negotiation was to call a statewide strike...Ted insisted that this was the solution... We need to have a strike. So we geared up for a strike and we held a special delegates, meeting at the Palace Theater in Albany, totally rigged. That's the way it was done in those days. All the speakers lined up were plants and the meeting opened and Ted Wenzl jumps up and says, 'I propose that since the negotiations are so difficult and the State is not doing anything to bring an end to this difficulty, we strike.' Someone who was planted at the microphone one said, 'I second the motion.' Someone at microphone three said, 'Me too.' You know, third and all like that. Ted says, 'Let's have a vote.' A few people said, 'Aye.' Ted said, 'Carried.' He didn't even ask for the nays. With the wave of his hand, he ordered the power to be cut off to the microphones and Ted ran off the stage,out the side door, into a waiting car and took off for Pennsylvania [to avoid jail]...

A legendary news reporter named Arvis Chalmers, for the then Schenectady Union Star, which was an afternoon newspaper, was in the audience and he ran out and got on the phone. He called in this story that CSEA had just voted to strike the state of New York.

[Meantime] [The] delegates, many of them jumped up and the stage screaming and yelling. They didn't even know what happened. They took over the meeting and most of the officers had stayed on the stage and they had a sort of an impromptu meeting, redo, and in the end decided to carry, on, of course, not to strike and to carry on negotiations.

The afternoon papers came out and by the time that meeting was out they were distributed to the delegates, World War III headline - 'CSEA strikes New York.' It didn't happen, of course, and the next day they had to have a major retraction on page 3. Ted Wenzl wasn't seen by anybody for about a week.

The following year, CSEA shut down mental hospitals, juvenile training schools, prisons, and other state institutions with another strike. This strike, involved 7,000 employees in a pay dispute. It might have been impressive except that the strike was scheduled for an Easter weekend. This was hardly an attention-getter. It was settled when the state offered new concessions.

A 40-hour strike in 1972 by CSEA had brought its members a 5.5 percent wage increase, but the strike action had been a relatively insignificant factor in the deal and as mandated under the Taylor Law, individual striking CSEA members paid the penalty of two days' pay for each day off the job.

IMPASSE

In our current negotiation, the State and CSEA went to impasse, the term used to describe a predicament with no escape.

Those of us in the labor relations business used the term less restrictively as a "hangout" at the bargaining table where further conversations between the parties appear fruitless and an interruption of services for production seems to be imminent or has already occurred.

PERB established a fact-finding panel which met on April 28, 1975 over the impasse between the state and CSEA and recommended a fairly typical solution of a 6 percent across the board raise. This was not acceptable to the State. Austerity called for no money to unions.

Union officials met internally to discussed PERB's recommended 6 percent salary increase while at the same time Gov. Carey, Peter Goldmark, and I met in the Governor's Capitol office to decide how to respond. Though some local entities had agreed on 6 percent wage increases, the State could not and would not accept the recommended increase. We had to accept that the unions were at least a partial cause of New York State's fiscal problems. The high costs associated with CSEA and other unions had to be brought down. We would continue the mantra, "No money."

I disliked number crunching, but I was determined to know who had done what, got what, and where and when as part of my new job responsibility. My investigation of voluminous budget-related documents revealed a number of additional costs related to labor relations that had not been accounted for, including numerous costs associated with practices inherited from the Rockefeller Administration that had not been reflected in the succession of agreements with CSEA and the other unions. My findings revealed the extent to which the state of New York had been footing a significantly large bill to help union leaders organize.

Nevertheless, Gov. Carey was fully committed to two-way collective bargaining as a viable way to maintain New York's standard of public services. He also cared about equitable pay for public sector employees while keeping a cap on tax increases. New York State residents had experienced too many tax increases under Gov. Rockefeller and were now headed for taxes of over 15 percent to pay for public services.

New York unions had their share of past pleas from the state that there was no money, which in some cases they had found to be untrue. The fiscal crisis we faced, on the other hand, was demonstrably real. The unions were going to have to listen because the state was moving toward a billion dollar deficit (which seems like nothing today, but it was large then). Fringe benefits associated with unions had reputedly absorbed 45 percent of the state payroll ($384 million in fiscal years 1974-1975). The total package cost for public employees was estimated to be around $770 million. This did not include the high administrative costs for handling all this.

Given the above considerations and with the awareness that things had to change, we rejected PERB's recommendation and allowed the impasse to continue.

Negotiations with CSEA continued into the spring of 1976. Finally, late in the evening on March 12, 1976, three months following CSEA's December 1975 strike threat and impasse, a tentative agreement on a two-year contract extension was reached with CSEA. It called for no salary increase in the first year. Instead, CSEA workers would received a one-time $250 bonus. There was pissing and moaning about this meager win, but the union ultimately ratified the agreement. It was understandable, but unreasonable, that CSEA had asked for a state prohibition of all layoffs. The state could never guarantee this with any predictability. I pointed out on several occasions that CSEA needed to look instead at the dichotomy visited upon their membership. Members were being laid off while the union wanted traditional raises for its working employees. Demands needed to be placed into the realm of shared reality.

It occurred to me that perhaps collaborating to meet the state's need to solve basic and persisting issues, e.g., job security would help construct this reality.

I used my private sector experience with the Armour Automation Committee to develop a labor/management initiative. The New York State Legislature agreed to invest $1 million in a joint labor/management committee to be called the Continuity of Employment Committee (CEC). The task of the Committee was to exercise foresight and figure out ways to avoid layoffs now and in the future, whatever the fiscal ups and downs experienced by the state.

The proposal was accepted by CSEA partly because union knew it had to do more to protect state employees and the outlay of a significant sum of money demonstrated the state was serious about helping public sector workers. Whatever the posturing at the table, the formation of the CEC represented a level of understanding that we were all in this together.

CEC's joint/labor management initiatives were separate from contentious negotiations between CSEA and the state. While CEC received little media attention, labor conflicts were frequently reported in the press. The reports of wage and benefit freezes by the state brought angry letters to Gov. Carey and to myself as the head of OER. One constituent wrote me, "Your attitude in the present negotiations of no salary increase and your insistence of [sic] taking away fringe benefits already enjoyed from previous contracts sounds like the ravings of a very sick person." The governor's fan mail wasn't any better. One employee said: "I would like you to know that I voted for you, but I would vote for my pet dog for governor before I would vote for you again."

I frequently used the press to respond to these passionate sentiments, for instance: "We're not asking state employees to wear hair shirts, we're asking for some reasonable changes." I defined "reasonable" as a measure of cooperation where the county and other local government levels follow New York City's lead and voluntarily accept a wage freeze and deferred raises for a year.

Clearly that wasn't going to happen.

Negotiations for the 1977 collective bargaining agreement began in late 1976. CSEA halted our Albany negotiations for a 1977 contract in December of 1976. CSEA broke off negotiations in January 1977. On January 6, 1977, I met with David Burke, Peter Goldmark, and Robert Morgado in the Governor's office and reported that based on my previous negotiations with CSEA it would probably be possible to reach an amicable settlement with the union for a 6.5 percent increase in wages and benefits with no confrontation and optimal gubernatorial credit taking as long as I had adequate access to the Governor during negotiations as mandated by the Taylor Law. This door was closed due to the Governor's preoccupation with New York City and changes in the executive chambers.

I renewed the above proposal to CSEA on January 19, 1977 in an effort to cool off the crisis and to head off a fact-finding hearing facilitated by Theodore Kheel. However, I failed to convince the union to accept the offer. There was a bargaining hiatus during the first three months of 1977. Both sides claimed in the media that the other side had refused to cooperate. We went to impasse again.

Meantime, the union experienced increasing pressure as CSEA members wondered how many more layoffs would occur. For its part, the state had an unhappy and stressed public sector workforce that threatened to take its toll on services.

This time I took a second CSEA strike threat seriously because its members had been without a real salary increase for almost two years and they now believed that they were losing what they had already gained.

A public relations nightmare I caused probably did not help the situation. Quoting John L. Lewis, I suggested that CSEA didn't have a head – "its neck just grew up and haired over." I had grown frustrated in my dealings with CSEA, mostly with its unresponsive leadership. CSEA leader, Ted Wenzl, was a barrier to successful negotiations. He had shown no interest in dealing with government representatives from Gov. Carey on down. His contempt for negotiations with the state was demonstrated further by the fact that he did not bother to attend any bargaining sessions. I personally believed that aside from his boorish behavior, he was genuinely confused about who he was supposed to negotiate with and why. I also believed that he really did not accept that there was a fiscal crisis.

My slur was widely reported in the press in the middle of January. I could not take it back or ameliorate it. Wenzl told the press that I should be immediately fired because I had rendered myself "useless as a negotiator." Nevertheless, as it turned out, my outburst did not have much effect on the bargaining process other than comic relief.

In contrast to Wenzl's outrage, manufactured or not, Roger Cole, director of CSEA public relations recalled to one interviewer in an oral history project,

> ...The governor's Office of Employee Relations on television was asked about the relationship between the state and CSEA and he said something on television, "CSEA doesn't have a head. It's neck grew up and haired over." It was the funniest thing I ever saw...I had to respond to that silly stuff. Ted Wenzl insisted that we show that tape to the very next action. So, when it was shown at the delegates' meeting the response was laughter.

When impasse between the state and CSEA came before a PERB fact-finding panel chaired by Ted Kheel in February of 1977, CSEA complained to the panel that the state of New York was indifferent to the layoff situation and that we had reneged on our commitment to a substantial across-the-board salary increase made in the last round of negotiations in 1976. This was blatantly untrue and so I responded that the state had never promised a substantial across-the-board salary increase to any union. We had been clear on that count. There would be no special treatment–no increases in salary, base salary, or fringe benefits–to any union.

Before the Kheel panel made its decision, the state offered CSEA a wage increase of $63 million. This was less than the 12 percent wage increase for the first year that the union had wanted, so we were still far apart. Alternatively, neither side accepted the panel's recommendation of a 5 percent increase immediately and a 3.5 percent increase in January of 1978.

There was no face-to-face bargaining following the panel's decision until April 15, 1977 when the union presented its demand of a 12 percent wage increase in the first year or a minimum of $1200. CSEA indicated that it was ready to be more flexible if there was a double-digit offer for the first year. The marching orders from the governor had been that no more than an aggregate of $80 million should be committed for salary and benefit increases, even though all of the collective agreements were scheduled for renegotiation. This meant an average increase of 4.5 percent for the 180,000 employees involved. This was an unrealistic figure for most of the unions and their units.

The allocation of monies within the scope of the negotiations was left to my determination. I offered CSEA either a 5.75 percent increase in a one-year contract or 10 percent increase spread over a two year-contract. This was a $170 million pay package for a two-year contract. Though not what the fact-finders had recommended, given the fiscal situation and historic wage increases, this was a pretty good deal for the union.

CSEA squatted on the offer with no communication and then announced it would strike the following Monday morning. Behind the scene, we began all-night negotiations. I knew before the all-nighter that the state had the money and was even going to sweeten the pot a little.

Why do this all nighter if I already I had some idea that this time the union would accept the offer based on what was really on the table? In the context of my bargaining philosophy I considered that part of OER's job in the broadest sense was to support a viable scheme for labor relations. As Fred Livingston had said, "there is always tomorrow."

From my perspective, uncertainties are important because the best bargaining chip is a desire for stability. CSEA was a developing union that needed validation in the face of an increasingly unhappy and worried constituency that had suffered through two years of uncertainty. Given unpredictable circumstances, if a fair agreement is to be reached, opposing sides have to appear as close to equal as possible. Helping CSEA achieve the appearance of tough bargaining was a good for all approach.

I have almost always acted on the belief that when both sides look good there is a better outcome in terms of sustaining relationships between the parties.

So, while there are real all night sessions that are exhausting, this was not one of them. Rather, it was implicit to both sides in the room that night that an agreement was ready to come on stage.

I guess Ted Wenzl, the president of CSEA, did not know this back-story because the union leader angrily walked out of the negotiations that night even though I had sent strong signals to him before that our offer on the table was not necessarily a bottom line.

Saturday morning we met with PERB to bring our sides back together at the table. The union kept its strike threat active until 6 a.m. on Monday April 18 and publicized its stance in the media. Just in case, the state prepared for a strike. It lined up supervisory personnel and took other actions as reported in the press on April 16:

> Beds were seen being lugged into the Capitol, and one woman reported that 'pound after pound' of coffee had been brought into her office during the afternoon. The Capitol police were instructed to disregard usual building passes for the weekend.

CSEA continued to play the press with comments and statements, but we had actually reached an agreement about 9 a.m. on April 17th. This event was well reported in the *New York Times* and other papers. A new contract was announced. The union would receive more than $215 million in increased wages and fringe benefits over the next two years for a total of 14 percent over the two-year period. This was 25 percent more than our previous offer. State employees earning less than $10,000 had a more equitable situation with the new agreement, and we had two years of a more stable workforce that deserved the wage increase. CSEA had achieved its first wage increase since 1974.

Politics and OER

In the two-year long process, layoffs had been minimized and no taxes had been raised, so the public was a winner. For our part, we had held a line on fiscal responsibility and done a credible job of building relationships with the unions.

Everyone was happy. Well, almost.

I believe that what transpired at this point regarding what was said at the table and what was said later was due mostly to lawyerly interferences that had plagued CSEA's leadership. CSEA lawyers held too much power within the organization. This eventually became a cause of internal dissension. It is important in negotiations to know whom you are dealing with and whether they help or hinder the process and the outcome. In this case, the lawyers were a negative influence.

The press was also a negative influence because it failed to do its homework. The press had generally expressed unhappiness with the state's stance toward unions. It was sympathetic to the idea that in the past the state had adjusted to rates that were not what was actually paid. There were notable exceptions such as the coverage by A. Raskin writing for the *New York Times*. He knew labor relations and politics well.

"Me tooism" also reared its head. The Police Benevolent Association (PBA) of State Troopers announced it would refuse to accept an earlier agreement with the state because the CSEA had received a better settlement.

Had we finally ended two years of strife? Well, almost.

Politicking went on in its own sphere, as is its nature. In an end-run in June the legislature passed the bill to implement the labor settlement, but with a few riders attached that offered special deals with no fiscal analysis, to some employees, and a lucrative pension plan to some legislators. There were a number of other items that had been previously vetoed by the governor. Gov. Carey was not happy but he was stuck. It is like asking your mother if a friend can spend the night while the friend is standing right there. Challenging these items would have risked the fair deal with CSEA. I commented to the press regarding this turn of events, "it's about 50 percent what we asked for and 50 percent stuff we never heard of."

Welcome to public sector collective bargaining!

REVISING THE TAYLOR LAW

Based on his experience with the Taylor Law, the notable arbitrator, Theodore Kheel (1969), said,

> ... [The Taylor Law] did not and is not likely to work as a mechanism for resolving conflicts in public employment relations through joint determination, whether called collective bargaining or collective negotiations. With skillful and responsible negotiators, no machinery, no outsiders, and no fixed rules are needed to settle disputes. For too long our attention has been directed to the mechanics and penalties rather than to the participants in the process. It is now time to change that, to seek to prevent strikes by encouraging collective bargaining to the fullest extent possible.

In my view, the "fullest extent possible" would have to include the uncertainty of a strike threat. Prior to 1968, I had fervently argued that public employee strikes should be impermissible. I made my opinion known in an article published in the *Labor Law Journal* that was frequently cited.

Four years later, I took the opposite view in my representation of a National Education Association (NEA) local affiliate that had gone on strike in Holland, Michigan. An injunction was issued and the local affiliate took its appeal to the Michigan Supreme Court. I wrote an *amicus brief,* arguing that the injunction against the strike was unconstitutional and an abuse of judicial discretion.

The defense lawyer for the school board supported his case by quoting my earlier anti-strike view published in the *Labor Law Journal.*

Luckily, my post-1968 pro-strike position proved more persuasive than my previous anti-strike prose.

One of the justices in the earlier case was also a justice in the Holland Michigan case. He asked me how I could possibly reconcile my opposing positions. I said, "Your Honor, I've learned a lot in the real world."

There are a number of well-cited arguments against a strike, but the threat of a strike to protect legitimate claims is a fundamental democratic and human right. It is also a matter of equity in labor/management relations which is essential to healthy collective bargaining. In this sense, the threat of a strike serves to prevent a strike more than punitive and reactive measures on the part of public management.

Jake Kelliher and I decided to make this perspective known.

We began our virtuous undertaking with a proposal that would effectively dismantle the Taylor Law.

We knew we were tilting our lance at a windmill, but even *pro forma*, we believed it was an important endeavor.

The average reader would not have caught the extent to which we gutted the statute with deft and apparently painless language and authorized strikes through due process-related clauses - even as they were wooed to our position - unless the reader was on the lookout for subversive content.

For instance, we wanted to eliminate interest arbitration for police and firefighter unions and abandon the Triborough Doctrine, which stated that in the event no collective bargaining agreement is reached between the public employer and the union, benefits under the old collective bargaining agreement would continue undiminished until a new agreement was reached .

We also would have eliminated the two-for-one penalty for individual striking public sector employees.

Being protective of the Taylor Law, and being an astute legal mind, Mel Osterman figured out what we were doing and immediately mounted a defense.

He called Jake. "Jake, do I read this correctly? If you read this section versus that section, you're legalizing strikes, aren't you?"

Jake asked me, "What could I say? I said, 'Well, you win the prize, Mel.'"

Jake recalled that Mel immediately shored up a defense:

One of my jobs was to go out and sell our proposal to school boards, associations of mayors, and associations of towns and counties. Once Mel understood where we were going with the bill, he wrote a memo to his client, the New York State School Board Association, and educated it on the ramifications of our proposed bill. The School Board Association quickly mobilized and sounded an alarm to all local representatives of municipal government… From then on we were in trouble and I was in the line of fire.

A three-column chart was produced attacking our proposal point by point. The headings were: "*Existing*" [law], "*OER proposed* [law]", and "*Consequences*".

Our changes to the Taylor Law were intended to protect rights that included due process and freedom of association. There was no reference to these fundamental concerns in Mel's responses to our proposal. In a March 1978 letter to the governor's counsel, Judah Gribetz, I delineated what we saw as non-responses to any constitutional concerns in "The Osterman Analysis."

Sometimes the old saying is true, "if it ain't broke don't fix it," but ultimately the Taylor Law was an experiment that survived because of inertia. Reacting to specific strike situations with what was another in a long line of punitive statutes did not equate with effective labor relations, including saving the state money in the long run. I had seen what an effective alternative without a no-strike provision could look like in California when our task force assumed the right to strike was both a human right and a reflection of human nature.

The argument that both collective bargaining and the right to strike is undemocratic is grounded in the supposition that unions are yet another "special interest" with unfair dispensations. They are not when they are at their best. Almost all of us work under different conditions that included powerless situations. I do not consider this need for representation to be a special interest. Secondly, historically unions have been well integrated into the rest of our social life in terms of social causes.

Justice Louis Brandeis elegantly captures why the right to strike is important to society:

> Because I believe in a future in which material comfort is to be comparatively easy attainment, I also believe that the race must steadily insist on preserving this moral vigor unweakened. It is not good for us that we should ever lose the fighting quality, stamina, and the courage to battle for what we want when we are convinced that we are entitled to it, and other means fail… There is something better than peace, and that is the peace that is when I struggle. We shall have lost something vital and beyond price on the day when the state denies us the right to resort to force in defense of the just cause.

INTEREST ARBITRATION REVISITED

Interest arbitration is found in the laws governing labor relations of most states. The public has little or no say concerning the outcomes of interest arbitration. In New York State, the Taylor Law did nothing to address this. One might have thought that the Taylor Law might have served as an experiment that over time addressed the exclusionary and opaque practices found in interest arbitration?

The advent of interest arbitration in 1974 had been quickly followed by experimentations with tripartite arbitration panels, final offers, and issue-by issue arbitrations. These arbitral experiments might have been applied to the parties' efforts to deal with a particular fiscal situation, or by a drive for reform, or by law, by inability to resolve intractable conflict, or by some awareness of the costs of poor labor management relations.

In the process of negotiations, PERB manages issues between the parties. If its efforts fail, an arbitrator as a third party is appointed by PERB or the parties to make a final decision.

There are problems of accountability associated with this role. The arbitrator or arbitral panels represented private actions involving persons who have no stake in legislative spending decisions that affect all of us. Yet, it is our elected representatives serving in the legislature that hold the purse strings, Consequently, salary increases might have to be funded by upward adjustments in taxes, leaving potholes in the street unfilled, roads unsanded during snow storms, fewer park hours, curtailed services, and laid-off workers, all of which cost the taxpayer who has little knowledge of these expenditures.

Interest arbitration is mostly exclusionary. The addition of interest arbitration to the Taylor Law reflected the powerful lobbying effectiveness of police and firefighter unions in a statewide election year. However, singling out one profession over another because of concerns about public safety is unfair. If binding interest arbitration is to be the final solution in lieu of the right to strike, then it should adequately protect all classifications and types of public sector employees' interests against unilateral terms imposed by the employer.

Binding interest arbitration brought a measure of labor peace, but one has to ask how much was it really worth in the face of constitutional concerns and inherent inequities.

COOPERATION AND CONFLICT

The adversarial legal system will not disappear and in fact we should hold on to some of its "moral vigor." However, real progress can only happen when cooperation exists. In other words, collective bargaining carries inherent tensions and a sense of immediacy that do not necessarily account for the bigger picture. Frequently, many of the largest issues are identified away from the table thanks to cooperative efforts.

Items that appear on the table in collective bargaining are usually the tip of the iceberg. Fundamental issues, e.g., lack of job creation or patterns of layoffs, do not surface easily. These issues do not get resolved through binding interest arbitration, strike activity, in court, by statutory mandates, political relationships, or even through the collective bargaining process.

If decades of arbitrating labor/management disputes taught me anything it is that issues are resolved as a result of trusted and tried one-to-one and group relationships that have been forged in the resolution of labor problems that are more frequently off the table, e.g. the selection of a foreman, who turns out to be a shitty foreman, or the problem of an incompetent teacher. Perhaps these issues are symptomatic of patterns representing gross inequities, industry ills, or agendas that are poorly articulated. Perhaps the elephant in the room is too big to see. The capacity to recognize fundamental issues behind the routine and to have the foresight to see these routine problems as a strategic and mutual concern comes with the understanding that adversarial approaches, while serving some purpose, will always have limited utility in the scheme of things.

Referencing Fred Livingston again, I would leave, but the parties would have to work together tomorrow. My relationship with Carl Gray, head of Council 82 exemplified that precept. The union head, representing correctional officers, and I built a relationship on earned trust. Acting on our mutual understanding was both advantageous and communicable to our respective constituents and members. This was in a sense the capital that allowed us to deal fairly and wisely with correctional officers.

We earned trust by making *in situ* visits together to the most long-suffering workers, which included mental health workers and correctional officers. This exercise allowed us to deal with sensitive and chronic issues away from the collective bargaining table, and it also gave us some foresight.

When it came to New York's correctional officers, we gained enough information to safely predict that the odds were that a strike would happen within the next couple of years and nothing would prevent it. We needed a plan to manage the strike and mitigate circumstances following the strike. In the meantime, we agreed to continuing consulting with each other in order to address emerging issues with some consistency. The strike occurred a couple of years later in 1979. Both of us had left the scene, however our legacy – a blueprint for handling strike – was put into use.

My active cooperation with Carl Gray was partially inspired by the intelligence gathering methods developed by Lemuel Boulware, though I did not necessarily share his motives behind the final offer negotiating strategy.

THE REMARKABLE CEC

Good labor relations requires informed relationships. In other words, it helps to carefully read who you are dealing with, what their needs and wants are, and what you want out of a deal. This in turn supports planning for contingencies. This exercise frees you from the fears surrounding the possibility of a strike, and hopefully from the tendency to make sweeping laws out of fear of social unrest. It helps if the leadership on both sides is principled and cooperative.

I ran into Bill McGowan, the CSEA president who succeeded Ted Wenzl, in an airport. We didn't know each other well, but we respected each other. I shared an idea with him for a joint labor/management problem-solving committee while we waited for our respective planes. Bill liked the idea and promised full cooperation. Thus the Continuity of Employment (CEC) was born as an interdisciplinary action-research program with a three-year lifespan. It was the first of its kind in the country.

I recruited Robert B. Mckersie, Dean of the New York State School of Industrial and Labor Relations at Cornell University, to provide leadership for the CEC. The Cornell professor later published excellent accounts of its processes and achievements. Beyond his writings, there is not much mention about the CEC and its origins in the journals, though it performed beyond expectations at a critical time in New York's labor history.

It is worth providing some detail on the CEC because though I have formed or observed labor/management committees in the past with good results, the CEC represents to me an ideal we have yet to achieve in labor relations. Some of the details below helps delineate why CEC was unprecedented.

The agreement for CEC, a three-year program between the state of New York and CSEA, was signed in March of 1976 as a quiet aside to tense negotiations between CSEA and the state of New York. Its mandate was to support state workers whose employment had been affected by fiscal and policy decisions in the short term and to develop long term solutions. The CEC mandate was funded by the State for $1 million in lieu of increased wages and benefits for CSEA.

Four CSEA regional presidents of CSEA and four members representing public management, along with an alternate for each, met monthly in Albany, New York. The state offices represented were the Department of Civil Service, Office of Manpower Management; Office of Mental Retardation and Developmental Disabilities; Employee Compensation and Relations Unit, of the Division of the Budget; the Department of Education's Office of the Budget, and the Employee Relations Office as a management alternate. Thomas Gibbs, Assistant Director of the Office of Employee Relations represented my office.

One could consider that the participation of any particular office or agency representing public management was only as useful as the measure of the leadership, the motivation of people involved, and access to actual decision making authority.

The facilitator's leadership skills and knowledge were essential to the success of the committee, which is why I recommended Bob McKersie to be CEC's neutral chairman. The labor and management officials accepted my recommendation based on his exceptional academic credentials and his reputation. Bob was appointed in September 1976.

He was a superior facilitator. Bob had the patience to allow trusting relationships to unfold and he knew how to share ownership of the problems and solutions that emerged with the committee members. Bob was also able to unobtrusively shift perceptions one degree or another in order to help the committee members cast enough light on a subject to reframe an issue or concern in some reasonable and actionable way that everyone understood.

The committee convened the first week in April of 1977. A mission and agenda were laid out. An action research methodology was chosen. Researchers and technical assistants were appointed to work on research and programming on a continuing and a single-project basis. Doctoral students coordinated programs and produced hard data to guide the committee in its decision-making.

Other experts conducted independent lines of research to be integrated into the committee's action research efforts. Some examples of these studies included investigating the content and adequacy of human resource planning and administrative decision-making by the state of New York and its agencies.

An expert arbitrator and mediator studied the value of a task-force approach following the Warwick School model and how to apply this model to state agencies undergoing similar disruptions.

A professor of Professor of Personnel and Human Resource Management at Cornell's ILR School studied the costs and benefits of advance notice. Another study involved the analysis of legal constraints on continuity of employment for laid off workers and reformulated layoff statistics. Other participants handled the wide dissemination of reports from the data that was collected.

CEC Topics

The committee had a three-stage goal which was: (1) exploration of novel problems which were defined as chronic, unsolved problems that had proven to be persistent roadblocks to significant changes. (2) the implementation of promising strategies to address problems associated with the re-employment of people laid off in the past and the prevention of future layoffs. (3) The institution of permanent solutions into the state's normal flow of human resource operations.

The joint labor/management committee reviewed chronic conditions that plagued labor and public management such as the use of normal and induced attrition (e.g. early retirements), job sharing opportunities, transfers, indemnification, (e.g. severance pay), and transition to work strategies such as retraining.

CEC was a precedent-setting committee unmatched by any previous or subsequent labor/management effort in the country because it placed the importance of process over form. It placed a high value on gathering intelligence while it remained independent of politics and

211

collective bargaining processes. It focused on the impact of programs, including changes in policies and laws on the people involved, rather than on rationales for changes made from a top down institutional perspective. In other words, it looked at the actual effects on individual workers of the " black box" of state government decisions about a multitude of programs.

Its members were willing to experiment with innovative approaches while dealing with the reality of a massive state bureaucracy. The above challenges required acts of faith on the part of CEC members.

This is particularly true when it came to agreeing to work with unfamiliar methodologies. Action research relies on some generally stated hypotheses to be shaped on the ground even as data from different sources are collected. This represents a risk of unpredictable results.

It is a testimony to leadership and the altruism of parties more familiar with competition that the committee unanimously agreed to commit most of its resources to action-oriented demonstration programs while continuing to invest heavily into research and technical assistance.

The above efforts involving broad participation yielded invaluable self-actualizing broad statements that applied to individual workers, the system, and specific public agencies.

Examples of the CEC's broad statements were: Agencies can mitigate discontinuous employment. Employees can use self-help if they have the right agency help from the agency's personnel function. A good system allows agencies to institute effective programs.

The CEC demonstrated changes agencies could reasonably institute as worker self-help initiatives that represented were humane solutions. These changes included advance notice of layoffs, effective vocational, career and personal counseling in the instance of disrupted employment, good resource planning through timely data, systematic approaches to help laid off employees, such as a well-designed skills inventory, and better official communications to address the common occurrence of rumors and misinformation.

Putting a system in place

The CEC's research initiatives were triggered by strong evidence that the state of New York had no system in place to serve its workers through fiscal ups and downs. In the words of the committee, "no statewide readjustment system existed." It concluded that a decentralized workforce plan was needed based on agency workforce assessments that reflected human resource supply and demand projections.

The committee looked at the persisting forces working against this proactive approach and concluded that items such as dealing inadequately with state budget cycles and problems with provincialism was partially responsible for a troubled system incapable of coping with layoff problems, particularly during a budget crisis.

With the adoption of the CEC, New York State became the first and perhaps still the only state in the country willing to invest in a longer-range view of workers' security in a tough budgetary environment.

Paralleling the committee's work, collective bargaining negotiations between the state and statewide unions continued over the three-year period.

Robert Mckersie wrote:

> … The work of the committee was viewed as supplementary to collective bargaining. While the mandate to the committee had come from collective bargaining (and indeed had been incorporated into the language of the agreement), the work of the committee was adjunct to the adversary process of collective bargaining (Change and Continuity Draft, 12/31/79).

The committee produced several reports identifying how the fiscal crisis affected different workers. An early report assessed the layoff experience of a broad spectrum of state workers, while a subsequent report sought to validate findings of earlier surveys to understand the impact of layoffs in relation to particular sites or agencies.

In one instance, authors Noonan and White produced a comprehensive statewide report based on questionnaires and face-to-face interviews and specifically a survey of white, married, union-affiliated, mostly male (72 percent) workers who had some college education.

The Noonan and White report substantiated an earlier report that showed a strong association between an individual's loss of earning and savings, and strong evidence of significantly increased stress in the personal lives of workers. It was a report that challenged the gauze of a bureaucracy that masks the true price of inefficiency now and in the future.

Noonan and White reported that many of the workers interviewed by the authors had been on a path of upward mobility, reaching out to the American dream of middle class living, when the tsunami of layoffs or threatened layoffs occurred in New York State's public sector. Workers experienced higher debt and savings depletions. This was associated with a greater range of health problems. There was a "significant association" between "blue or depressed feelings, sleeping, tiredness, increased drinking, etc., and the stress of layoffs due to lost savings and incomes to manage debts such as installment payments.

The authors noted, as had other CEC reports, that the employees interviewed were unprepared for a layoff and they were uneducated as to their rights. In addition, they no longer trusted their respective unions or the state.

Significant disparities that had remained unresolved or ignored by unions and public management had led to a general condition of inequity in New York State's public sector workforce.

Nonwhites were more adversely affected by layoffs, especially in terms of financial buffers. Women were also more likely to be negatively affected. The authors reported that compared to men, women had less seniority in the occupational structure of the New York State Civil Service System and less mobility in terms of finding new work elsewhere in the event of a layoff.

These reports, based on extensive interviews, helped direct the committee's selection of demonstration projects. Mental health was a particular focus since it was one of the most contentious topics between unions and the State because of facility closures and resultant job losses, as well as the issue of deinstitutionalization in terms of the welfare of patients. The mental health agency and facility closures happening around the state affected the most vulnerable workers, who were mostly nonwhite and female.

Following its mandate to serve workers first, the CEC members agreed to focus on a particular mental health agency that was slated for closure because of the financial crisis.

CSEA agreed to "hold its fire" on its protests against deinstitutionalization and to give the CEC a chance to provide relatively low-paid mental health workers the means for continued employment. The union's condition was that the demonstration should not include layoffs or the forced transfer of employees to non-state employment (McKersie 1979 12-14).

CSEA requested that the legislature conduct a comprehensive study of staff supply and demand within the mental health system. The state legislature then requested that during its third year of operation the CEC conduct a major analysis of workforce prospects for the state's mental health agencies.

A special advisory committee was formed within CEC. Its members conducted hands-on field research. Two CEC staff members worked full-time on the project for several months. The CEC also involved all affected state agencies.

Two laid-off employees who had previously worked as counselors for a drug abuse agency met with laid off mental health care workers and worked with them on options and alternatives for re-employment.

The demonstration project supported the CEC members' research hypothesis that closures did not necessarily mean layoffs. It demonstrated the capacity of both parties to think long-term and yet act with immediacy.

McKersie [2]recalled,

> The Committee walked into [a] complicated crunch and ended up deploying all three hundred workers, many of them to other units operated by the Office of Mental Retardation.

> Most fundamentally, the cooperation and earned trust between the CEC parties, regardless of negotiations or circumstances happening outside of the group's activities, led to achievements that would not have been realized outside of the Committee.

> Their cooperation with each other depended upon a shared belief among CEC members that continuity of employment meant caring for the life of the worker in practical ways whether in terms of unemployment or under employment. The initiative of the Committee to act on this belief, and even institutionalize some of its practices within the New York bureaucracy and political environment, was unprecedented and unique in the country's public sector.

The CEC was clear about what it was designed to do, how to do it, and why. The CEC had worked at a human level inspired by the workers themselves.

The CEC was designed to go out of business after three years, which is what happened. The era following was focused on the catchword of productivity that swept the nation, but not necessarily in the context of the CEC's findings or from the perspective of individual workers and at-risk groups.

"Productivity," rather than job security or job creation was spoken of in isolation rather than as part of a whole system, and that is where federal and state money and expertise went. What makes or motivates a worker to be productive became secondary.

On a positive note, there were residual effects from the activities of the CEC according to Jim Northrop, my former deputy at OER. Jim

---

2   Change and Continuity 12//31/79 (draft)

continued on in the new administration under Gov. Mario Cuomo. He observed that the CEC and collective bargaining experiences during the Carey Administration had elevated cooperation and thus improved relationships between the state and statewide unions, including a willingness to try out different kinds of joint labor/management committees.

My vision for a statewide more effective collective bargaining apparatus may not have been fully realized, but OER could boast of significant accomplishments.

Like other agencies, the OER had been swept up by the fiscal crisis. It had met this challenge and improved labor relations in the process. The OER had complied with Gov. Carey's "no-money" marching orders and across the board statewide unions achieved no increases in salary schedules or fringe benefits with minor exceptions. Some financial concessions were made to address employee concerns if they involved little or no cost, required no job actions, and if they fell within the collective bargaining system.

Summarily, largely thanks to OER's experienced and skilled staff, the Governor's austerity-driven bargaining mandate had been met with a much lower than average across-the-board increase during his first term at a time when statewide unions, particularly CSEA, were under increasing membership pressure.

Working in concert with the Governor's office, OER had set New York on a path toward a rational compensation system including a best test for compensation levels, the accounting of all compensation components, and compensation component trade offs for wages.

With the formation of the CEC, the young office had successfully established an unprecedented joint labor/management initiative unique in the country. A positive relationship between labor and management had been established through a desire to serve workers. The trust and willingness to solve social problems and protect workers on the part of the CEC members demonstrated that there were other paradigms for effective labor relations beyond adversarial relations.

Political heat

I believe that the feared threat of a strike is less of a threat to public services than political end runs that undermine contractual rights and obligations.

I had conducted my first set of negotiations as the director of OER when Albany was hit by a blizzard on February 2, 1976. Employees were unable to get to work, so the Director of State Operations decided that state offices in the Albany area should be shut down.

There was a question as to whether or not the day of absence should be counted against employee leave accruals, specifically their five-days of personal leave.

Historically, so-called "snow days" had been counted against leave. Time off was recorded as personal-leave time, and employees who managed to get to work were not entitled to compensatory time off. One of the Governor's key advisors, in the belief that reversal of past practice would redound to the Governor's political advantage, persuaded him to reverse that position.

Since we had a proposal on the bargaining table to reduce the five days' personal leave time to three days, and since the effect of the Governor's decision was to add a day, our position at the bargaining table was irreversibly compromised.

CSEA had lost an arbitration decision that held that leave provisions of a labor agreement did not entitle the state employees they represented time off with pay when work was unavailable because of snow conditions. The statewide union put enough pressure on the governor, who was tooling up for his reelection campaign, to get him to direct the Civil Service Commission to award paid leaves for such days, in effect gaining a retroactive amendment to the collective bargaining agreement.

If collective bargaining lacks the authority and the capacity to deal with workers' real concerns, unions invariably turn to legislatures and focus their resources on political decision-makers to offset built-in political disadvantages.

The political lessons I gained from this experience were that collective bargaining is only as strong as the parties honestly agree it should be and this should be reaffirmed in each bargaining round.

Collective bargaining should be viewed at all levels as a protected constitutional right if there is to be a viable labor environment or even a democratic government. If one or the other party says we'll go ahead and agree now, and then undertakes an end run to the legislature to get what it really wants, that is a serious blow to this right.

End runs are never easy to swallow for an administrator. I was disappointed when our final labor settlement with CSEA came before the legislature, the fruits of our negotiations were saddled with riders for special deals that had little to do with the collective bargaining process that we had struggled through.

In 1977, for instance, there were 39 bills related to terms and conditions of employment that passed both houses of the legislature and wound up on Gov. Hugh Carey's desk. Thirteen of these were classic end runs, which unions had won through legislative proposals. These were benefits that they had either traded off or otherwise lost at the bargaining table.

In 1978, the problem worsened, and the Democratic Assembly did little to protect their governor against the political disadvantage of being placed in this position.

Approximately 40 bills, manifesting more than an incidental relationship to the terms and conditions of employment, went to the governor for approval or veto. Ten of these were end runs. These included such matters as time off with pay (without charge to leave credits), for absences due to severe weather conditions or power failures, and employee participation on certain boards or panels, as well as greater benefits than had been negotiated in such areas as tenure or retention of employment, retiree dental insurance, and continuity of employment.

In addition, approximately 30 bills were sent to the governor that involved subjects that had either been excluded from the collective bargaining process by statutory or decisional law, or rendered inappropriate for the bargaining table because of the multiplicity of the parties of interest and the functional structuring of government. Included among these were various retirement proposals, employment status changes, and other civil service law amendments.

Furthermore, as had been the case in 1977, there were a number of bills or mandates or authorizations by the state to local governments to increase expenditures to improve benefits (principally retirement) for or on behalf of local employees, particularly police and firefighters.

If the terms and conditions of state employment fixed by legislation include the influence of special interests to the extent that public employment organizations can manipulate political processes in ways detrimental to state administrative budgets we all lose. Collective bargaining is intended largely to displace this way of doing business, but it only works if all the parties, the governor, the legislature, and the unions, appreciate that collective bargaining becomes a sham if it is politicized.

POLITICS AND PUBLIC ADMINISTRATION

Political end runs contributed to the transformation of the OER as an authoritative agency, possessing moral vigor and insight, into an overly bureaucratized, marginalized agency that barely had a mention in the press or elsewhere when New York State experienced yet another fiscal crisis with the associated labor issues in 2008.

Gov. Hugh Carey has been depicted as "the man of the hour" during New York's City's fiscal crisis. Indeed, he was. He was a good governor. The premise, however, underlying his second term in particular was that if the city was saved, so was the state. Unfortunately, things were not that simple because the state lost its governor to the city. No matter how bad the situation might have been for New York City, that should not have happened.

As Gov. Carey divided his time unequally between city and state, with a greater portion of resources going to New York City, he redirected his top advisors in the executive office, who had been my primary and trusted contacts for labor relation matters, to resolve the city's woes.

Given the fiscal situation, Gov. Carey became increasingly dependent upon a bright young man named Robert Morgado whom he had wooed away from the Ways and Means Committee in 1975.

In order to fill the void in Albany created by his work in New York City, the Governor made Morgado Director of State Operations, a nebulous and now powerful position that had not existed for years, and put him in charge of negotiating the 1976-1977 legislative budget. The Governor was drawn to people who took the initiative and Morgado was smart, brash, and ambitious.

In a memorandum to department heads, Gov. Carey went to considerable lengths to clarify the extent of the unprecedented authority delegated to Morgado.

The Director of State Operations will be the central contact in the executive chamber for the integration of administration policies, the maintenance of day-by-day liaison with all departments and agencies and the resolution of interagency matters. I expect each of you to take into account this new organizational arrangement in your direct, daily working relationships with the executive chamber... (New York Times, November 5, 1975).

The press depicted Morgado as the Governor of Albany. Some members of the press even called him governor of the State. In 1977, Robert Morgado became Secretary to the Governor., i.e., his Chief of Staff.

Whatever good Morgado might have accomplished, states do not run on politics alone. State administrators both manage the routine state operations and find themselves in positions of immediacy where they have to make critical decisions based on their special knowledge. This requires close contact with their superiors.

However, Morgado had little time for state administrators. OER, like other agencies, found its phone calls to Morgado unanswered. What had been OER's duties, which was to manage labor relations with its knowledgeable staff, became an ad hoc game of political football under the direction of Robert Morgado and his associate in the governor's office, Meyer Sandy Fruscher. Neither had labor relations experience, yet they bypassed OER and dealt with the unions directly without consultation.

Because of this end run, OER as an administrative agency directly responsible to the Governor, lost the capacity to build on successive negotiations at its most sensitive stage of growth.

As the situation worsened, I decided to leave. I sent the governor a formal letter of resignation along with an outline of upcoming issues facing public sector labor relations in New York State.

I was not shy about including the OER's loss of authority and warned that a strong Office of Employee Relations with good leadership was essential if the goal was to develop a viable structure of labor relations that could withstand the inevitable fiscal crises that would be experienced in the future. I recommended that my successor possess the courage, knowledge, and leadership skills to uphold administrative responsibilities despite political interference in order to give the OER the continuity it needed and to signal to the unions that OER would not be held captive to politics.

I recommended my deputy, Jim Northrup, as that person because he was an experienced administrator with a long history in government. He knew New York's labor relations history, and he was relatively immune to political machinations.

I also recommended re-establishing a Personnel Policy Committee to ensure coordination among the governor's senior staff members to avoid what had become embarrassing and hapless ends to union negotiations under the new regime that now occupied the executive chambers.

Many of my recommendations would have been relatively easy to put in place by borrowing what has worked for the private sector and through the use of the existing Executive Law, which specified the authority of the Director of OER to have direct access to the Governor.

Jim Northrup stayed with the office as the only remaining labor relations expert through Governor Carey's second term. However, he was not offered my job. Instead, Fruscher became my successor as Director of OER in 1978, I believe this appointment was primarily to give him a spot in government. He was good at public relations, which is not labor relations.

The governor's decision to hire an administrator with no history related to collective bargaining with New York State unions and no labor relations experience in general was partly responsible for the reversal of deals with the unions that had been fostered by OER. This opened the door for the 48 agencies in the Executive Department of New York's government to conduct autonomous negotiations with unions in which an increasing use of end-runs which further weakened OER.

I know what I achieved in furthering good labor relations as an expert in labor relations and an adequate administrator, however, I have wondered over the years, would I have been able to ensure a strong OER and perhaps even have eventually realized my vision of a sustainable collective bargaining system that weathered fiscal ups and downs if I had not been in the red when it came to achieving political capital. Or, as a state administrator working under the Taylor Law within a willfully politicized bureaucracy, whether my efforts would have amounted to no more than pennies on the dollar.

CALIFORNIA DEVISED A NUMBER OF STATUTES STARTING WITH THE GEORGE BROWN ACT IN 1961. PUBLIC SECTOR WORKERS WERE ALLOWED TO JOIN UNIONS, BUT UNION AUTHORITY WAS CONFINED TO A MEET AND CONFER MODEL. SUBSEQUENT TO THE BROWN ACT, OTHER PROPOSED STATUTES WERE PUT INTO LAW THAT CONTRIBUTED TO AN INCREASINGLY FRAGMENTED AND UNCERTAIN SYSTEM.

IT IS POSSIBLE TO LIVE UNDER THE UNCERTAINTY OF STRIKE THREATS.

15

DEVISING A BARGAINING SYSTEM

During the years I was on the law school faculty at the University of California, Davis, I was involved in efforts to remedy California's fragmented and almost nonexistent legal structure for labor relations.

In 1972, 80 persons, from the Western states and Washington, D.C., including myself, met on May 11 for three days at the Highlands Inn located in Carmel, California. The name of the conference was the *Western Assembly on Collective Bargaining in American Government.*

Conference participants included unions, federal, state, county, local branches of government, business interests, communications experts, and representatives of the legal, and academic professions.

These diverse participants shared a common concern. They were experiencing to one degree or another the ramifications of California's lack of progress in clarifying laws and policies for collective bargaining.

California was not the only state to be behind the times in terms of legislation but it might have been the most important one because similar to New York, its legislation would influence other states.

The participants had a number of concerns. Perhaps the most

pressing concern was the failure of most states to enact adequate legislation. This failure could too easily result in the regulation of state employees by executive order under a species of the Taft Hartley Act, which held the premise that public sector labor problems were the same nationwide and should be dealt with uniformly. The act was antithetical to a belief shared by most, if not all, of the participants that state statutes should be relevant to diverse government employees within particular geographical boundaries.

There were lively and engaged in-depth and intensive discussions surrounding this and other concerns related to public sector collective bargaining. The participants found many issues in common. For example, it was noted that an exponential increase of ordinances regulating relations between counties, cities, and municipalities was occurring across the country. This was a reflection of the fragmentation and contradictions associated with the majority of state laws affecting public sector labor relations.

The assembly produced a plenary session report on May 14th that contained unifying principles that could be adopted by the western states.

- The endorsement of the principle of collective bargaining for employees at all levels of government.
- The scope of public sector collective bargaining should be defined by state legislatures to include wages, hours, and other terms and conditions of employment.
- All federal, state, and local employees (except for members of the armed services) should have the right to strike in order to make genuine collective bargaining possible.

The assembly's report contained the hope that this product of an unprecedented meeting of minds from different public sectors would inform California's policy formulation.

Following my participation in the assembly, I committed myself to advocating for a legislative committee as a followup to my participation in the assembly.

With input from me and Joseph Grodin, that year the California State Legislature approved the formation of the Assembly Advisory Council on Public Employee Relations. I was encouraged by my contemporaries in the labor relations field to ask Joesph Moretti to sponsor a proposed bill based on the council's work. He agreed.

I had an ulterior motive. I did not want Jerry "Moonbeam" Brown to be California's next governor. I thought Senator Moretti would make an excellent governor. I believed his name on a bill derived from the Council would help him in his bid for the office just as the work of New York's Taylor Committee had benefited Nelson Rocke- feller.

I recommended UCLA law professor Benjamin Aaron to chair the Council. Joe accepted my recommendation. Ben, in turn, recruited Howard S. Block, Morris L. Myers, Don Vial, and me to serve as a Council members. We had all participated in the earlier Assembly so we had a good starting point.

Our staff members were Leah Cartabruno; Associate Consultant, Assembly Office of Research and Philip Tamoush; Administra- tor, Public Sector Management Programs, Institute of Industrial Relations, University of California, Los Angeles.

The council was referred to as the Aaron Committee.

The job of the Aaron Committee was to:

(1) provide expertise on policy questions relating to the resolution of disputes between California's public employees and their employ- ers,

(2) review the effectiveness of current California statutes pertain- ing to public employer-employee relations,

(3) assess the statutory solutions adopted by other states,

(4) and appraise current trends in California pertaining to collec- tive negotiations.

The Aaron Committee would then produce a framework for settling disputes between the State's public jurisdictions and public employees by December 1972.

Ben never seriously expected that the committee's end-product would pass the California legislature. However he believed that a diligent, apolitical committee of labor relation experts could produce a blueprint for California's public sector labor relations that might have far-reaching value. Ben recalled in a letter to me:

I was asked by Bob Moretti, Speaker of the California Assembly, if I would serve as chairman of the Advisory Council, I looked on the invitation as an opportunity to make an impact on the debate over granting expanded rights to public employees not only in California but in other states as well. I hesitated to accept his invitation because of two considerations. First, I knew that even in the unlikely event that the California legislature could be persuaded to adopt the kind of public employee collective bargaining law I favored, it was a 100 percent certainty that the then Governor, Ronald Reagan would veto it.

Second, I was worried about who else would be appointed to serve on the Advisory Council. Aware of the penchant of politicians to select such persons for reasons unrelated to their relevant experience or competence, I feared that the effectiveness of the council might be fatally undermined by members totally unsuited for such an important task.

For those reasons, I told Moretti that I would accept only on certain conditions. One was that I be delegated the sole authority to select the four other members of the Council.

I also explained why there was no possibility of securing enactment of a comprehensive collective bargaining law for public employees at this time, and said that my only interest in serving on the council would be to draft a bill that could serve as a model to emulate in the future. I therefore asked him to promise that he would introduce the bill exactly in the form submitted, without regard to the possibility of its acceptance by the legislature or the Governor. Insistence on these conditions must have seemed to him insufferably arrogant, but to my surprise, he accepted my terms.

For the next five months of 1972, the advisory council held public hearings in Sacramento, San Francisco, and Los Angeles. Written statements were received from a range of stakeholders in July and August. The committee's analyses of the needs and recommended reforms from this data gathering revealed sentiments that closely reflected the recommendations made by the earlier Western Assembly.

Based on numerous interviews and testimonies we came up with some solid elements for a proposed California statute.

A PROGRESSIVE PROPOSAL

The committee proposed one system for collective bargaining covering all public employees which would be modeled after the National Labor Relations Act (NLRA). This system would be administered by a three-member board.

Other recommendations included a repeal of all existing public employee labor relations statutes (except those covering public transit districts which were a part of the Public Utilities Code enabling statutes) and the replacement of these statutes by a comprehensive preemptive state law.

The committee agreed with the Assembly's conclusion; the right to strike is democratic and inherent in human nature and should not exclude public sector workers. For the sake of public safety and welfare we meticulously included adequate safeguards that included exhaustive and reasonable procedures.

Statewide findings from the committee's data gathering had shown that it was possible to live under the uncertainty of strike threats. The articulation of this view challenged the belief that strikes by public sector workers were dangerous to the public welfare. The committee said that the majority of governmental services were either nonessential or their essentiality did not depend upon whether the employer was public or private.

In answer to the argument that the right to strike would cause distortions of decision-making in regard to allocation of public money and that strikes would give stronger unions greater advantages over weaker unions, which would interfere with an orderly representative government, the committee responded that the same was true of politicized processes within a representative government.

The committee said that while collective bargaining is viewed as an adversarial process, it is more usefully characterized as a process of negotiation based on uncertainty. Therefore, the committee members favored a prescription that would encourage public employers and employee organizations to reach voluntary settlements or agreements on procedures that they themselves devised, preferably without third-party intervention. This more voluntary process would naturally produce uncertainty among the parties as to the consequences of not reaching an agreement. Neither party could predict with any accuracy what might happen if the dispute persisted to the point of impasse. We considered this sufficient enough motivation to reach agreement.

The committee's report provided an effective blueprint for policy and verbatim it was good enough for us as a council appointed by the legislature to present as a proposed statute.

Robert Moretti was impressed with the committee's effort. We had produced comprehensive law applicable to public employee relations at all levels of state government. The final 267-page report with appendices was published on March 15, 1973 as the *Report and Proposed Statute of the California Assembly Advisory Council on Public Employee Relations*. Our report with very minor changes became the Moretti bill.

Following Ben Aaron's prediction, bills containing the council's recommendations were introduced in 1973, 1974, and 1975, but each was defeated, though some elements of the bill eventually became law.

There was no further reference regarding the right to strike in its successive versions. Without a specific statute, the prevailing view was that public employee strikes were unlawful.

In 1985, the California Supreme Court issued a decision in *County Sanitation District No. 2 of Los Angeles County v. Los Angeles County*. After reviewing the common law understanding of prohibitions to strikes, including a careful review of a long line of case law and policy arguments the court held, that.... The common law prohibition against all public employee strikes is no longer supportable.

However, since the California Supreme Court decision was not explicit enough it had little impact on sanctions and statutes that worked against the right to strike in California. As Grodin (1985) observed, "things went along contractually."

The *City of San Jose v. Operating Engineers Local Union No 3 et al* brought some clarity in 2010 with the decision that California should allow public employees to go on strike to enforce their collective bargaining demands unless the striking employees performed jobs essential to public welfare. But whether a particular employee's job is so essential that the employee in question may not legally strike remained a complex and fact-intensive matter.

My hope that Bob Moretti would achieve governorship of California were dashed. Jerry Brown won. It turned out that he was not that bad as a governor. Bob told me later that he was pretty sure he had lost his bid because of ethnicity. He said, "I am Italian, which is fine, but I look like a Libyan and that is a very small group in California."

In terms of the void created by California's inability to articulate an adequate legal structure for labor relations which became a determination for policy, one has to turn to Harry T. Edward's observation. He noted that even though public employees might occupy essentially the same position vis a vis the employer as their private counterparts the largely unchallenged view is " that the "king is always right" regarding a "prevailing and outdated" sovereignty concept that workers cannot challenge the authority of the state.

THE LAW IS ALWAYS ABOUT RELATIONSHIPS

16

THE ELEPHANT'S TAIL

My interest as a grievance arbitrator or a neutral arbitrator on a panel was to make a fair decision, but also to safeguard future workplace relationships between labor and management when possible.

I have decided around three thousand labor law arbitration hearings over a 50-year period Sometimes a case involved a hefty file with processes that dragged on. Other cases went quickly and were a few pages, or in the case of expedited or short-form hearings, a few paragraphs

Disputes representing group interests might involve issues such as seniority, bargaining unit work, reassignment issues, fair pay and benefits, and other issues.

Grievance arbitrators weigh the rights and responsibilities of the parties based on different criteria. They then provide a remedy.

Grievance procedures are found in most collective bargaining agreements. These procedures serve as an irreplaceable pressure valve and contribute to a consistent and predictable relationship between labor and management.

An experience involving my seven-year-old daughter casts some light on the reasoning that might go into an arbitral decision.

My daughter was in a boarding school for girls located in Feather River Valley in Northern California. If the students had no demerits, they were allowed to come and spend every other weekend with their parents.

Students who signed up for a visit had to appear at a designated time and place on a late Friday afternoon to meet the bus.

One Friday, my daughter missed the bus and was unable to visit my wife and I. She was outraged. She had counted on the bus being a half an hour late, but it left on time for the first time in several months. She angrily said it wasn't fair.

I told her reasoning made no sense. She just didn't get there on time.

When I thought about it, I realized that my daughter had a valid point. She had good cause to reasonably expect the bus to be late.

Had past practice acquired the force of law? Had the bus driver and the institution that tolerated his practice, implicitly brought a rule into being? My daughter reasonably relied on this past practice "as a rule", but her reliance proved to be a mistake because the exception was the formal rule, e.g. the written bus schedule. She had in arbitral terms a "just cause."

Labor arbitrations have their own nomenclature representing technical or substantive considerations for working out questions such as these. One could say that without recourse to grievance procedures,

Suppose an employer acts permissively and the employees consistently get away with some act or practice and then one day the past practice is no longer okay, at least for some employees or a particular employee. The employees, or employee, are punished. They might not "know" the law; they only know customary practice. By the way, in the face of a debates about the nature of law, that is about the only thing I learned in law school that had much to do with jurisprudence. And that is a crude version of it.

LABOR GRIEVANCES

The courts have held that arbitrators have a special knowledge of the workplace and labor relations more generally. Arbitrators might have a basis for judgments that are frequently foreign to the court's competence, Because of this the arbitrator is imbued with expansive legal authority with the understanding that a judge cannot be expected to bring the same experience to bear or give the same weight to the intent of an agreement.

A particular arbitrator is usually chosen because of each party's confidence in the arbitrator's knowledge of the common law of the shop and their trust in the personal judgment of the arbitrator to wisely interpret the collective bargaining agreement and to bring to bear considerations that might not be expressed in the labor contract.

The employer's common response to employees' behavior, barring any heinous act, as spelled out in most collective bargaining agreements is generally progressive discipline. The underlying principle of effective progressive discipline is to use the least severe action that necessary to correct the undesirable situation. This involves increasingly severe steps or measures if an employee fails to correct a problem after reasonable opportunity to do so.

The arbitrator considers whether management delivered this workplace form of due process effectively and fairly.

Compliance with workplace rules would be a factor of an arbitrator's judgment as to a remedy, but not the only factor. In reality, rules that govern behavior in the workplace as a predictor as to how a case can come out do not exist. In terms of best practices, experienced arbitrators rely on facts peculiar to the grievant.

The arbitrator might deal with questions of intent. As a guiding principle, the intention to do an act is the same thing as performance of the act. In one case an employee was discovered in a bar about to raise a glass to his lips when he was supposed to be working. Despite his denial in the face of the obvious, it was clear that he intended to drink an alcoholic beverage but was prevented from doing so by the fortuitous intervention of his supervisor who happened to walk into the same bar. In another case, an employee offered a pretty girl a seat in his cab in violation of company policy. His intent was clear but he didn't actually perform because she said, "No." His intent was a good enough cause for discharge.

REMEDIES AND UNCERTAINTIES

A body of law known as equity was developed in response to the inability of the English common law courts, which strictly adhered to rigid writs and forms of action, to entertain or provide a remedy for every injury. The king, therefore, established the *High Court of Chancery*, the purpose of which was to administer justice according to principles of fairness in cases where the common law could give no or inadequate redress. From this development grew the maxim that every right has a remedy.

In seeking a remedy, grievance arbitrators follow the law of equity more closely than the courts do. This can be challenging. It is recognized that arbitrators have broad authority to order any type of relief", even beyond what the courts would do. What people abstractly know about the law is that there is a remedy somewhere. It is up to the arbitrator to find it.

However, finding the right remedy is perhaps the least understood and most challenging subject for grievance arbitrators for a number of reasons.

The culture or past practice of a workplace might contradict the formal rules or policies of the employer. Acts of "permissiveness" on the part of the employer or a "practice" has no legal standing but the employee assumes it is all right to perform a certain act. The power of the employer over the employee might be an issue. The employer might unpredictably and opportunistically enact an existing rule. Maybe an employer wants to get rid of an employee by any means possible and a violation of a rule, though frequently ignored, becomes one of several charges.

Perhaps it is a situation, as in my daughter's case, that is relatively innocent of power. Who knows what might make the bus late or on time and who knows when someone is going to behave uncharacteristically and challenge the status quo? Who actually knows the rules of the workplace when they are cast in elusive or bureaucratic words and phrases within a thick employee manual?

There is a lot of uncertainty in the workplace today, more so since the boundary between workplace behavior and private lives of employees has become blurred. Critical knowledge of workplace rights has not kept up with either dramatic changes in the workforce or contemporary inequities that exist between labor and management in both the private and public sectors. One could argue that the current milieu of labor relations has placed an even greater responsibility on the arbitrator to define just cause in human terms in the face of uncertainties that bring about dog law.

HUMAN-SCALE JUSTICE

One day I pulled my car up to a gatehouse and verified my identity to the security personnel guarding a high security facility above the campus at the University of California, Berkeley. The facility housed something like research into nuclear fission; I don't remember exactly what it was. The guy at the gatehouse looked over my credentials. He stared at me, and then asked,

"Mr. Wollett, did you used to be the umpire deciding SAMSTRANS cases?"

Wondering what would come next, I said I did.

"Well, you fired me."

I said without thinking, "My God, I'm sorry."

He said, "Nothing personal, you did me a favor – that was one of my worst jobs ever, driving buses for SAMSTRAN from Palo Alto to San Francisco and vice versa. God, that was hard work having to deal with traffic every night and every day. I had to worry about not only driving, but also collecting fares. I had to watch my passengers to make sure they didn't fall down. That was a very hard job. I was exhausted at the end of every day. Now I've got a job where I can sit down all day. I'm in a covered facility where I'm out of the rain. So thanks very much Mr. Wollett for firing me, I really appreciate it."

I had another case involving a U.S. Marshall who was fired because of his alcoholism. I had developed a full record and put a lot of time into the case. There was no doubt he was an alcoholic and no doubt that he had misbehaved on the job on the day in question while under the influence.

I puzzled over this case. The employee had a fine record as a US Marshall until he started seriously drinking and developed a record of not showing up sober. The time came when the enough was enough rule came into play and he was fired.

The employer had been permissive and tolerant of his alcoholism for many years so I thought the employee deserved another chance, especially since he appeared to be sober now. He seemed on the road to recovery by the time he appeared before me.

Would he stay that way? I did not know. I attached some conditions and put him back as a U.S. Marshall anyway, despite my reservations. He had been with the U.S. Marshall's service for many years and he had a good record when he was sober.

I remained nervous about my decision and the U.S. Marshall's office was so outraged by my decision that they terminated me. That was my last case with them.

Two years later, I received a handwritten letter from a woman who introduced herself as the wife of the employee. She wrote, "thank you Mr. Wollett for saving my husband's life. He's been dry for over two years now, he goes to AA meetings and I think he's on track. We're getting along and our three kids are happy. Anyhow, thanks for saving my husband's life. If you'd upheld his discharge, I don't know what he would have done. But he had one more chance. You gave him that, so thank you, sir. My kids thank you. I thank you. And of course, my husband thanks you, too."

Taking away someone's livelihood is a tough call. It is rewarding when it works out for everyone.

BACKYARD JURISPRUDENCE

I have arbitrated in many places, whether in the wilds of Oregon or the center of San Francisco. Wherever I practiced, I created my own court of law wherever I landed– no guns, take off your hat, any extraneous lawyerly acts should remain outside of the process whenever possible. These were my standards of conduct that demonstrated respect for the law and the direct testimony of clients in the arbitral world.

CHOOSING AN ARBITRATOR

The arbitrator serves the parties and more fundamentally the contract between the parties. Their behavior in that regard should be accountable to the parties, even before an arbitrator is selected.

Is the arbitrator faithful to the collective bargaining agreement, which is a voluntary contract entered into by the parties? If the language is unclear will he or she go the extra mile to address this? Is the arbitrator knowledgeable enough about the workplace at issue? How does the arbitrator frame collective good in the public sector? How does an arbitrator address the respective strengths of representation on both sides since there is often an inherent inequity? Does he or she see more to law than glory or splitting the difference between the parties?

Then there is a kind of accountability or set of skills and knowledge I consider most important. Can the arbitrator question, assimilate, and determine the most relevant facts. Grievance arbitrations almost always turn on these questions of fact, as might be applied by judges in certain kinds of civil proceedings. The matter at hand based on a full evidentiary record trumps *stare decisis*. In fact, precedent is a low priority in grievance arbitrations.

I can't think of a better way to express this than the following quote:

It has been said that too much intelligence is harmful to a judge, but I do not subscribe to this. I do say, however, that the best judge is the one in whom ready humanity prevails over cautious intellectualism. A sense of justice, the innate quality bearing no relation to acquired legal techniques, which enables the judge after hearing the facts to feel which party is right, is as necessary to him as a good ear is to a musician; for, if this quality is wanting, no degree of preeminence will afford adequate compensation" (Calmandrei 1942)[1].

An arbitrator or mediator might be a lawyer or a non-lawyer, depending on the particular state. I believe that professional legal status matters less than the arbitrator's character, capacity, and knowledge. However, I also believe that there is an absence of effective training when it comes to training arbitrators to decide grievance arbitrations. This training is different in a number of ways from that found in other areas of law.

EXCUSING IGNORANCE

"Ignorance of the law is no excuse," might work in the courtroom but not in arbitral law. Ignorance of the law can be excused. For instance, what if an employee does not have reasonable access to a workplace rule or a law imposed from outside the workplace.

A staff nurse in a large California hospital had a big heart and did what she thought was right by informing the patient on some matters pertaining to her health. As it turned out, her act was based on misinformation. She was accused of violating the hospital's confidentiality policy and the new HIPAA law (the Health Insurance Portability and Accountability Act). The employer claimed that her actions had harmed the reputation and integrity of the hospital. She was terminated.

I put her back to work because the hospital had sent her verbal and written warning, but these warnings were not framed adequately or formally in the context of key policies and rules.

In fact, HIPAA confused everyone in the workplace. Even today, HIPAA causes breakdowns in communications and its uncertainty has a chilling effect on providers concerned with their patients' or clients' welfare.

Most commonly, ignorance of the law can be excused in the case of permissiveness on the part of the employer. In another case of mine, a large company permissively strung out a low-level employee

---

1   Calamandrei,Paulo, et al, Eulogy of Judges, Princeton University Press, 1942.

and then, in response to a particular incident, leveled a previously unapplied confusing series of sequential moves and timeline procedures for reporting absenteeism.

The employee had been with the large company for almost 22 years without any problems until at some point her performance in regard to absenteeism became spotty, possibly due to physical problems. The employer tolerated this for some time with no warnings.

The time came when she needed a hemorroidectomy. In a five-day period she had surgery and then took several days to recuperate. During this period, the employer claimed she had abandoned her job and she was terminated.

She had obeyed almost all of the rules in terms of reporting steps surrounding this event. However, overall communications between management and the employee over her condition and medical needs had been poor. There were several possible explanations regarding the mutual inadequacy of some of the communications over her medical issue. The employee barely spoke English. She was resistant to discussing her condition and resultant surgery in the workplace for cultural reasons related to the privacy of particular body parts. It also appeared that the management environment was not conducive to such confessionals in any case.

None of these factors excused her performance in terms of the evidentiary record. I could have terminated her based on the employer's claim that she had abandoned her job as evidenced by poor communications. That would have been a proper decision, but was it fair or just?

A discharge requires a particular diligence to find the truth since this is the loss of someone's work with all its attending benefits. I took this responsibility seriously.

As I reviewed the facts of the case, I could not see in any evidence that the employee's missed steps had been intentional nor did I see evidence that would lead me to conclude that she had abandoned her job. Finally, there was not enough evidence or proof to support either party's claims of contact related to mandated reporting steps.

While an arbitrator follows the evidentiary record which often contains missing pieces to a story, the human side of this grievance is worth relating as a matter of equity involving a class of worker. The employee had worked for the employer for over two decades. She was not literate and did not come across as particularly bright. She was not particularly valuable from the employer's perspective because she had few skills. Her seniority would not have helped.There is something called management rights, which is usually referenced in a collective bargaining agreement. However, as an inherent right it is not a bargainable part of the collective bargaining agreement. This can be frustrating in deciding cases when I know that I am seeing a case of poor management, but must decide based on management rights. In this case, while the older employee had served her employer well for over 20 years, the system internal to the company had not served her as well. It was not my job to tell management how to run their business, but it was clear that her case was badly mishandled. There was an unmet management obligation and responsibility on the part of the employer.

I suspended the employee for six months. I ordered that she was to be given her job back with her seniority rights intact when she returned to work.

The employer ignored the decision and upheld her termination. In this case, the employer wanted to maintain the authority of its prerogative to be arbitrary (which is not a management right in all fairness) by ignoring the established arbitral process. That was not going to happen. I had that authority to reinstate her and pursue compliance, and that is what I did.

EXTERNALITIES

The arbitrator has a duty to abide by the collective bargaining agreement and to follow the evidentiary record. However, the arbitrators primary responsibility is to determine the question of just cause and this frequently requires an independent judgment on the part of the arbitrator that can supercede other factors. In the early case involving the U.S. Marshal I had reinstated, the employer had asked me to reconsider, stating that I might not have understood the rules of what was called the Merit Systems Protection Board (MSPB). I understood the rules. In response to the employer's petition for modification of my award, I answered that while the congruency of the many kinds of law that can be brought to bear in a particular arbitration was important, the meaning of just cause as I determined it wins the day. If I had followed the dictum of the MSPB in the absence of my judgment of just cause, the act of arbitration would have been pointless.

Workplace issues can appear turn on outside interests. This can be dangerous if it strays from workplace considerations.

One discharge case became a racial issue, more manufactured than not. A Hispanic bus driver assaulted an African American rider who had said on the bus in a loud voice that "they shouldn't let 'spics' drive buses."

The insulted bus driver had a 20-year unblemished record and was ordinarily good at dealing with people. That particular day he lost his cool and slugged the rider. The NAACP demanded his termination for hitting a passenger. The bus driver received a six-month suspension.

I decided on no suspension in favor of the bus driver, though both had been at fault. I put it this way: deciding a popularity contest, e.g. by accepting pressure from the NAACP, was not a management right and so there was no basis for management to suspend the bus driver.

However, the next case demonstrates some of the complexity and some of the boundaries underlying arbitral judgments. For instance, popularity can be a factor in a decision in the context of collegial workplace relations. This is a mandate involving getting people back to work so operations can run smoothly. It is an area of expertise the courts decided belonged to arbitral processes. There were other layers to this case related to the rights of a whistleblower that might have been important but were not part of my decision. In my view, this case also had a moral question about legal practice that I used with my students over the years.

A reporter with a newspaper that serviced an area of northern California, containing one of the few public hospitals within a radius of at least 100 miles, wrote an article about some charges leveled against the hospital that its operating room was careless and sloppy in its sanitation procedures. The implication was that the hospital had problems with diseases that should have been controlled.

The reporter interviewed an operating room RN about the charges. She was a good source because she was a fully qualified member of the California Nurse's Association and was considered to be very competent. She told the reporter that she wholeheartedly agreed with the charges against the hospital.

The hospital officials immediately suspended her when they saw her quoted comments in the newspaper.

My concern with the workplace arbitration was did the hospital discharge an employee in order to uphold discipline in violation of the collective bargaining agreement, which requires just cause? If yes, what shall the remedy be?" I held that the hospital had violated the collective bargaining agreement by discharging the nurse. She was guilty of misconduct, but her misconduct did not constitute just cause for termination. I decided that the appropriate remedy was a two-week disciplinary suspension.

However, when the physicians and nurses who worked in the operating room discovered that she was going to get her job back after she had served her suspension, they voted that having to work with her under the circumstances was incompatible with notions of collegiality. They went so far as to refuse to work if she came back.

The hospital board had an emergency meeting and decided that since they were faced with a potential revolution and insurrection by their hospital room staff, physicians, and nurses, they would increase the severity of her punishment from a two-week suspension to termination. Nevertheless, while the hospital board had the authority to manage the hospital and to effect whatever punishment they deemed to be appropriate, they could not change the remedy I had imposed. They could not upgrade from discharge to termination on the basis of a popularity contest. So, the hospital management had to face the issue of whether or not discharge was appropriate.

Under the collective bargaining agreement the nurse deserved some discipline. However, while it is true that reinstatement as a remedy for a wrongful discharge is fashionable, it is not always appropriate. What I had to consider as an arbitrator was the repugnancy of a popularity contest in terms of an individual employee's rights versus the concept of collegiality in the workplace, which also holds an important meaning.

Given the latitude I had to find a remedy, I devised an alternative remedy for the wrongful discharge which was to substitute money for reinstatement. I awarded the nurse a sizable amount of money covering her out-of-pocket losses and damages such as pain-and-suffering for her loss of reputation.

Was she a whistle blower or was she shooting off her mouth, rather than righting a wrong in the sense of whistle blowing? It is an interesting question given some of the facts of the case, but the issue for me as the arbitrator was narrower than that.

In my view, her actions after receiving a large reward from me caused me to doubt her intentions. She subsequently proceeded with a civil suit against the hospital independent of the collective bargaining agreement. Her tort claim was based on a breach of contract in association with her termination which would not have stood up in the arbitral process. She also claimed wrongful injury to reputation and character, granting that it would be difficult if not impossible, to obtain re-employment anywhere else as a nurse.

On this theory, the lawyer obtained a substantial sum of money for the RN. Her suit bothered me primarily because her double dipping came out of the public pocket. Labor agreements contain common law concerns like any court in the land, particularly when it comes to the rudiments of procedural due process. I feel I had rightfully, and generously, delivered her rights in my award.

A CRIMINAL IS OFF THE HOOK

Another example shows how constitutional rights prevail in workplace arbitrations. A deputy sheriff stole a credit card which he subsequently used. The sheriff relied on the theft as a reason for termination. However, he did not follow the collective bargaining agreement that stated, like most labor agreements, that an employee on probationary status can be terminated at will. If the sheriff had followed the contract the matter would have quickly ended because the employee's only recourse would have been under civil service law, which had potentially harsher penalties.

The sheriff violated the procedural due process rights of his employee. Since the accused has the right to face the accuser in any court of law, he was entitled to be confronted with the specific charges against him, to cross examine his accusers, to rebut documentary evidence, if any, to present testimonial and documentary evidence on his own behalf, to be represented by council, and to have a decision made by an impartial decision maker. Because of the sheriff's inappropriate action, that did not happen. Consequently, the damage to the employee's reputation was assumed and therefore he was entitled to a remedy according to Court of Chancery.

Based on the contract's memorandum of understanding, I referred this case to the administrative appeals board for redress to harm inflicted on the employee's reputation and left it to this entity to find a remedy while I retained jurisdiction. The employee continued his life of crime and eventually went to prison.

AN EXAMPLE OF MANAGEMENT RIGHTS

There was a drug problem in a local high school. Members of the sheriff's department had earlier set up a sting operation to deal with a previous drug problem in the same school. The sting operation was aborted when a leak appeared to come from the sheriff who carelessly "talked to much" about internal matters. This time the officers under him did not want the sheriff involved. Bypassing the sheriff's authority, several employees and the sheriff's deputy assistant, a 15-year veteran of the department with a good record, decided a female undercover agent should be sworn in as a reserve deputy sheriff without the sheriff's knowledge. These employees conspired to put together a palpably phony arrangement to fool the sheriff in order to have her appointed as a reserve deputy.

The employee achieved this by going to the sheriff's office when he knew he was not there. When the receptionist told him, that the sheriff was not available, he made it clear that he was now in charge by saying, "as acting sheriff I am appointing an acting deputy."

But the power to appoint is a cherished management right.

I acted as a neutral arbitrator in this tripartite hearing. The sheriff's testimony and his predecessor's testimony made it very clear that both of them held the power to appoint. The evidence showed that the veteran sheriff's deputy assistant had knowingly assumed a power that was not his.

In terms of just cause, I did not consider his offense dischargeable because of his many years of distinguished service to the department and the community, but the remedy had to be severe enough to address his hierarchical responsibility as a public servant.

He had been off duty six months before the hearing date. I concluded that there was no way that the employee could return to the department at his present rank of assistant sheriff. I re-instated him as a deputy sheriff. I gave him a three month-suspension and directed the department to pay him for three-months back pay minus net earnings from other sources. The public need was met by providing a remedy for violating a critical need for command for a well-functioning force. At the same time, I acknowledged the value of a highly skilled employee who had provided good service to the public.

LEAVING A LEGACY

Arbitrators do not set astounding precedents, but they do influence systems of law, including other arbitrators operating in the arbitral system as they engage the work lives of people and organizations. There are principles associated with organizations such as the American Arbitration Association (AAA) and the Federal Mediation and Conciliation Services (FMCS) that apply to all arbitrators registered with these organizations. There are also principles created by individual arbitrators that are adopted by other arbitrators.

I had several principles that I followed to the best of my ability in my years of practice.

These principles represent my legacy. They are:

(1) different standards for public sector workers,

(2) adherence to, or if necessary expansion of the discipline of the record,

(3) consistent support for non-adversarial and empowered outcomes,

(4) following facts peculiar to the grievant as established by the best of arbitrators.

Some of the standards I set were adopted by other labor arbitrators, particularly in relation to public sector disputes. I have also shared my practices in university classrooms and in my papers and presentations. I chose the following cases to exemplify some of the challenges related to implementing these kind of standards.

THE WORKPLACE AND PUBLIC GOOD

The "public" is a precept that escapes a large number of arbitrators when they render decisions in the public sector. This is a gross oversight in my view because the public is a third party with the right to adequate, consistent, and safe public service. The responsibility to protect this right falls on both labor and management as well as the arbitrator. Some cases are easier than others, for example, when there is a clear potential risk of danger to the public due to a particular employee. Others are less easy to decide.

By a higher standard in the public sector I mean that sometimes otherwise good public employees with good records cross the line. Even if it is only once, the potential for public harm could be great enough that there is just cause to terminate an employee. I have had fewer cases where the loss of a misbehaving but otherwise valuable public employee poses an even greater potential harm to the public, and I might decide that the employee be reinstated, as in the case above where the deputy violated the chain of command. In other cases, there might be factors that cause me to decide for termination.

A good officer serving in a small ocean side town in a municipal police department was part of the K-9 (canine) unit. The officer had done an excellent job training the dog assigned to him. He obviously cared about his charge. However, no matter how talented the dog was or how good a job the officer had done, K-9 unit dogs have to be continually trained and retrained to remain effective.

The officer had failed to give his dog sufficient training as required by the rules of the police department, which involved a refresher course for the dog every six months. But for me there was an even greater issue which was he had lied about training his dog. Lies are common in arbitration hearings, but I was predisposed to weigh his lie in relation to his responsibility as a public employee and the potential for harm. In my mind, the officer's behavior with the dog coupled with his lying held enough consequences for public safety and welfare that I decided for the employer and the employee was terminated.

Why such a strong emphasis on the employee's and management's responsibility to the public? The duty of the public sector agency is to first serve the public through its employees. My decisions could have a direct effect on the quality of services provided by the public agency. Public sector work is commonly labor-intensive and while the same can be said regarding service industries in the private sector, the services performed by public sector employees are regarded by the body politic as essential. Yet, consumers of public services, have no choice as to who is hired, and funded with public money for these essential services, and the quality of their work. If members of the public need a service, they take what is available. There is no market play. There is only one fire department.

THE POST-9/11 WORKPLACE

I terminated an ill employee. This decision was a harsh reflection of the perceived need for greater safety in the post-9/11 world.

The incident took place shortly after 9/11 at one of the nation's largest airports.

One night a security guard who controlled airport access at a critical gate went to his immediate supervisor as soon as he came on shift and said he needed to go home because he did not feel well. His request was denied. He asked the supervisor if he could take a short nap during his break. That request was also denied.

He fell asleep. While he was sleeping, two contractors waited to be let through the gate that was his responsibility. As the Access Controller it was mandatory that the security guard physically touch the badge of each person who entered the gate.

When no one showed up to let them through, the contractors reported the unsecured gate to the supervisor who discovered the employee asleep in his car with the gate still unsecured.

The grievant had not contacted anyone before he fell asleep nor had he locked the gate. By the grievant's account, he had probably been asleep for around 20 minutes.

This was not a pleasant decision. The poor guy was sick and he had tried to go home, yet in a *Loudermill* hearing, he was terminated. Where was the fairness in this?

The heart of my decision involved the security of a major public facility. The risk to the public by violating this particular workplace policy following 9/11 was too high.

I took into account not only the failure of the employee to adhere to proper performance standards, but the level of services that the funding public is entitled to expect. An arbitrator must address the operational responsibilities of a public agency when it recruits, trains, retains, promotes, reevaluates, disciplines, and makes other decisions concerning the quality of the workforce. Such decisions go to the heart of the disciplinary function, as it did in this case. So, my decision was based on operational rather than disciplinary criteria, in other words, a determination of the quality of an essential public service.

In cases where the arbitrator is asked to second-guess management funded with public monies, he or she must find the nexus between the behavior of the employee and the quality of the public service provided and make a second finding. If the decision is to restore the employee to the workforce, the overriding judgment is that forgiving the conduct at issue or lessening the penalty will not adversely impact the quality of the service.

Within this framework, I would have had to make a finding that if I forgave the conduct at issue or reduced the penalty, it would not have a serious adverse on the public service which the employee was obligated to provide. I could not do that because such a conclusion would send the wrong message to other employees with serious responsibilities performing similar services. I said in my opinion and award:

> [The grievant] did not behave badly. He made reasonable efforts to terminate his service early on that day. He knew he was not in the physical condition to perform at optimum levels. If his job had required a subset of lesser responsibilities, his decision to stay on shift might have been acceptable, at least in avoiding the ultimate penalty of termination. However he did not hold a lesser job. And the choices he made affected not only him, but also the security of the airport. Under these circumstances, it was just for responsive management to hold him to very high standards, as I do. The discharge was sustained.

One does not particularly think of establishing new law in grievance arbitration cases because that is not common. However, this case received more attention than usual. It became a precedent used by other arbitrators who had cases involving the public sector's responsibility to the public.

There was another element to this case which might have shifted my decision. What if the grievance had not focused on disparate treatment? That is a question I might have presented to a classroom of law students because given changes outside of the workplace, including influences on the workplace by the event of 9/11, it becomes a very complex question.

Unfortunately, disparate treatment was his primary defense and I could not change that. His disparate treatment defense was weak. He argued that other employees discovered to be sleeping on the job were not terminated. The employer responded that the other cases were not similarly situated.

The disparate treatment rule has always had significant appeal in labor arbitrations. It was my view that management has no obligation to run its disciplinary affairs so perfectly that if it is tolerant in one or two cases, it must be tolerant in others. The permissiveness must be pervasive and known to the grievant, which was not the case here. If management's permissiveness is widespread and known to the employee, the employee may sensibly conclude that the violation of the rule will not be the basis for termination. But this takes solid evidence, which was lacking in this case. There was little I could do to strengthen the evidentiary record and thus possibly mitigate my decision which I would have preferred to do. The employee would have had a far stronger case based on the fact that he was sick and that he had asked for permission to go home. Perhaps this would have given him a chance at reinstatement.

The question of higher standards because of the need for public safety is a ubiquitous one in the public sector arbitrations, particularly in relation to transit authorities. I had many such cases.

In the transit industry for instance, there might be issues such as weighing access to medical information in the name of public safety versus an employee's right to privacy. The decisions that are made in these cases are critical to ensuring the safety of the public from, for instance, a sudden heart attack or an unreported loss of vision.

A bus driver transporting the elderly did not want to give up his right to privacy. He asserted a privilege not unlike a self-incrimination privilege when he refused release of his records to the company from a physician to his employer.

The key issue was that the employer wanted him tested for more than one condition. The employer's demand for all medical records, which could be considered an invasion of privacy in other circumstances, had to be weighed against passenger safety.

The employee was cited for insubordination and was issued a warning. He continued to refuse the agency's request and was discharged.

While recognizing the issue of safety, the employer's demands appeared to me to be nebulous at best.

There was another concern I had in relation to this case. An arbitration hearing is not a typical courtroom. It is not uncommon for the parties' representatives to have unequal skills and knowledge levels in terms of basic knowledge and their briefs. This was the case here.

The employer had a sharp lawyer as opposed to the union representative who was intelligent and full of heart in her fierce defense of her client, but she had little legal background. It was my practice to level the playing field whenever possible by being as hands on as possible in my questioning, which can be viewed as part of the evidentiary record.

Despite the excellent brief submitted by the employer's lawyer in this case I also found it necessary to spend a lot of time trying to sort out what specifically the conflict was about. Precisely what information did the employer want that warranted further medical evaluation.

I concluded that there was nothing in the collective bargaining agreement that supported the employer's claim of insubordination. I returned the employee to work with back pay contingent upon a medical exam where the physician determining the employee's fitness for work would supply the transit company with relevant information. The contingencies I imposed satisfied my demand for a higher duty from an employee of a public agency.

There were occasions when I was not able to meet a higher public sector standard as I would have preferred because I must follow the principle of management rights.

A deputy sheriff in the state of Nevada apprehended and arrested a young man and his passenger for speeding. Both flunked the alcohol test. (The accuracy of the blood readers became a central issue in this case which I will not go into here.) The departmental policy was that if a suspect fails what is called the (Preliminary Breath Test (PBT), he or she had to be removed and kept off the road.

When the deputy sheriff responded to another call he made the driver and his passenger promise that they would not go back on the road and left them there. In the meantime, he called dispatch and asked them to send a two adults to take the two boys home. He then told the boys that two adults were on their way and that neither was permitted to drive. The two teenagers ignored his order and took off.

I could sweeten this case up with a number of facts, but the essential point is that the two teenagers went back on the road at a high speed and collided head-on with another vehicle, apparently the lead car in a caravan. The young driver and a person in another vehicle were killed instantly.

The employee had broken departmental policy, which was that he was to stay with the two juveniles until relieved. Despite the horrendous consequences of his failure to do his duty, he was merely suspended with loss of pay for 20 working days.

The winner in this case was management rights.

There were public sector cases where I required a higher standard of duty while recognizing a myriad of laws designed to protect the public such as certifications versus fairly interpreting the contractual arrangements between labor and management.

The question was by what authority did the employer, Bay Area Rapid Transit (BART), operating in Northern California, set standards for employee exams.

BART had established a first certification plan several years before and then implemented a second plan a few years later.

The second plan included 13 categories of employees specifically responsible for passenger and employee safety, including equipment use and maintenance. Four years later, it revised its recertification plan yet again to include those employees identified by the appropriate department managers.

The union claimed that this last policy rendition was too vague.

The employer claimed that the arbitrator could not issue an award on the merits of the case because it was under statutory law which BART was mandated to follow in reference to the California Public Utilities Commission (CPUC).

The union responded that nevertheless an application of the

"employee certification plan" was a violation of the collective bargaining agreement which called for mutual consent in matters that directly impacted members of the bargaining unit.

The appropriate remedy was for the district to stop requiring re-examinations until the CPUC order could be implemented on a fair, equitable, and non-disparate fashion based on evidence that there was a difference in the chosen employee classifications. At that point, I said that they should then immediately begin to re-examine all employees in the classifications specified under the CPUC order.

In my mind, the question of merit was the discretion of BART to determine which listed job classifications should be selected for medical re-examination and recertification in a way consistent with provisions of the collective bargaining agreement. I could not understand how job classifications with varying impacts on safety were subjected to the same standards as the medical recertification program. BART refused to comply with a cease and desist order until a determination could be made.

I ruled that if BART refused to comply, the program should remain dormant. In my second finding, I ordered BART to cease and desist from the program by a certain day or until parties reached an agreement on compliance, whichever came sooner. I directed the parties to meet and bargain in good faith to reach an agreement on the question. If they did not, there would be another hearing.

THE PRIVATE SECTOR AND PUBLIC SAFETY

In my practice of arbitral law, the public received a special entitlement in arbitral considerations, However, I do not want to neglect the issue of safety in the private sector. I have had private sector cases where I felt the potential impact caused by an individual worker or a company on public safety was too great not to impose a stiff remedy as opposed to a lighter penalty where safety was less of an issue.

A maintenance mechanic working for a manufacturer of corrugated shipping containers had neglected to follow the rule regarding a lock on a steam valve for a soak tank. This rule involved the right application of glue. If it was not applied properly, corrugated box products might be defective. When the lock was found missing the employee was questioned. The employee argued that he found no reason for a lock because he found no work order to explain why the lock was there. He claimed he had searched for a note without success. He said he had then tried to contact his supervisor, including the person whose name was next to the lock on the soak tank.

He further justified his position by saying that he was hard of hearing and he thought he had heard a supervisor say, "Yeah, remove it." So he did. What he had actually heard was a radio. He subsequently reported that he fixed the lock and the soak tank.

He was terminated for a violation of plant safety rules.

I did not doubt the employee's veracity nor did I believe that he was careless about safety. Nevertheless, I decided for the employer. Careless or not, his circumstance still did not justify violation of a safety rule which had been put in place to deal with a very dangerous substance.

He was guilty of poor judgment or faulty reasoning as we all are. But this was shaky ground. The tag said, "danger lockout ... do not remove." The injunction seemed clear enough.

The supervisor involved had also fostered a permissiveness that encouraged the employee to believe that he could ignore the requirement with impunity. But in this case even the fact that the supervisor might have been careless was irrelevant based on the maxim that "One man's carelessness does not excuse another man's."

This was a tough and unhappy enforcement of a rule, as it was with the sleeping security officer and as it was with the officer who neglected to train his dog consistently and lied about it, but as I said in the opinion I wrote for this case, "...we are dealing ... with safety. Steam, which is very volatile... can be a deadly force."

THE DISCIPLINE OF THE RECORD

By a disciplined record I mean ensuring a record that is complete enough to discern something close to the truth. The evidentiary record is most closely bound by the collective bargaining agreement or contract. Then there are statutes, civil services rules, and so forth to be considered. The arbitrator is also bound by the grounds chosen by the parties, even if they are poorly constructed as even the collective bargaining agreement might be. Not the least, there is the judgment of the arbitrator in determining facts.

What if just cause is not represented explicitly in a collective bargaining agreement?

In one otherwise routine and unexciting case, the determination that a worker could be properly categorized as unsatisfactory took 294 pages of transcripts, 10 witnesses, and additional records central to establishing just cause in order to conduct a reasonable investigation, followed by an extensive analysis, to determine that the employer did not confront an employee with the charge against him.

What if there is a *prima facie* case that requires inference as to facts to achieve a fair and just decision? The labor arbitrator has latitude regarding the power of judgment in these instances. One could take it further and say the arbitrator has an obligation to exercise this latitude.

At the same time, labor arbitrators have an obligation to decide the case with as much speed as possible in order to get people back to work for the good of the workplace and the good of the industry. Getting people back to work quickly is also a way to minimize the bad effects of a dispute.

So this tension exists. However, regardless of the need for expediency, the arbitrator should rest on a complete and accurate transcript - as complete and accurate as human beings can make it. This practice leads to remedies that are more thoughtful, even creative, and almost always accepted by the parties, and without splitting the difference as, unfortunately. some arbitrators do.

Toward this end, while the evidentiary record must be adhered to, individual arbitrators can define (1) what evidence is acceptable or not, (2) the extent of the parties' involvement in the evidentiary record, and (3) how hands on the arbitrator is as he or she expands the record toward a better understanding of facts or a closer interpretation of the facts, particularly when items in the collective bargaining agreement are unclear.

Some evidence is not acceptable. For example, extraneous facts, while perhaps representing a broader sense of justice outside of the hearing room, are not appropriate and any subset of evidence receives the consideration it is worth. For instance, I would not accept "sub-evidence" as having probative value. My view, which I habitually communicated in advance to the parties, was that affidavit evidence was worth less than most evidence. The same held true for declarations. A declaration is a fancy affidavit with a magic little paragraph at the end, I understand I am offering this evidence with the understanding that if I state anything falsely, that I could be prosecuted for perjury. That simple magic phrase is assumed to contain probative value, but it does not.

I once asked a former student who had worked in a district attorney's office for over 20 years, "When did you last prosecute anyone for perjury following a declaration?" He answered, "We've only done it once and that was 20 years ago in an insurance fraud case."

The reality is that a declaration is only as good as its relative speed compared to sworn testimony.

I had a spirited exchange of ideas with a friend who was a County Superior Court judge. He was a very competent guy and an excellent judge. He defended the receipt of declarations with the argument that we don't have enough judges. Declarations were one way to speed the calendar along. I understand the need for practicality given scarcity, but what kind of excuse is that?

In terms of more actively involving the parties, an arbitrator can always sit idly by and simply compare two briefs for intrinsic merit, while leaving the development of the record entirely up to the parties. The respective parties might do a good job or a bad job.

I did not find this passive role good enough in terms of an arbitrator's obligation to the parties to seek the truth. I was often directly involved when it came to development of an insufficient record. My involvement might include a direct interrogation of witnesses or the grievant if the record required that kind of substantiation.

I cannot always play that role. For instance, in the case of the airport security guard sleeping on the job, the employee had chosen a poor defense that I could not change or mitigate.

THE STICK MAN

In yet another memorable post 9/11 story, my actions as an arbitrator represented a giant leap into the testimonial evidence in search of the inexplicable – motive. Given the fearful world we live that affects our lives, including the workplace, this case involving high anxiety deserves a fuller account.

After years of satisfactory service, a U.S. Marine returned to civilian life and took a job as an aircraft washer with a corporation, dealing with intelligence systems for national security purposes, that held large federal government contracts.

The former Marine was a grunt who prepared airplanes for launching. He re-covered them, parked them, and serviced them with fuel, oil, and oxygen. His work merited relatively low security.

The employee had received a number of promotions over a five-year period. He had been considered an excellent employee until "boredom" during a break in a lunchroom lead him to create a three-dimensional doodle.

Shortly after 9/11 occurred, the employee was charged with violating general work rule number 10 which contained the following language: "threatening, intimidating, coercing, harassing, discriminating or interfering with fellow employees, supervision or customer."

He was charged because a fellow employee had observed him making what appeared to be a "mock" bomb and reported the incident to the site manager saying, "I don't know of anybody who would sit there and do something like that especially with the situation in the world…" A closed briefcase sitting at his feet was also suspicious.

This report led to a high alert within the supervisory staff and among some of his fellow employees. Testimony that emerged about other events involving the employee indicated suspicious behavior. This fueled increasing concerns that perhaps he actually had been developing a prototype for a bomb.

Questions floated around the workplace. What would the employee do? What was he capable of? What were his thought processes?

His supervisor and fellow employees thought he had seemed angry and resentful lately. Some in the workforce said they were afraid of him. One fellow employee claimed that his wife was "scared to death... "She's scared he'll find out where we live and might kill us."

The investigation into the employee's behavior took place over a three-day period. Encounters on the day in question demonstrated that the employee was clearly angry and perhaps even threatening.

The day the prototype bomb was discovered the foreman reported to the site manager that an altercation had occurred between the employee and the crew chief. Another employee saw the former Marine and his crew chief "out on the flight line having some kind of confrontation. They were real close together...[He] was up in [the crew chief's] face. I can see him waving his arms and moving his mouth...I could not hear what he was saying."

The crew chief testified in the hearing that during the incident the angry employee warned him "he had experience with explosives and could 'blow this thing up' if things did not go right" and that he was "pushed to the limit." Then the employee said to him, "I'm through with you, Motherfucker." The crew chief said he was "kind of frightened" partly because the employee kept referring to his military background..."I was kind of shocked... he is a man full of anger...I don't know what he will do."

He was insubordinate because his immediate supervisor said his actions " involved not only cursing, but clear threats of disobedience and assault." For instance, he was asked to tie down a plane because bad weather was coming, a job that only job only took a few minutes. The employee responded that it wasn't his job.

Another employee testified to an incident the day the mock bomb was found that the employee under investigation confided after discovering a loose tool in the plane, "Man, I'm so mad, I could just punch someone out." The employee thought about throwing the loose tool it in the engine cowling, but he decided he might get caught and besides putting it in the engine cowling "might hurt a pilot or anybody." The employee asked the angry employee if "everything was okay" and the response was "No, everything is not okay. I don't want to lose my job for grabbing or punching somebody or doing something else to somebody." His fellow employee was worried about "vengeance" and quoted the bible to the former Marine. Then he decided to distance himself from his fellow crew member because "He had a lot of anger in him and everyone else saw it."

It was reported for the record that he told a fellow worker that he wished he could kill everyone. Well, I suppose that is threatening enough.

DEFINING A TERRORIST

In my mind, key questions emerged. What is a terrorist and what would be the possible relevance of the term in this grievance arbitration? What is the context of his reported angry statements? What motivated him to make such outrageous statements?

The purpose of a grievance arbitration surrounding an employee's behavior is to determine whether the behavior is grounds for some form of discipline, which might involve the question of whether he committed a criminal act when he purportedly made a mock bomb? Was he manifesting a criminal intent to kill somebody or hurt somebody or do something crazy? That was the real question, not whether he was a terrorist, although that would be the popular issue.

What was troubling to me personally was a further question: what rights would a suspected "terrorist" actually have? What would the just cause provision in the collective bargaining agreement entitle him to?

As a subtext, were his workplace rights diminished because of the horrors of September 11? In the event of foolish and intemperate remarks, were the odds of losing his job greater? Was his job in greater jeopardy in this environment because he complained about the way in which the supervisor carried out his job duties? Did a good record as an employee, unblemished by any disciplinary action make less of a difference in this post 9/11 world? Did his background as a US Marine actually work against him?

These were questions I asked myself since I was well aware of the haunting effects of 9/11 on workplace relations, especially in a large company with government security related contracts. But this factor was not part of the evidentiary record. Still, the amount of testimony as to his behavior and the reports of fear or, at the least, the uneasiness it evoked, *were* part of the record, as was my uneasiness about the situation evidenced by a decision to expand the record.

There were other questions regarding the record that were within my jurisdiction that bothered me. I saw an absence of procedural due process rights based on the testimony I received. Additionally, I could not understand based on the protestations of some sense of imminent danger, why the U.S. Navy, the prime contractor, was not alerted since the evidence showed that was standard procedure. Finally, I wanted to know, given the extent of the reported fears, why no one asked him what was in his briefcase.

I also had problems with the testimonies involving a sense of a threat. The wife of an employee was afraid? My bullshit radar was on notice. Besides, I rarely accepted hearsay in my hearings.

Then there was the Rorschach test - the perceived depiction of a bomb or perhaps idle twisting of wires. No one in my household, for instance, including myself, found a semblance of a bomb in the images of his creation.

Importantly, it was difficult to understand why the employer did not communicate directly in face-to-face communication with the employee to ascertain why he said some of the things he said, as I ended up doing.

I found nothing in the record where management warned the employee to cease and desist from inappropriate language. I found no evidence that the employer had attempted to find out why an employee with an exemplary record was behaving in such a strange way.

262

There was some small evidence that the termination involved an unstated motive on the part of the employer. Was the employer's desire to terminate the employee over the incident a preemptive strike in support of the employer's obligation to maintain a safe workplace? Perhaps he should be discharged for this alone. How else is an employer going to protect itself against an employee who is "going postal?"

In any case, I felt that this case involved something other than an operational concern, which meant I had to address motive. I could not introduce the topic of why the employee appeared as a threat to others in this new world. I would have to leave that kind of interest to my anthropologist co-author, but what I could ask and wanted to know was why this employee was so angry. Did we in fact have an employee who was going postal or did we have an employee frustrated by legitimate concerns surrounding the safety of operations? After reviewing the existing facts I concluded that just cause for his termination rested on this assessment.

The employee had indeed made a number of remarks which at the least indicated to me some state of generalized rage. However, while he made general threats, he did not threaten any particular person. I felt that a proper inference could be drawn from some of his remarks that he was very angry about something.

In order to learn more about the source of his apparent anger, I conducted a direct interrogation that became part of the evidentiary record. As I did this facts emerged about his state of mind.

The veteran marine had recently lost his wife and was raising two young daughters. This had been a stressful time for him, but he had managed overall.

ARBITRATOR QUESTIONS EMPLOYEE

During my interview with the grievant he addressed my concerns calmly, honestly, and openly. He never failed to look me in the eye, which admittedly impressed me.

Still, was he making a bomb prototype?

He told me that he had arrived at work on July 19th and waited for the arrival of aircraft when he would perform his duties as a member of the engine rinse crew.

He chose to sit at a table in the break room until he received an assignment from his lead man. While he waited he made an imitation clock face from a 1-inch roll of masking tape and some .025" diameter pieces of safety wire. He also made a wire "stick man" from another .025" diameter piece. He did this openly with no effort to conceal what he was doing from anyone who cared to look. In reviewing his final artwork, its character appeared to be consistent with the grievant's testimony that he was "doodling," meaning thereby that he was dealing with his boredom during downtime, keeping his hands busy.

Q All right. Can you tell us what happened on the day you were in the line shack seated at the break room table on the day of July 19th?

A We had come into work. I believe that's a Friday. We had come into work and we were sitting waiting, we as in myself, G and T, but T normally gets up and fills the rinse cart with water, so he's in and out checking on that. G was sitting across from me just like you're sitting there and I was sitting where the lawyer here is sitting and G was eating. We had been waiting for about anywhere between two and-a-half, three -- more like three hours, I believe.

While we were sitting there, I just was getting bored. So, I'm usually drawing and I was drawing that day. We normally have these towels, what we call canopy towels, that I normally sit there and I draw on waiting to go to work, but they had run out of those. So, there was a round piece of 1-inch masking tape that was sitting on the table. I grabbed that and I drew the face of a clock on it, you know, and then I said, well, let me get some safety wire out of the toolbox which was sitting on the window.

I got up, walked around G over to the toolbox, took out the safety wire, twenty-five thousandths of an inch, and came back over, sat down and proceeded to make the hour and the minute hand just sitting there. Then I had an extra piece left over, so I just made a stick man and laid it right on the table.

Shortly after that the plane captain, G, walked through the building, because on this side of the building -- I want to call it the west side of the building -- is the entrance off the flight line. During that time on the west end of the flight line, which is about this is an estimate, about fifteen hundred meters to the left where the Blue Angels park their jets is where we were parking the T-34s that day because they were working on the flight line. So, none of the plane captains were in or around that area. They were all on the far end.

G walked through on his way through other parts of the building. Where exactly I don't know. I was sitting there again making the clock.

Q Okay. Tell us about the stick man.

A The stick man, it was just an extra piece of safety wire that was left over after I had done made the hour hand and the minute hand as the lawyer provided on that example that you have.

Q This exhibit?

A Right. See, this was just actually one long piece right there. If I can show everyone, it's just one long piece that I pulled off the roll and I snipped it and then I cut it in half and out of that half I made the hour hand and the minute hand and if you look closely, you will see from the 9:00 o'clock position to the 3:00 o'clock position a piece that went across in order to hold the hour and the minute hand in place. You know, I had that one extra piece after doing that and I made a stick man and put it on the side.

Now, this is what's bothering me is this part here. I did not do that. I did not do that.

Q: What part are you talking about?

A: This right here, I did not do that.

Q You're talking about the paper towel?

A Yes, sir. I did not do that. This piece of paper towel here, sir, at the bottom of the stick man, I didn't do that. I did not do that.

Q: What about your anger …? Let's talk about it directly. You have heard all this testimony about, to use my words, which is kind of a vulgar word, but that you're really pissed off about a lot of things, angry.

A: No sir.

Q: No?

A: Dismayed. … We attend these ethics meetings every year and they push down our throats that The Company stands here, this is what you're supposed to do, and then, sir, then you go and do these things, they do nothing about it. I have inside the folder right there signed documents stating that I underwent these ethic classes and that we're to follow these to the letter because they are grounds for termination. So, when I do this, I'm laughed at or I'm being told, aw, you're just overly reacting.

THE ONE HUNDRED PERCENT EMPLOYEE

There was a history of substandard practices in the workplace that bothered the former Marine, especially in terms of pilot safety that he had tried to address through proper channels. He had followed protocol carefully and filed ethic complaints against his employer for improper work procedures with no results.

He then lost it for a few days and appeared threatening.

Was he a terrorist? Was he going to go postal? Was he even insubordinate? I decided no on all counts, though he didn't seem very happy.

In the labor relations' world insubordination refers to defiance of an order given within the authority of the supervisor, which is deliberately ignored by a subordinate. It takes more than acts of disrespect or remarks that are offensive to supervision or other employees to support a finding of insubordination. I found no insubordination.

Did the employee threaten, intimidate, coerce, harass, discriminate, or interfere with fellow employees? The answer seemed to be "no" although one can argue that his intemperate remarks about violence might have interfered with the ease and comfort of some employers, there was not enough there to say that he was threatening to the workforce.

I concluded that his break room action did not look like an act of terror unless the mere appearance of the object is shocking enough. This finding was consistent with the employer's failure to alert the United States Navy as a prime contractor that expressed concern over "acts of terror." The employer did not report its concern to the U.S. Navy that it had a "mock bomb" manufactured on company time and property by an employee of doubtful stability. The inference that I drew from this negative fact is that the employer was primarily concerned with maintaining order in the workplace (certainly a legitimate concern), not with the "mock bomb" as an instrument of terror.

The action of the grievant in making the so-called "mock bomb" did not support the conclusion that he was a terrorist, a potential terrorist, or that he had engaged in an act of terror. The burden was on the employer to establish that it was something other than what the employee said it was and that burden had not been sustained. I had found nothing in the existing record to suggest a weapon of terror and in expanding the evidentiary record; I believed the employee's innocent explanation of the manufacture of the "prototype bomb."

It was as I suspected after so many arbitrations. There is always an employee that follows the rules and expects others to do the same. An employee with his military background might be more likely to have trouble with breaking the rules.

Aside from his personal life, could his angry references about his military background relate to the fact that as a U.S. Marine he was dedicated, single-minded and depended on discipline when it came to maintaining equipment. In contrast, he now found himself working for a company servicing the military that possibly engaged in some unsafe practices. Because, as it turned out, this was a source of his frustration in alignment with many of his remarks which were misconstrued in a climate of hypervigilance at the least, and fear at the most.

The evidentiary record included the the testimony of a psychologist who evaluated the employee. According to the psychologist, the employee's military experience was a critical factor in his over reactions to what he saw in the workplace. He testified that the employee was simplistic, idealistic, and psychologically naïve. He tended to view the world in extremes - black or white. The expert witness added,

He's rigid in that he's sold on it. He's a hundred percent. He's gung ho. He thinks things through and then he arrives at a conclusion. He's there for the duration and that makes him somewhat rigid.

Sometimes he was sorely disappointed because his expectations are unrealistically high." He internalizes and becomes disgruntled, disappointed, withdrawn. If his reaction was extreme enough he would harm himself, not others.

This evaluation sounded very much like a young military recruit returning to a civilian life with different rules and standards, a story of thousands yet to be told well enough. He kept his job.

LABOR LAW IS INNOVATIVE

Work of some kind is something we all have in common. Most of us work for others. That is why we have labor and employment laws. I view labor law as the unsung hero of law primarily because its focus is on relationships that must be sustained tomorrow for social and economic reasons. This demands innovations in law. I view non-adversarial approaches in that category. These approaches in my experience must engendered a capacity on the part of the parties and the arbitrator to recognize what I call enlightened self-interest.

Committee or task force work can be one approach. I had a number of examples of this successful approach in my career such as the story of the Armour Automation Committee, the example of the Continuity of Employment Committee in chapter 14, and the committee experience of the Cinncinati Galvanizing Company. Other examples of non-adversarial approaches where labor and management work together are expedited arbitrations drawn from the transportation industry. I was a neutral arbitrator for more than a thousand expedited arbitrations, mostly to do with discharges and suspensions.

With some exceptions, many private and public sector arbitrations I conducted over the years, some drawn out for months, could have followed an expedited procedure and saved time, money, and good will.

Arbitrations or civil trials can be costly in different ways for the employer and the union. For example, bad feelings are more likely to linger and fester because of extended processes. Union representation is managed by small locals with comparatively little money to cover costs. Employee witnesses get time off from work to testify, instead of being paid to work.

For the most part, expedited arbitrations were decided by tripartite labor/management panels where I served as a permanent neutral arbitrator. One would worry that expedited arbitrations would mean a loss of due process. That was not my experience. I saw no loss of due process or procedural due process rights. I found that partisanship or a serious disagreement between the parties was rare.

Employer and union representatives on tripartite panels were usually familiar with their industry. This not only quickened processes, it judged a grievant based on a working knowledge of the workplace and brought understandings that were sustained by the two sides that had a common desire to preserve their industries for the greater good.

No decision by any tripartite panel I participated in was ever successfully challenged or collaterally attacked before the National Labor Relations Board or in any court, despite the absence of some procedures and safeguards that lawyers prefer such as discovery.

Some expedited systems were extraordinary because of the number of cases that were efficiently and fairly processed in a short amount of time. Two of the most notable examples are the Bay Area Rapid Transit (BART)system and SAMSTRAN, both are major transportation systems in California.

SAMSTRANS

SAMSTRANS was the principal community bus line between Palo Alto, California and San Francisco. This transportation system realized demonstrable cost-savings through increased efficiency thanks to the Amalgamated Transit Union (ATU) and SAMSTRANS' mutual support of expedited arbitration procedures.

There were no lawyers and no briefs. There was no forum for discovery. If there were witnesses, they were sworn in and heard without fuss. Most of the testimony in the expedited process consisted of offers of proof under oath. Decisions made from the bench were later confirmed in short form opinions. The objective was not necessarily to always get the decision right according to the parties' perspectives of what was right, but to get the case decided as fairly as possible and get people back to work.

The ATU and SAMSTRANS worked collaboratively to reduce miss-outs, which had become a serious and costly problem. The parties put together a strict expedited arbitration process that was unforgiving. A contract arbitrator (myself) administered cases involving miss-outs on a case-by-case basis with the advice of representatives of the employer and the union. Both parties worked to avoid cluttering the expedited process with frivolous grievances and meritless cases. Looking at my records, I see that in one day we arbitrated seven miss-outs, one of them involved intent to terminate for a multiplicity of miss-outs in a circumscribed time frame. That was a fairly typical caseload.

Because of the labor/management cooperation between the ATU and SAMSTRANS, miss-outs and other forms of absenteeism were reduced from about 10 percent to 3 percent in the course of a few years. The results, which can be directly attributable to the expedited procedures, were a measurable improvement in service to riders and consequently improved morale and consumer support, which led to improvements in public funding, which paid for wage increases. Both parties benefited. Consumers received better service. Bus drivers got more money. This was an example of enlightened self-interest.

BART

The BART system, where I served as a permanent neutral arbitrator for a number of years, was a clever system that used a five-member panel put together by BART and a local of the ATU to ensure the orderly and safe operation of train stations and trains in the Oakland-San Francisco area. The expedited procedure operated smoothly and fairly. Among the expedited models I became familiar with, I think this one was the best.

Of the five members on the panel, two were selected by the union, two by management. I was the fifth member. The cases that came before us were usually major discharge cases. The proceedings associated with a grievant were confidential, which meant that each panel member voted freely without fear of attribution or retribution on interim or final decisions.

This was a stable system for many years. Both sides were committed to preserving, particularly the 2/2/1 panels. One day an administrator who had been recently hired to manage labor relations, expressed his dissatisfaction with a particular decision. He used this incident to criticized the way the tripartite board used consensus to reach decisions.

The case that caused his unhappiness involved a train operator who was fired for incompetence. The employee wanted reinstatement to his position and then decided he would follow the union's recommendation and accept assignment to a lower classification as a station agent trainee. He would put in time as a trainee before being hired back full-time. The new administrator's challenges to the decision and the process was responsible for the elimination of a successful practice that had been sustained between labor and management.

The case was not complicated, except for the fact that one tripartite board member was also a witness and the rule was that witnesses must be sequestered. BART's new hire wanted the board member to remain in the hearing room and not be sequestered as a witness, The union wanted him sequestered to preserve the sanctity of the 2/2/1 process.

While BART had hoped to terminate the employee, it accepted the consensus of the panel members, which was to give the employee a trainee position in a lower classification that did not endanger the safety of passengers. The question of a conflict of interest involving the board member/witness should have been moot.

The labor relations administrator refused to accept either the sequestering of BART's representative on the board or its method of consensus in the case.

He focused on me with a vengeance. He wrote in an angry letter that members of an arbitration panel are only representatives of a point of view. They are not neutrals capable of enacting consensus, which actually is how we operated. Though I had the title, it was an egalitarian and neutral process.

The administrator saw a more adversarial context: "Their job is to persuade the neutral arbitrator to adopt the view advocated by counsel by the party that they represent…"

Following a barrage of vitriolic speech directed at me over the 2-2-1 process, the new labor relations administrator terminated my services, not an uncommon fate among "permanent" arbitrators.

BART's 2-2-1 consensual process as it had evolved and refined itself over the years, had lent itself to unprecedented cooperation and consistently resulted in fair decisions. It was not an uncommon practice for the neutral arbitrator to follow a partisan line by throwing the deciding vote with the union or alternatively with management in a 2-2-1 proceeding. BART's democratic approach had clearly benefited both labor and management over the years.

BART's expedited system while not appropriate in some cases, would apply in many grievance arbitrations. It represented a consistent judicial decision-making structure. Further study of expedited arbitration systems might have some value for reforming the overly adversarial U.S. legal system.

THE CASE FOR MED-ARB

Sam Kagel, a native of San Francisco, California, was not the most brilliant lawyer, however, he played an important role in shaping modern labor arbitration and developed a well-deserved national reputation.

Sam was smart, witty, caring, and inventive when it came to methods for resolving disputes. He could be a roughneck, which paid off in tough disputes between labor and management whether it was the NFL or longshoremen. He could also play on the opposite side of the coin and conduct delicate mediations. He knew when to step back and when to assert his authority as a neutral arbitrator.

Most perceived Sam as fair and honest. He was those things, and more. Whatever the parties' identity or affiliation, Sam steadfastly maintained that arbitrators should always be ready to mediate when they conducted an arbitration.

For Sam, mediation carried a kind of empowerment where the parties experienced what I have describe as self-enlightenment.

Empowerment means a process where the parties take on a degree of shared ownership of a particular issue. This kind of empowerment was the objective of Robert McKersie when he chaired the Continuity of Employment Committee (CEC) in New York State during Gov. Hugh Carey's administration.

Along those lines, Sam invented "med-arb." Med-arb is a collaborative model that operates to resolve workplace grievances. It could be described as related to a litigation settlement where the dispute is turned over to the parties.

Though Sam practiced mostly in the Bay Area region, he held a national reputation, partly because of his concept of med-arb.

I was sent to Honolulu by NEA to bail the union out of an ill-conceived, lukewarm strike. Sam was the arbitrator in the case. There must have been 50 or 60 parties at the collective bargaining table representing waterfront employers and the waterfront workers, as well as several other interest groups, including the Attorney General of the State.

As was my style at the time, I intentionally said something disruptive in the middle of the hearing in order to throw things off-center. Everyone was popping off, so why shouldn't I.

My pre-Sam thinking in relation to multiple parties was as an assumed adversary. If I was not called upon, I had better get in the act. I would identify myself, who I am, why I'm there. I'd make it clear that I was a noisy representative advocating for my client and so worry about me at all times. I had planned to be a pain in the ass. That was my frequent strategy.

Though his back was to me and he was preoccupied with another matter, Sam was fully aware of my disruption as well as my intentions. He turned around to me, and glared. To the surprise and shock of everyone at the table, he said, "Wollett, if you can't say anything constructive, keep your fucking mouth shut." As far as he was concerned, the matter ended there and he went on with whatever he was doing.

Sam was a fundamental kind of guy who never hesitated to bluntly say what he thought. Sam got away with this kind of show-stopping latitude, whatever the audience, because he was an engaging personality and he inspired a level of trust. He was *sui generis*, one of a kind. People listened to him. I did, and I did not forget the lesson. He was one of those life changers in terms of how I looked at the world.

Sam's med-arb model while it has been adopted in different countries, is still viewed as neither fish nor fowl. Critics view med-arb as impossible to evaluate as to its effectiveness. They say that it doesn't have shared standards of practice equal to that of mediation or arbitration.

The relevancy of these opinions seems off the point to me. People make med-arb more complicated and academic than it needs to be. I think they fail to see the relevance of the process and are inclined to think categorically.

Having frequently used the approach myself, I've never seen med-arb as particularly complex or worthy of extended analysis. It was simply a very handy tool, as adaptable as a Swiss Army knife, that accounts for multiple perspectives and methodologies.

274

Informally, you could say that med-arb represents an inclination toward peaceable resolution where while the arbitrator retains a particular kind of authority.

Some of the ideas behind med-arb and its basic premise were a good match for my belief that the parties would still have to relate to each other long after I was gone. This thought encouraged my ongoing desire to empower the parties that came before me whenever possible.

I believed that if the parties could reach an agreement with some facilitation, while retaining the authority to step in or finalize particular details, they would be more likely to concede that the outcome was fair.

One such case involved a university's claim that a security officer, a sergeant represented by the guild, abused the use of a university credit card provided to him for other purposes.

Ordinarily, I would not interfere with the parties in the midst of arbitration. After all, they came to arbitrate. But an experienced arbitrator has a sense of the direction a particular case is taking. In this case, the record was incomplete and the parties' presentations were poorly constructed because the bottom line was they didn't know what they wanted out of the deal. After listening to both sides for a while and looking at the evidence, I decided I needed to go off the record and take an action inconsistent with the concept of a neutral arbitrator.

I said to the parties, "at this point, what I would like to do is go into recess and I would like to have an off the record meeting with counsel for both sides. I would also like to have the reporter join the group not to record anything necessarily but just to be available in case she's needed."

After everyone else vacated the room, I told the remaining lawyers and the reporter,

What I'm about to say, it's not at all binding on anybody. We're just conversing, but the following seems to me to be true regarding where we're going and what the proofs are likely to be. If I'm right, the probability is that I will decide the case as follows..." I then gave them the scenario. I said, "before I do that [give them my decision] in a definitive way, however, I want to remand this case to the parties for a serious discussion on the question of whether or not a settlement along the lines of the decision I'd like you to make makes sense. It's certainly a cheaper route than the one you're on. There are other advantages to my proposal, as well, not just money. During this recess you think about what I've proposed. You talk about it in light of where I'm going with it, the way I see this case. I understand that there could be more to come on both sides if we continue on, but this is the way I view it now. So, think about the question of whether or not reaching a settlement between you makes good sense.

I presented the continuance of arbitration as a threat. If the parties did not go for a settlement, I would arbitrate.

THE LONG LUNCH

Empowerment sometimes means leaving the room, so I took a long lunch. When I returned, I was advised informally that the impasse was over and that the parties had reached a settlement, which meant they would not be going on to arbitration. I asked them to advise me of the terms and the grievant's lawyer, outlined the agreement. Later, we put the settlement in writing and the parties signed off on it.

They had concluded that a settlement was in the interest of both parties and no one had to admit to wrongdoing. They were better off settling than going forward. This was usually spelled out in the settlement agreement. The first part of the settlement was that the agreements are based on the unique facts and circumstances in each of three grievances that had been put forward by the parties.

The second point was that the parties agreed to standard release language, releasing the university of any claims or matters associated with the action taken.

So, I had become more of a mediator than an arbitrator.

The parties did an excellent job after some minimal guidance. They had only left out one important item. They did not stipulate that this action was not precedential.

They saved themselves some money and left with a better relationship. I subsequently concluded the case with the usual arbitral processes, which includes receipt of the testimony of a couple of witnesses and reviews of direct examination and cross-examination. Though I had accumulated a lot of documents into evidence as part of the record, the parties still realized a savings because the documents they had initially submitted had not actually reveal what the party wanted, which they subsequently figured out in a couple of hours while I had enjoyed my lunch.

The hearing followed Sam's general meaning of med-arb, which was good enough. There was just enough information for me to get an evidentiary feel for the case so that I could communicate the upcoming hardship for the parties if the case continued into a full-blown arbitration.

I did this in a number of cases. It probably cost me some business but if you're going to be any kind of labor arbitrator, you have to remember that most fundamentally you are incidental to the ongoing relationship between the parties. The parties will be living together. It is much better if they learn to settle disputes on their own. That is your ultimate objective.

FACED WITH RAPIDLY CHANGING WORKPLACE CONDITIONS, I PLUGGED HOLES IN A LEAKING SIEVE WITH MY LITTLE FINGER.

17

EXTINCTION

Sometimes there is no easy workplace resolution or remedy when industries die or dramatically change.

I have always had a romantic attachment to the idea of being a newspaperman or maybe a broadcast journalist. I wanted to be like Walter Cronkite.

Earl English fostered that desire. Earl not only taught a course in journalism, he also ran the print shop that printed the weekly high school newspaper when I was Editor In Chief for the paper.

Earl never taught me how to run a Linotype machine, but he taught me about grease sheets and, as a reporter, to not clutter copy with excess verbiage, especially adjectives and adverbs.

I lacked the eloquence of Mr. Justice Jackson, but I was able to unload a few adjectives and unnecessary adverbs and that was good enough.

Earl never went beyond high school, but he was literate. This was appreciated immediately following the Great Depression as jobs opened up in higher education and people like Earl were in demand to run journalism departments. Earl took a job with the University of Missouri as head of the journalism department.

Earl English had introduced me to machines and literacy. The two were romantically co-joined in my mind and I was determined to be part of that profession.

Aside from my high school experience, I had a brief stint in the newspaper business with Peoria's daily newspaper, the _Peoria Journal Transcript_ and I did grunt work on the proofreader desk at another paper. I came to know the players on a newspaper. If I was puzzled about a word or phrase, or the way in which a sentence was written, I might go to somebody on the copy desk; but the best advice came from the guys who worked the Linotype machines. They were mostly self-taught and frequently more literate than the reporters.

I did not become a newspaperman, but over the years I decided a number of newspaper disputes, most frequently to do with work jurisdiction matters.

I came to know one union in particular. My first introduction to the International Typographical Union (ITU) happened when I represented a commercial printing business. Thanks to the ITU, When it came to work jurisdiction issues I learned early on who was boss.

Torchy Torrance, a prominent University of Washington alumnus, upstanding citizen, and a friend begged for my legal advice concerning his commercial printing business.

Torchy was an excellent wheeler and dealer when it came to his many business ventures, but he was stymied over his dispute with his printing foreman. The foreman had strayed and done some journeyman's work, which got him kicked out of the ITU. The upshot was that Torchy would have to fire an excellent foreman.

Torchy had the impression that he was the boss over these kinds of decisions because he owned the business. It took some convincing on my part, but Torchy finally realized that the powerful ITU was the real boss in this matter.

With the de-skilling of an industry and a re-skilling to address new technologies, the territory owned by a skilled workforce is gone.

The dirty, messy, massive, cumbersome, and potentially danger-ous Linotype machine of many parts was once viewed as a machine anyone could operate. (In reality, it took at least four years to master.) Then came the electronic transfer of images, which became increas-ingly easier, faster, and more broadly distributed, but also more complex in terms of defining workers' jobs and union territory at the dawn of a new age. I should note that in the spring of 2011. Amazon claimed that its "eBooks" were outselling the "old-fashion" printed version 105 to 100. In 2012 it was 114 ebooks to 100 printed versions (more independent authors are only online so that also has to be considered).

The print industry was once the most labor intensive industry. It was built on crafts and knowledge owned by the workers. Newspa-per employees within this industry, including "back shop" employ-ees such as printers and typesetters represented critical democratic principles to increasingly broader audiences. A pride of literacy carried through several generations and was fostered by a healthy competition between small newspapers.

My hearings on work jurisdiction issues starting in the 1960s. The number of work jurisdiction hearings peaked in the 1980s and 1990s. The inevitability of extinction was clear. Some younger people would be retrained in new technologies., Some workers, many representing the last of their kind, would be protected by seniority. However, it was over for an entire group of industrial workers. Unions could only try to maintain traditional work jurisdictions and demand some "fair" share of new technologies. Hopefully, this would mean retraining or new jobs for their members. However, ultimately there was no fair share.

Cases dealing with creative employees are tricky because the most challenging issue with these employees is that they like to think that they define their job to an extent, not that the job defines them. The problems they face are operational and economic priorities that fall under management rights.

I grew to understand the more personal meanings behind the loss of freedom of expression thanks to changing market demands.

An over-zealous food editor, like many highly creative people, could not do anything less than follow her muse. The highly skilled editor and writer worked for the San Francisco Chronicle. She made judgments as to the food, recipes, and methods she would introduce to readers. One might think that well-crafted opinions and innovative ideas by well-liked writers and respected editors would sell newspapers, so her desire might be seen as an economic benefit for the employer.

Some of her ideas were viewed as esoteric and involved overtime. Putting in hours to do something extraordinary as a respected food editor might have been reasonable. However the managing editor told her to present the kind of foods and recipes that his superior, the publisher, believed the newspaper readership really wanted.

The managing editor explicitly told her not to pursue her judgment because the order from above was that it was not in the budget. The managing editor told her to comply or she would be terminated.

Unable to resist the strength of her ideas, she put in the overtime anyway. She was not fired, but she was demoted to a non-creative position. She lost the freedom of expression she prized so much.

She was insubordinate and the newspaper's management had a right to call her on it. But, was there some intangible loss to the newspaper's readers and in the final analysis to the newspaper?

A copy editor worked for one of the most revered newspapers in Northern California; a newspaperman's newspaper. The regional paper had a nationwide reputation because it set a standard for good journalism and it was a nationally acclaimed training ground for journalists.

Like other papers, it was going through significant changes because of economic forces and the introduction of new electronic media. As a reader, I felt that its editorial content began to decline during this period.

The newspaper attempted to reinvent itself to fit a new age, though it was not clear how it would achieve this.

There were rumors the paper was preparing itself to be sold and this could have been associated with a general uneasiness throughout its departments. No one was sure what would happen next, or whether they would keep their jobs.

None of this background entered my evidentiary record as relevant to the case, but, of course, it probably was relevant.

One day, a copy editor was asked to fill out and turn in a mandatory performance evaluation.

True to his training, after carefully pulling the mandatory performance evaluation out of its envelope, he quickly focused on an offending line of type on the signature page. He "corrected" a statement that came before the employee's signature line that said, " Note: The employee's signature is an acknowledgment that the employee has received the evaluation *and* discussed it with the supervisor. It does not represent agreement with or endorsement of the *content.*" The copy editor stopped after the word "evaluation" and crossed out the rest.

He refused to acknowledge reading the document or that any communication had actually taken place by refusing to sign the document.

He was charged with insubordination. He refused to defend himself against the charge and calmly said, he was ready to be terminated.

Good copy editors are not that easy to find and he was excellent at his job. The conundrum frustrated his supervisors. With one possible exception, no one wanted to lose him. All he had to do was to sign the original document without his editing and be done with the matter. His answer was that he didn't mind being fired.

It was clear by the excellent work that he did that his job and his skill were important to him so why did he passively accept the situation without a defense? Was this some kind of passive death by firing squad, which is not that uncommon in the workplace? The only reason the copy editor offered was that the mandatory performance evaluation did not used to be mandatory.

I upheld the employee's termination for persistent insubordination based on the principle that management has a right to manage and that ended the matter.

But I do not always walk away from hearings intact.

While this is getting into more philosophical depth than I usually do, I concluded that copy editor who refused, or perhaps could not, explain his cause was Herman Melville's *Bartleby the Scrivener* brought to life. Maybe the copy editor "preferred not to…"

Perhaps, the ink in his veins after many years in the newspaper business was running out of a cut artery. This consideration reminded me of a poem by Emily Dickenson.

> *There's a certain Slant of light,*
> *Winter Afternoons,*
> *That oppresses, like the Heft*
> *Of Cathedral Tunes—*
>
> *Heavenly Hurt it gives us—*
> *We can find no scar,*
> *But internal difference,*
> *Where the Meanings, are—*
>
> *None may teach it—Any—*
> *'Tis the Seal Despair—*
> *An imperial affliction*
> *Sent us of the Air—*
>
> *When it comes, the Landscape Listens—*
> *Shadows—hold their breath;*
> *When it goes, 'tis like the Distance—*
> *On the look of Death—*

There was, as is often the case, a back story regarding workplace relations that did not make it into the evidentiary record. It might have if the copy editor had chosen to defend his actions .

A call had gone out from the administration department asking for employee participation in coming up with creative ideas for pulling the newspaper up on its feet.

The copy editor was a thinker and he was full of ideas. He brought 21 suggestions to his supervisor. She summarily dismissed him and his ideas, and rudely asked him to leave. This incident, the latest in a series of negative interactions between the supervisor and the employee, heightened a pre-existing tension between the copy editor and his supervisor. These facts were not part of the evidentiary record.

My personal impressions were that the supervisor did not come across as well versed in human relations, while the copy editor seemed to narrowly live for his job perhaps at the expense of practicing some social skills.

My decision to terminate the copy editor was reinforced by the fact that his own union was reluctant to represent him since he had offered no defense for his insubordination except to imply that he had a "cherished right" not to sign his performance evaluation. If he signed, he said cryptically, "I might as well steal a car."

"Cherished right?" The only logic I could come up with was that the copy editor sincerely believed that if communication did not exist why should he sign something agreeing that communication did exist.

Nobody, including myself, knew what had actually happened. Sadly, the newspaper lost a valuable and skilled employee with years of training who had consistently produced above average work and had caused no trouble in the past.

He was Bartleby the Scrivener, and his signature was his only defense.

THE WORKPLACE AND FREEDOM

The changeover to the digital age represented more than the disappearing feeling of a book in hand. It represented a loss of pride in work that had been owned by generations of workers. This ownership defined the character of a worker and solidarity.

The history of many unions reveals their part in society as effective social organizations. In an era when unions and benevolent societies provided essential social services, the ITU was among the best at providing services to its members, from mortuary services to homes for the sick.

For this and other reasons, the International Typographers Union, was an excellent model for industrial democracy.

This included its capacity for advocacy. The print industry was frequently perceived as a threat to centralized government. Newspapers and the print industry were key defenses for freedom. The ITU was one of the most militant and progressive unions in the 19th century defending workplace rights within the industry, including the constitutional right of freedom of association. This was partially preserved by ITU through means such as unprecedented strike actions and its printing of bold words of protest.

The ITU also championed equal pay for women and the eight-hour workday. Its support of these causes set the ITU apart from most unions. It also successfully defended a proprietary right to employment.

Over the years ITU managed to maintain control of workplace jurisdictions to the benefit of its workers because of its extraordinarily effective organization which did not neglect the rights and responsibilities of the individual. Historically, highly skilled pressman and compositors had to maintain " high character" if they were to argue for wages. Holding to one's craft and exercising freedom of expression were inexorably linked.

There was a time when ITU represented literacy as pride in one's work. In more recent times, ITU's focus has been to delay the irreversible incursions of rapidly changing new technologies that has threatened the collective notion of a proprietary right to employment.

The inevitable fate of the union culture as it exists today is to an extent promoted by unions' responses to marketplace influences. I cannot see, at least not yet, how the digital age will emulate the union heritage of solidarity, literacy, and pride.

So, I wonder. When the copy editor righteously deleted the assumption in the performance evaluation that communication had occurred, his comment was "I might as well steal a car." Did his protest mean more than words spoken by a disgruntled employee?

A GROUP OF YOUNG LAWYERS BEGAN AN ODYSSEY TO TEACH OTHERS ABOUT THE UNKNOWN FIELD OF LABOR LAW.

18

Coming of Age

My coming of age as a practicing and perhaps more principled lawyer happened because of The Labor Law Group, which exists today.

In 1947, a group of labor lawyers informally met for the first time. Led by Robert Mathews and William Wirtz, the group of young lawyers began an odyssey in a little known area of law which represented an untried profession. Their ambition was to teach others about the field of labor law in the belief that the methodologies of the time that drove legal education would not work in this area of law.

I joined shortly after the Labor Law Group was formed. I had been inspired by a round table discussion chaired by Robert E Matthews, a law professor at the Ohio State College of Law.

The early members of the LLG included those that became close friends for the remainder of my life, Benjamin Aaron, Charles Morris, William Wirtz, and other fellow labor lawyers. Bill Wirtz summarized the LLG's aspirations.

...Labor law...questions how a free society, wanting to stay that way, handles problems in which individual and system interests frequently conflict and human and economic values often compete... [Teaching labor law] affords a unique superior opportunity to inquire into how we can see to it that the future will continue to be a good idea.

Toward that end, the group advocated for a constructive role for lawyers as advisors and facilitators rather than as "hired guns" on the scene after employment and collective bargaining relationships fall apart.

The LLG used participatory approaches by distributing published books and teaching materials to classrooms and then soliciting feedback, revising, and redistributing these materials based on what they learned.

This approach as well as their philosophy of law drew critics. The production of collaborative works turned away lawyers who believed in individual achievement over collective interests.

In 2009, shortly before his death, my friend, Ben Aaron said that the LLG saw labor law as the only area of law that contained all aspects of law and human relations. He said to me once that his membership in the LLG changed how he taught, what he taught, and his entire research direction.

Dog Law when I was 17

From my perspective, the LLG gave me further insights into what I had learned as a student, which was to think critically and talk plainly about all the facts in a situation based on human-scale reasoning. I can only hope that I achieved some of this in my career.

I only hope that some of this legacy breathes in law schools. As Richard Whately said in the 19th century, if we can only reverse our optics, we just might produce a few good lawyers.

The aspirations of the LLG still exist but the question of a free society remains open. We do have conflicting systems. If I were still teaching constitutional law, I would present new challenges to my students, specifically the *U.S. Supreme Court v Social Justice.*

My identity as a constitutional lawyer is inseparable from the practice and teaching of labor law. This does not mean that this is a practice found in the workplace beyond rudimentary common law understanding. In fact, one can argue that there are massive violations of constitutional principles in the workplace setting. Some of this is in the name of industrial peace. It is also a matter of corporate greed.

Since WW11, U.S. Supreme Court's 5-4 majority decisions have increasingly favored corporatism and militarism, often outside of representative government. The costs of this trend are felt by social programs and the workplace. These are often inseparable issues.

Duke v. Walmart is one of many cases related to the workplace that demonstrate how the U.S. Supreme Court's lack of world understanding persists in 2013.

When I was 17 my mother gave me a book titled *Nine Old Men* which I used as a basis for an oratory speech titled "The Supreme Court of the United States v. Franklin Roosevelt and The New Deal." Her persistence won me a state championship in a 1937 event sponsored by the National Forensic League in Lincoln Illinois.

For those who have forgotten, or perhaps never knew those times, the country was in terrible shape as it struggled through the Great Depression. There was 25 percent unemployment. Political activism was rampant and often viral. Characters like Father Charles Edward Coughlin – a nutty Catholic priest - fomented hatred.

President Roosevelt continued to push Congress, to produce legislation after legislation in response to domestic ferment.

The Hughes Court called Roosevelt's proposed bills unconstitutional and knocked down key provisions of the New Deal meant to create critical social programs.

A distinguished law professor at Northwestern commented "So senile has the Supreme Court come in its judgments that even a grade-school child can tell beforehand how at least four of the justices will rule."

Prior to 1937, there had been only nine 5-to-4 decisions by the U.S. Supreme Court. Within eight months of the New Deal, a parade of constitutional challenges resulted in five 5-to-4 decisions, and this trend has grown stronger, particularly on matters related to large social concerns.

No matter how far the Court strays from common sense and in the process violates the principle of equity stated in Article 3, Section 2 of the U.S. Constitution; no matter how eloquent the Court's dissents, the Supreme Court effectively ends up with near absolute power over all branches of government. This is a dangerous and unaccountable anomaly in a representative democracy.

The Last Mile

Enlightened self-interest

Justice Learned Hand wrote in the *Spirit Of Liberty*,

It is a mistake to rely excessively on written words to tell us how we can behave. We have to rely on other things that rely elsewhere in deciding on how we behave. The codes don't do it all, just as the common law doesn't do it all.

"We have to rely on other things that rely elsewhere..." I finally figured out the right question. The question is not *how* much power, but *where* power resides.

It lies in the middle ground. This is where the innovation and good will happens. Will we make this common ground a wasteland or rich estuaries of possibilities?

The island I live on in the Northwest has two culturally distinct north and the south communities with different needs. The northern part of the island has an army base and all the attendant problems that come with transiency, including a large number of low income single mothers, domestic violence, and drugs. It is predominately Republican. The southern part of the island has fewer of these problems. It is known for its progressive politics and cultural amenities and more expensive real estate. It has a strong democratic contingent.

Rural problems, such as Methamphetamine labs and domestic violence afflict both sides of the island.

Two excellent judges preside over these two distinct parts of the island. They deal with all the problems inherent in the American fabric, including the fate of children and their families who for one reason or another enter the criminal justice system.

Unlike the U.S. Supreme Court, these judges' decisions do not reflect their politics.

I met the two judges when I became involved with our Island County Court Appointed Special Advocate (CASA) program.

Formed in 1977 by Seattle Superior Court Judge David Soukup, CASA represents abused or neglected children in court proceedings. More than 70,000 CASA advocates volunteer in state and local programs.

Judges are informed by CASA's firsthand knowledge of family situations. There are many testimonials from judges that this different knowledge base informs wiser, more humane, and more relevant decisions.

The local CASA applied for funding to hire a part-time attorney. The organization's volunteers needed advice on particular cases and they needed to become more familiar with legal terms to use when necessary in their communications with the two judges.

CASA envisioned seeking legal counsel perhaps once a month for two or three hours. When the county denied their funding request, I offered my services, *pro bono*, with the caveat that I did not know much about the CASA program, or dependency courts, which do not have the protections of criminal courts.

I thought it was pure genius that CASA volunteers drew on legal consultations and in turn offer judges and legal counsels relevant and informed facts along with their own understanding regarding a child's welfare. I wanted to be a part of this process.

I attended weekly court hearings as well as monthly CASA meetings. These meetings were in-service training opportunities that gave me a chance to acquire knowledge and insight into the details and challenges involved in advocating for the best interests of abused and neglected children.

I asked many questions and read a wonderful book on decision-making that was handed out to each volunteer, *A Question of Balance.* There were also case study sessions using the collective wisdom around the table to help volunteers who were stuck on a particular case. When I felt more comfortable, I increasingly offered suggestions and recommendations.

CASA volunteers face all kinds of situations. They lose some cases, and I like to think, win more. The following case was a learning lesson for every one involved.

During divorce proceedings, a father sought limited visitation rights for his wife who had been diagnosed with a mental illness.

His attorney subpoenaed a volunteer's notes. Unfortunately, the volunteer fancied herself a novelist and wrote prolific notes. She had not listened to the director's warnings during her training about the importance of brevity and circumspection in her note taking.

To make matters worse, the father had the financial resources to hire a local attorney well known for go-for-the-throat tactics in divorce court. The mother did not have a chance. She was deemed mentally unstable and had no money with which to defend her interests

We knew the subpoena of the CASA's notes was a fishing expedition to benefit the father's parenting plan. He would be the custodial parent and would give the mother limited access to her children.

I advised the CASA members that the only option was to turn over CASA's notes and in fairness give the notes to the mother's public defense attorney, and the state's attorney.

We did that. The father filed his parenting plan and the dependency action was dismissed. The state could not argue that he was not providing a safe, stable home for his children.

However, there was a back story that should have been introduced in the proper light. He had previously abandoned his children when they were very young when their mother began to exhibit bizarre behaviors. He also denied his family financial support.

In our CASA eyes, which had an intimacy with the case, he had chosen to leave his children to an unknown fate with their mother, who he now argued was unfit.

Despite her hallucinations, which it was shown could be treated, the mother had demonstrated love and nurturing toward her children.

Since the children deserved and needed to continue to have more of a relationship with their mother than the parenting plan allowed. We all felt badly about this outcome.

We used this harsh experience as a learning opportunity to provide further training so that volunteers would not be faced with such testimonial issues again. Volunteers learned to keep careful track of all dates and times of contacts with all stakeholders and make relevant "CASA-only" remarks where needed to jogged their memory in case they had to take the stand.

Both the director and I knew that the volunteers' confidence and proficiency, in what could be an unrelenting world of difficult cases for CASA volunteers, would continue to grow with this procedure. I told the volunteers that they knew an amazing amount about their cases, more than they realized. With enough knowledge and some basic legal acumen ordinary people can do extraordinary things.

I have read about the healthy reciprocal relationship between judges and CASA volunteers found in courts across the country. This exemplifies the concept of enlightened self interest. Judges working with CASAs around the country have said they could not handle domestic cases as proficiently without CASA volunteers. Some say that their relationship with volunteers made them much better judges which meant more hope through more relevant decisions for juveniles and their families. Judges began to buy into the realization that there are alternatives to immersion in the criminal justice system.

The CASA volunteers also taught judges something about the meaning of law. Their efforts are transformative within the legal system.

The current U.S. Supreme court could learn from the two judges on my island because they are trapped in a whirlpool of their own understanding.

Past U.S. Supreme Court majority decisions and dissents have acknowledged that the law must talk to ordinary people. The Court has frequently relied on phrases such "not so vague that men of common intelligence must necessarily guess at its meaning", or a "common sense" interpretation of rules and behavior. This phrasing represents more than a nice thing to do, it is a right. This is a message that every lawyer who practices law should send, along with a blueprint for the next generation. I did my best in my practice and teaching of law.

www.ingramcontent.com/pod-product-compliance
Lightning Source LLC
Chambersburg PA
CBHW051626170526
45167CB00001B/72